To Lea Simonds,

whose consistent support and friendship
have kept *Creative Nonfiction*
going—and growing—for 20 years.

CONTENTS

the first 20 years of

CRE ONFICTIONMAGAZINE

TRUE STORIES, WELL TOLD

Edited by
LEE GUTKIND and **HATTIE FLETCHER**

Introduction by **SUSAN ORLEAN**

PITTSBURGH

Requests for permission to reproduce material from this work should be sent to:

Rights and Permissions
In Fact Books
c/o Creative Nonfiction Foundation
5501 Walnut Street, suite 202
Pittsburgh, PA 15232

Cover and text design by Tristen Jackman

ISBN: 978-1-937163-16-7

Printed in the United States of America

YOU'LL KNOW IT WHEN YOU READ IT

Susan Orlean

First of all, don't worry about what it's called. Call it narrative nonfiction, or literary journalism, or creative nonfiction, or long-form narrative, or feature writing. Does it matter? How about: *I just learned something really fascinating and now I'm going to tell you about it.* Or how about: *I am going to write this so vividly that you will feel you are experiencing the story with me.* And: *Everything in this is true.* And: *Life is just so damn interesting.*

Like pornography, you don't need a definition, anyway, because you will know it when you read it. I did, right from the start. My first encounter with creative nonfiction came when I was a kid. At the time, I was pawing through a copy of *Life* magazine, which was my favorite periodical back then, mostly because it always featured cute pictures of baby animals. I don't remember the year or month. I do remember sitting on the floor of our living room, flipping through the pages of the new issue, and coming across a story that described a day in the life of a small-town doctor, a general practitioner in Minnesota or Kansas or someplace like that. As much as the pictures of baby animals in the back of the magazine beckoned me, I lingered on that story. I can still recall one photograph of the doctor, exhausted and rumpled after a long day of delivering babies, bandaging skinned knees, and telling a few people some bad news about their health. In my mind's eye, I picture him slumped against a cabinet of medical supplies. He might have been smoking a cigarette.

There was no obvious reason for the story to have been written—that is, there was nothing extraordinary about this doctor or this town, no significance to the particular day that was examined. The story simply detailed the ebb and flow of the day and the dozens of little dramas that the doctor encountered, and it implied, without saying it in so many words, how important the doctor was to his community, and how the stories of all the lives of the town could be seen in cross-section by observing his world. The story also implied, by the mere fact of its existence, that it was important to know something about other people, whoever they were, and not only when something newsworthy—in the conventional sense—had happened to them.

I was really young at the time, but even so, I was fascinated by the story. I remember thinking, *you can really write stories about things like this, just stories about life?* And then I thought, *I want to do that!* I really did. I never wanted to be a ballerina or a movie star or any of those other fantasy careers little girls often have. I wanted to be a writer, and as soon as I saw that story, I dreamed about being able to write stories like it—stories that seemed like they didn't need to be told. That meant, of course, that they urgently needed to be told, because learning something new about the world or about someone, and then telling it to other people, is essential, crucial, transformational, and therefore urgent.

And now comes the hard part. If you can't really define what this is—this hard-to-name, difficult-to-define practice of telling true stories—how are you supposed to learn how to do it? How do you do it right? Since it doesn't have the rules of typical journalism—no inverted pyramid of information, for instance—how do you know what makes it work? There's no simple answer, since it's not a simple form. The best piece of advice I ever got was from my first editor, who explained to me that writing nonfiction of this sort was a three-part process. First, you report, he said, and then you think, and only then do you begin to write. I knew about the reporting and the writing parts, but the thinking part was a surprise. I'm not sure I understood what he meant at the time, but as I dug into bigger stories and more challenging narratives, I started to appreciate what he meant. Gathering information is where you start, and disseminating it is where you end, but if you don't spend the time in the middle processing what you've learned, putting it in context, questioning why you cared about it, and assessing how learning it has changed you, you can't write a great story. This means you should spend a lot of time as a writer looking like you're not working because thinking doesn't really look like much to an outsider. (The closets of writers around the world get extremely well organized during that thinking phase, because we feel like we're not being productive since we're not reporting and we're not yet writing, so we panic and we organize our closets.) That thinking part is so important and so easy to shortchange. In fact, if I could do anything differently with stories I've written, it would be to have given myself a little more time to think about them before I wrote a single word.

Other wisdom I've collected over the years: Don't over-prepare. Be willing to jump into stories naked; you'll listen harder and learn more authentically. On the other hand, do over-report. Follow bits of the story that aren't quite on topic; you'll probably find something unexpected and fascinating. Don't obsess about your notes. Take good ones, and make them accurate, but most of what you learn is taken in and recorded in your brain (or should be), and your notes really are just there as prompts. Also: read and read and read and read. Keep your favorite pieces of writing on your desk and imitate them. I don't mean steal from them; I mean use them as models, the way you might model your golf swing on a video of Tiger Woods. Write what you want to learn. Then learn it well enough to teach it, which is really what writing is. Choosing your own stories is a luxury that not every writer has, and often you will find yourself assigned to write about something you honestly don't care about and it seems impossible to pretend you want to learn about it. In that case, think of it as a writing exercise in which you will practice the art of inquisitiveness. Also, is there really nothing at all in the subject you wonder about? If so, question your choice of careers, since I can't think of a quality more essential for a writer than curiosity. Make beautiful sentences, but don't worry about making them fancy. Read everything out loud, either to yourself or to a willing listener. Cut out the boring parts. Put in a few jokes. Do not fear the editor's pencil; almost every story gets better when it's tightened up. Anyway, it's better to leave readers wishing your story kept going than to have them bail out halfway through because it got too long. This list could go on and on. Every story is so different; every interview, even, is so different, that there can't be—and shouldn't be—an instruction manual for how to do it. That's what makes it such a maddeningly addictive profession: it's new all the time. That's also why it's hard. That's also why it's wonderful.

I suppose sometime I should look up that *Life* magazine story in their archives to see if it still moves me the way it did back when I was a kid. I mean, the whole story of my life unrolls from that moment, really—who I am, what I do, how I see the world. I think about looking it up, and then I think, *Nah, better leave it alone and just hang onto the memory of what happened that day.* It's enough to know that a story can mean that much, linger in the mind, shape a future, or simply create a tiny moment when you see something for the first time in a new way. You know it when you see it. That's enough for me.

SUSAN ORLEAN is the author of *The Orchid Thief* and *Rin Tin Tin: The Life and the Legend* and a staff writer at *The New Yorker*. She lives in New York.

WHY CREATIVE NONFICTION MATTERS

Lee Gutkind and Hattie Fletcher

Unlike big, glossy magazines, "little" or literary magazines like *Creative Nonfiction* are often labors of love— underfunded, understaffed, and often, for these reasons, short-lived. A while back, Charles McGrath pointed out in *The New York Times* that "the typical lifespan for a literary magazine appears to be roughly that of a major household appliance: anything over 10 years is gravy."

Incredibly, as we write this *Creative Nonfiction* is celebrating its twentieth year of publication. That's pretty good for a magazine that started at a dining room table in Pittsburgh and which, even today, is put out by a small, part-time staff with the help of a few unpaid interns. It's not been easy, and in fact, there's more than a little heartache in our history; Lee tells the story of the struggle at the end of this book, in "The Fine Art of Literary Fist-Fighting."

If you're unfamiliar with *Creative Nonfiction*, allow us to offer a brief introduction: *CNF* is a quarterly magazine with nearly 3,500 subscribers around the world, and a total circulation of 7,000. Every issue includes between five and ten new works of creative nonfiction (often addressing a specific theme), as well as experimental work, micro-essays, interviews with writers and editors, and more. At the moment, we're working on the 52nd issue of the magazine—and we have plans for many more issues beyond that.

Creative Nonfiction is more than just a magazine, though; it's a community—a home not only for the writers whose work has appeared in the magazine's pages, but for anyone who loves this incredibly compelling and versatile genre. Unfortunately, despite our best efforts over the past twenty years, "creative nonfiction" is still not an entirely mainstream term, and we've been happy to welcome the many writers who've shown up at our virtual doorstep, arms flung wide, proclaiming, "I've been writing this stuff my whole life, but I never knew what to call it!"

We believe that more important than what you call it is what it *is*—and that's actually pretty straightforward: true stories, well told. You can't make stuff up and the writing has to be top-notch, but beyond that, creative nonfiction is tremendously flexible, allowing for plenty of experimentation in voice, style, subject matter, and structure. There aren't many rules around here.

In twenty years, we've published brand-new nonfiction by more than five hundred writers—some of them famous, but more of them not (or, rather, not yet). We're especially proud of our track record in giving writers their first significant byline; you'll have a hard time finding a literary magazine that *doesn't* say it's "looking for new voices," but almost every issue of *Creative Nonfiction* has included someone's first publication. How does this happen? Here's how a little magazine generally works (or how ours works, at least): writers send unsolicited submissions—essays and stories they've struggled through and sweated over, work they believe in—and we read them. All of them. And then we publish what we like best. There are, after all, some advantages to being little; we're not beholden to any big organizations or corporate interests, which means we can more or less do what we like.

(That said, if you know of a corporation or a big organization that would like to sponsor a literary magazine . . . call us!)

Now, in this book, we're publishing the very best of the best—the stories that have stuck with us and that we've been unable to forget. Some of them—Brian Doyle's "Two on Two," Jim Kennedy's "End of the Line"—make us a little weepy, even after multiple readings, while Harrison Scott Key's "The

Wishbone" has not yet lost its power to make us laugh out loud. Jennifer Lunden's "The Butterfly Effect" and Chester F. Phillips's "Chasing Lions," both originally published in a special Animals-themed issue, make us grapple with our place in the world, while other stories, such as Pria Anand's "Far, Far Away" and Caitlin Horrocks's "Pesäpallo," take us to far-away lands. Marilyn A. Gelman's "Scrambled Eggs" and Meredith Hall's "Without A Map" and Jerald Walker's "The Heart" and Jane Bernstein's "Rachel at Work" help us experience and maybe even understand, at least briefly, other lives. There are even a few stories here—Todd May's "Teaching Death" comes to mind—that have quite literally changed our lives.

Perhaps they'll change yours, too. That's what a good story can do. And that's why magazines like *Creative Nonfiction* matter—even if they are little.

THE BUTTERFLY EFFECT

Jennifer Lunden

METAMORPHOSIS

It was cold in Maine. Cold. And the snow was heaped in dirty piles on the side of the road. And the sidewalks were icy. And it got dark at 4:30 in the afternoon.

It was the dead of winter, and I wanted out, so I flew to California—to Pacific Grove, a.k.a. Butterfly Town, USA, to see the monarchs. It was a journey home, really, though I had never been there.

I grew up in a box-shaped house on a well-manicured lawn in the suburbs of a mid-sized Canadian city in Ontario. Across the road and abutting the river was a patch of city land, untended, wild, a field of tall grasses flecked with milkweed and Queen Anne's lace. There, I discovered my first monarch caterpillar. I was nine years old, and I had never seen anything like it. Boldly ringed in concentric stripes—black, yellow and white—it was stretched out on a milkweed leaf, eating. I plucked it off, held it in my hand, touched it with my fingers. Its skin was smooth, leathery. It did not roll up in a ball. It did not seem afraid. Docile. I broke off the milkweed near the top and carried my find home.

I scoured the fields in search of more. I filled jars with milkweed and caterpillars. I pounded nail holes in the lids. I spent hours watching them.

They ate voraciously. I could see their mandibles working. I could see the chunks they took out of the leaves, bite by bite. They grew fast, and before I knew it, they were climbing to the lids of their jars. They spun small mounds of silk and attached themselves to the mounds and hung there in the shapes of J's for a long, long time. And then, when the moment was right, they split the skins on their backs, wrestled with themselves and turned inside-out, and, suddenly, there they were, something wholly different: an emerald green chrysalis with little golden flecks and a gold crown.

Miraculous.

They would hang for days, for what seemed like forever, and nothing changed. And then one day, I could see the darkening. The butterfly was forming. Soon, I could see the outline of a wing. The orange. The black veins. The white polka dots.

The waiting for what would come next. . . . It seemed interminable.

I didn't want to miss it.

MIGRATION

When a monarch butterfly sets off on its journey to its winter destination, it does not have to pay a $100 fee because its suitcase is twenty-five pounds over the limit. It does not have to take off its shoes, its watch, its coat and scarf, in case of bombs. It does not have to put its carry-ons in the overhead compartment or under the seat in front of it. It does not have to watch the flight attendant demonstrate how to put on a seatbelt or an oxygen mask. It does not worry about going down. It does not worry.

It's eleven degrees Fahrenheit and a cold, clear day when my flight departs, and it's hard to imagine what a monarch does experience on its own winged migration. It experiences, certainly, the view. It experiences a silence I cannot imagine. It experiences, I think, a certain peace, a free tilting. It knows nothing but how to ride the waves of the wind.

It is the opposite of me, crammed here in the stale air of this "Freedom Air" Embraer EMB-45.

HABITAT

I have a carbon filter mask. If I were to give it a name, I think it would have a male name. Tom. Something strong and protective.

My mask is battleship gray. It shields me from perfumes and colognes, air fresheners, cleaning products, pesticides, fumes from fresh paint. I carry it in a baggie in my purse, and I take it out now, on this airplane, and strap it on.

I wear it when I can feel the headache coming on. When it hits, it feels as though my brain has swollen inside the cradle of my scalp. A fog rolls in. My capacity to juggle a number of thoughts at once, an ability most people take for granted, dwindles. It alarms me when this happens, when my brain gives way.

I have it easy compared to some people. I know people who suffer seizures when exposed to chemicals. Closed airways, joint and muscle pain, nausea, insomnia, disabling fatigue. Panic attacks, mood swings. I know people who could never hazard the bad air on planes. Some of them live in ceramic trailers in the deserts of Arizona. Some of them are homeless; they live in their cars or tents. They can't find anyplace safe to breathe. They can't find habitat.

We call ourselves "canaries in the coal mine." We have multiple-chemical sensitivity, and our numbers are growing.

BUTTERFLY TOWN, USA

Everywhere, all over the little town of Pacific Grove, population 15,522, there are butterflies. And not only the real live fluttering kind: There's a monarch emblem in bas-relief on the Chamber of Commerce plaque hanging at the Butterfly Grove Inn; there are twenty-two wooden monarchs of various sizes adorning the town's Shell station; even the bakery's cookies come in the shape of monarch butterflies. This place, this magical little place, is indeed Butterfly Town, USA.

I did not know, when I was nine years old, that it would come to this. I didn't know that the magic would stay with me, all these thirty odd years. That I would fly across the country to see the monarchs. That I would finally—or ever—get to see the overwintering monarchs clinging together in their clusters of thousands.

TORPOR

When the monarchs hang clustered together, paralyzed by the cold, that is called "torpor." They are clasped to each other, holding the heat between them. They wait for the sun to warm them. You wouldn't know they are so beautiful, hanging in the trees like dead leaves. Wings closed, their brilliance is disguised. They wait for the mercury to hit fifty-five degrees, and then they open their orange wings to the sun. Some of them flutter aloft; others stay together, warm and close in their safe clusters. They cleave to each other like family, like best friends, like a community.

The earliest record of the monarchs in Pacific Grove dates back to 1875, the year the town was established as a Methodist resort, when several hundred people first assembled there in worship. But as far as anybody knows, monarchs have been migrating to Pacific Grove for thousands of years. It is their home.

As recently as 1997, there were 45,000 monarchs overwintering in a little 2.7-acre grove of eucalyptus trees behind the Butterfly Grove Inn. When I am there in early January 2008, however, we count only 4,000. It is a bad year for monarchs.

In fact, annual counts show the monarch populations all over California in a rapid downward spiral. What is happening to the monarchs? Why are their numbers plummeting?

THE BUTTERFLY LADY

In 1987, Ro Vaccaro was a high-powered secretary at a high-powered law firm in Washington, D.C. She could type 130 words a minute. She typed for four lawyers and answered the phone for nine. She made a good living.

But four years earlier, Ro had been diagnosed with lupus, and her symptoms—joint pain, sensitivity to touch and depression, to name a few—were flaring. It had gotten so bad she had to wear braces on one arm and one leg to get around, to keep going. The stress was aggravating her symptoms. She worked in a twelve-story building, and she was thinking of jumping off it.

One day, her sister Beverly called. Beverly knew how butterflies buoyed her sister. Twelve years earlier, at an estate auction, Ro had found her first butterfly—in the shape of a beautiful, jeweled pin. She was in the middle of a divorce at the time, and she told Beverly, "I feel better just holding it." In that moment, Ro Vaccaro was transformed.

So when Beverly learned of the Pacific Grove monarchs, she called her sister and suggested they make a pilgrimage.

That October, the sisters found themselves celebrating the butterflies' return with the rest of the town at its annual Butterfly Parade, a Pacific Grove tradition since 1939. There were all the kindergarteners decked out in their bright orange monarch wings. There were all the town's children dressed in costume, marching down Lighthouse Road. There were the school marching bands, the baton twirlers. Monarch cookies! Monarch cinnamon rolls! There were all the happy people, celebrating the return of the monarchs.

Ro was touched by the magic. She knew she needed to come back to this place.

A year later, she did just that. And when she looked up into the butterfly trees, she told her sister it was like a cathedral. Later, she wrote, "They are nature's stained-glass windows, flying high between us and the sun."

She found a job there and took a ten thousand dollar cut in pay. Appointing herself Pacific Grove's first butterfly docent, she joined a small cluster of monarch aficionados, and, together, they organized Friends of the Monarchs, an education and advocacy group. Many years later, one February, she told a National Public Radio (NPR) reporter her story:

I surprised even myself by sending my letter of resignation by Federal Express. I said, 'Consider my two-week vacation your two-week notice. I'm moving to live with the butterflies.' And I did. As you can see, there's no brace on my leg, there's no brace on my arm, and I haven't wiped this silly grin off my face since I got here.

MIGRATION

How do they know where to go? How is it that they trace the same route, the great-great-great-grandchildren, year after year, and end up in the selfsame trees? Scientists have found forty genes that help monarchs use the sun as a compass to guide them to warmer climes. Still, it seems to me there is mystery in it.

It's possible that some of the monarchs I raised as a girl migrated down the coast and all the way to Mexico. East Coast monarchs flock to Mexico by the millions, as they have for thousands of years. Until recently, only the Mexican locals knew about the magnificent "magic circles" where the butterflies overwinter. There, millions of monarchs hang from the oyamel firs—Latin name: *Abies religiosa.*

They fly about twelve miles per hour, forty-six miles a day and as high as 11,000 feet. They migrate as far as 2,200 miles. In early November, millions of monarchs stream into Mexico.

On Nov. 2, my birthday, Mexicans celebrate "Día de los Muertos," Day of the Dead, honoring friends and relatives who have passed on. In Michoacán, where the monarchs come to roost, the locals say the spirits of their beloved return in the shape of bright, fluttering butterflies.

The locals call the butterflies *las palomas*, which translates as "the doves" or, according to Robert Pyle in "Chasing Monarchs," as "the souls of lost children."

DIAPAUSE

There are approximately two hundred roosting sites along the coast of California. None of them attracts the millions of monarchs that the Mexican sites see. One or two may count as many as one hundred thousand in a good year. Pacific Grove averages twenty thousand. The monarchs cluster there for five months, arriving in time to be fêted at the annual butterfly parade, then mating and departing around Valentine's Day. These butterflies live as long as eight months, much longer than the summer generations, which enjoy the bright flowers and summer breezes for a mere two to six weeks. They are in a state of diapause, these migrating monarchs: Their reproductive functions are switched off. They are conserving their energy. They are waiting for the right moment.

Around Valentine's Day, as milkweed starts poking through the earth north and east of Pacific Grove, something changes in the small enclave where the monarchs have spent the winter. The butterflies come to life. There's energy in the air.

Here is how Ro Vaccaro, the Butterfly Lady, described it on the Valentine's Day 2005 NPR broadcast:

They chase in spirals up into the sky, and there are chases going on all over the grove as the male butterflies try to choose their Valentine sweethearts. And when he finds the girl that he thinks would be just perfect, he zooms in front of her, and he sprinkles her with this wonderful perfume, and she is just dazzled. And he grabs her in midair with his feet, and so, like a little maple seed, they come twirling down out of the sky. He strokes her body, and then he puts his head right down next to hers, and it looks just like he's whispering sweet things in her ear. But he's going to trick her. He stands on his head and flips her, and if he does it correctly, he'll have the abdomens aligned, which is the only way he can make the connection. Then she becomes very docile, and she folds her wings together. He runs two or three steps. He lifts her up underneath his body, and he carries her all the way up to the top of the trees where they'll be the warmest, and they'll stay together till the sun comes up the next morning.

CHRYSALIS

One day this past summer, at the park where I take my dog, I spotted a monarch fluttering around a milkweed plant. I stopped and watched. The butterfly dropped down to the top leaf, touched the tip of her abdomen to it and then flew off. I bent over the leaf and beheld something I had never seen in all my years of monarchs: an egg, gleaming like a small gem.

The butterflies lay them one at a time—four hundred in all—on milkweed all along the migration route north. They mate repeatedly. Each egg is sired by the female's most recent mate. Each is fertilized only when she deposits it on a milk-weed leaf. Only milkweed. Nothing else will do.

When the caterpillar hatches, three to seven days later, it is two millimeters long. Tiny. Its first meal is the egg it comes from. Then, the fine, hairlike filaments of the milkweed. Finally, as soon as it is large enough, it begins its leaf-feast. It eats and eats. It's as though the monarch caterpillar was born to eat. It grows two inches in two weeks, fattens to 2,700 times its birth weight. It outgrows its skin four or five times and molts to accommodate its expanding girth.

And then, one day, it is time. Who knows how the caterpillar decides? It attaches a little silk fastener to the underside of a leaf. It pierces the silk with its "cremaster"—a small, hooklike appendage at the end of its body—and wriggles hard to make sure the connection will hold. It hangs . . . still . . . in the shape of a J, and then, when the moment is right, it splits the skin on its back, miraculously transforming itself into an emerald green chrysalis with a crown of gold.

MYSTERY

What happens inside a chrysalis?

One day, I decided to find out. Nine years old and aching with curiosity, I took one of my chrysalides to the side of the house and set it down on a large rock. I held it gently with my thumb and forefinger as I cut into it with my jackknife.

No butterfly, no caterpillar: just black ooze.

I'd made black ooze out of something that could have become a butterfly.

What I didn't know, what I was trying to find out, was what Kathryn Lasky describes in her lovely little book, *Monarchs*: "The body of the caterpillar melts away into a solution of transforming cells and tissues."

Something magical happens inside.

ECLOSION

It hangs, this gem of nature, for nine to fifteen days. When it is almost ready, the "imago," or butterfly, can be seen in outline.

The orange wing, the black veins, the white spots—they darken. The chrysalis is now translucent.

Finally, one day, in one small moment, the butterfly breathes. Its intake of air splits the chrysalis open. This is called "eclosion," when the butterfly emerges from its chrysalis. It hangs there, stunned, perhaps, by its new form. The world looks different through its new eyes. Its abdomen is fat with hemolymph, which it pumps through the veins into its wings.

FLIGHT

A nine-year-old girl is closer to the ground. She sees things up close. She watches. She waits for miracles to happen. And sometimes, when she is really lucky, she witnesses one with her very own eyes. The chrysalis cracks open. The monarch, fat and wet and crumpled, bursts into the world.

A nine-year-old girl takes the time to lie down on the burnt orange rug in her parents' living room, holding the new monarch on her finger above her. It clings to her. It hangs, drying. Her arm gets tired, but still, she holds the butterfly aloft. She wants to watch its wings unfurl. She wants to see its abdomen slim. She wants to watch it get strong.

When it starts to open and close its wings, it is almost ready for flight. The girl stands up. The butterfly clings to her hand. Carefully, gently, she walks out of the living room, pushes the screen door open, carries her monarch to the middle of her weedless, grassy yard. She holds her hand out to the sky.

She expects the monarch to fly away in an instant, glad to be set free. But it clings to her hand for a long time, opening and closing its wings, waiting. And then, suddenly, it lets go. It lifts itself up into the blue sky and flutters off into the distance and out of sight, leaving the girl down below with her hand over her brow, shielding her eyes from the sun.

MICROCLIMATE

Ro Vaccaro decided the butterflies needed an advocate. So, she began showing up at city council meetings, using the three-minute public comment period to talk about the butterflies.

Soon, everybody was calling her the "Butterfly Lady." It was here, at these meetings, that she first laid eyes on Mrs. Edna Dively, the woman who owned the Butterfly Grove Inn and the land beside it—the magical place where the monarchs roosted every year. Mrs. Dively was fighting for permission to develop her property. She wanted to build houses and an apartment building. And one day in 1989, the city granted her wish.

Mrs. Dively swore that she had no intent to take down the butterfly trees, that she would build around them. But Ro Vaccaro was dubious. Any change in the microclimate might make the monarchs decide the grove was no longer fit for their needs.

So Ro Vaccaro set about to stop Mrs. Dively.

CHRYSALIDES

I can't help it. When I see milkweed, I look for monarch caterpillars. And when I find them, my heart leaps with that familiar joy and excitement, and the impulse to take them home is too strong to deny. One year, long before I flew to California to see the monarchs, I found three caterpillars in the park and brought them home. Despite all my best intentions, I killed every one. Each died in a different stage of metamorphosis. The first, a caterpillar, got sluggish and simply stopped eating. The second died with only a little triangle of green on its back where the splitting had begun. I found it, finally, hanging vertically, its J depleted: done. It simply didn't have the strength to complete the transformation. The last died in chrysalis. It simply turned black. No orange of the wings, just black, and finally, I gave up waiting and took it outside, laid it in a pile of brush.

The next year, I found two caterpillars munching away on separate leaves of the same milkweed. My heart leapt. Then I hesitated. What if I had become, somehow, an angel of death for monarchs? I should not take these caterpillars, I thought. But.

I uprooted the entire milkweed and brought it, and them, home.

What could it be? What was killing my monarchs? Was it my loss of innocence—the simple fact of my adulthood—that left me incapable of supporting the magic to completion? Or was it something more sinister?

I built a screened cage for them. I avoided city milkweed. I doted. A few days later, both caterpillars hung themselves in J's and turned into green chrysalides. I waited. I waited.

And once again, the chrysalides turned black.

MEMORABILIA

She saved monarch memorabilia the way a mother saves all of her firstborn's artwork and school assignments. Boxes and boxes of letters, handouts and newspaper clippings. If it had to do with the monarchs of Pacific Grove, Ro Vaccaro put it in a box and kept it.

"I wear a butterfly every day, at least somewhere—but usually multiple butterflies," she told the NPR reporter. "I have a butterfly watch, butterfly earrings, butterflies on my shoes and socks."

She had monarchs on her hat, monarch pins, and buttons and patches on her coat. She decorated her house with them. The walls, the pillows, the rugs, the shower curtain. And she blazoned her car with bumper stickers about saving them.

Ro Vaccaro, the Butterfly Lady of Pacific Grove, lived and breathed monarch butterflies.

BREATHING

My other mask—my special occasion mask—is a flowery, lacy affair, skin-toned, with a little rose appliqué by its left strap. Feminine. Or as feminine as a fume-deterring mask can be.

It's not any better, really, this flowery, lacy mask. What I really want is a mask bearing an appliquéd symbol that stands for "your toxic products are making me sick." It would be nice if the symbol could point out, too, that 62,000 chemicals used in the United States have never been tested for safety. That we are human guinea pigs. That while we think our government would surely protect us from egregious toxins, we are wrong.

But what would that symbol look like?

If I have to wear something that makes me stand out in a crowd, I'd rather it not be something that stands for "crazy" (think Michael Jackson) or "communicable" (think SARS). I want people to know that this mask isn't about me so much as it is about us.

THE BUTTERFLY GROVE INN

The Butterfly Grove Inn is a pink motel nestled right next to the stand of eucalyptus trees where the monarchs have been overwintering for generations. In the lobby, someone has cut out a newspaper article about the monarchs and posted it on Bristol board next to the front desk. There are butterfly pins and postcards for sale. I buy an extra-long postcard depicting, in five photographs, the stages of metamorphosis. I have arrived at dusk, too late to find the monarchs.

I have always loved motels. The thrill of opening the door. Fresh space. But my love for an empty motel room comes fraught, now, with doubt and anxiety. Will the room be safe? Or will it be toxic?

I swing the door open and take a whiff. Inside, the walls are painted beige, and framed photo prints of waterfalls hang over the two beds. The room smells fresh at first sniff. But is that chemical fresh or clean-air fresh?

I drag my big suitcase through the door. Inside my head, the alarms begin to sound. Get out! Get out! The air is not good. But I have paid to stay the night at the Butterfly Grove Inn. There's nothing to do but open the window and let in the cold, clean air. The room is frigid. I put an extra blanket on the bed. The brain fog rolls in; the glands in my throat swell; I'm rubbing my eyes. The headache is on its way. Cleaning products, must be.

THE BUTTERFLY EFFECT

In the 1960s, meteorologist Edward Lorenz made a discovery that would change the way we view the world. He found that even minute discrepancies between two starting points could produce vastly disparate outcomes. For instance, if a little boy took two identical balls to the top of a hill and released one just a fraction of an inch away from where he let go of the other, they would probably end up in two very different places. The scientific term for this was "sensitive dependence on initial conditions." More poetically, it came to be known as "the Butterfly Effect," and Lorenz suggested the possibility that something so seemingly innocuous as the flap of a butterfly's wings in Brazil could create changes in the atmosphere leading to something as momentous as a tornado in Texas.

What happens, then, when there are no butterflies left?

MONSANTO

Almost fifty percent of this country's landmass is cultivated for agricultural purposes. Not so long ago, Midwestern corn and soybean fields furnished about half of the breeding grounds for the Eastern monarchs. No longer. Now, thanks to crops made "Roundup Ready" by genetic-engineering monolith Monsanto, one hundred million acres of monarch habitat have been annihilated; milkweed has been virtually extirpated from American farmland.

Roundup, advertised on TV in mock-Old-West-style, with suburban "cowboys" wielding Roundup "guns" while a little boy rides past them on a bicycle, is the herbicide of choice not only for homeowners and public works departments, but also for farmers. "Roundup Ready" crops can withstand heavy doses of the herbicide, which kills most every plant it touches, including milkweed.

Over eighteen million pounds of glyphosate—Roundup's active ingredient—are sprayed annually on U.S. crops, sidewalks and yards. The "clean field" ideal of industrial monoculture farming—no weeds, no insects and no diseases, thanks to insecticides, herbicides, and genetically engineered crops— is wiping out the monarch caterpillar's only food source.

GLOBAL WARMING

California is heating up. Most areas in the country, in fact, are getting hotter. Insect ecologist Dr. Orley R. "Chip" Taylor, director of Monarch Watch—an educational outreach program whose mission is to create, conserve, and protect monarch habitats—has demonstrated a correlation between rising temperatures in California and lower West Coast monarch populations.

Taylor reports that monarch numbers crash every time temperatures above 90 degrees combine with low water availability for a week or more. The hotter it gets, the shorter the lifespan of flowers, so nectar is less available. And while the need for water increases in hot weather, availability decreases. So monarch butterflies don't live as long in the heat, and they lay fewer eggs. This is called "decreased realized fecundity," and what it means is that populations take a nosedive.

Temperatures have increased 1.4 degrees Fahrenheit; nine of the ten warmest years on record occurred in the last decade. Precipitation has declined 0.25 inches per decade.

I feel a weight in the pit of my stomach when I read these numbers.

DEFORESTATION

In 1976, a National Geographic article revealed, for the first time, the location of the East Coast monarchs' Mexican hideaway. All of the East Coast monarchs, millions and millions of them, flock to the oyamel firs and other trees in seven to twelve sites (depending on the year), spread across the state of Michoacán's Transvolcanic Mountains. But there is a problem: logging. Although 217 square miles of these mountains are now a designated Monarch Butterfly Biosphere Reserve (MBBR) and protected by government decree, still, at a rate of two percent to five percent a year, the trees keep coming down.

Illegal logging strips away the butterflies' particular roost trees; it also puts gashes in the forest canopy. As Chip Taylor describes it, "These gaps are like holes in your winter coat, as far as the monarchs are concerned. They let in snow and rain, and the roosting monarchs are more vulnerable to freezing." In 2002, millions of monarchs froze and dropped to the ground. Witnesses described wading through dead monarchs, knee deep.

Shortly after he took office in December 2006, Mexico's new president, Felipe Calderón, promised to protect the MBBR, and in December 2007, the government conducted what amounted to the largest illegal-logging sweep ever seen in the vicinity of the Reserve. Nineteen sawmills and lumberyards were raided, and at least forty-five people were arrested and charged. Logs and lumber from as many as 1,750 trees were confiscated.

Of course, those trees could not be taken back to the forest. And although the World Wildlife Fund in Mexico and the Michoacán Reforestation Fund have planted a combined total of more than 4.8 million trees over the past ten years, even these aren't enough to keep up with the rate of deforestation.

HABITAT

Every day in the United States, new subdivisions, malls, condominiums, and parking lots consume six thousand acres of natural habitat. This adds up to 2.2 million acres per year. At this rate, an area of habitat the size of Illinois is razed, then paved, every sixteen years.

Soon, the butterflies will have nowhere to land.

WAYSTATIONS

Chip Taylor had an idea. It was a simple idea, really: If enough people would create waystations in their backyards or on their rooftops, then perhaps, despite the clear-cutting and the Roundup and the development, the monarch migration—one of the great natural phenomena of the world—might be saved.

The Monarch Waystation Program encourages people all over the country to create garden sanctuaries to sustain breeding and migrating monarchs. Monarch Watch sends starter kits that include seeds for six kinds of milkweed and six nectar plants favored by the butterflies. The nonprofit's Web site, http://www.monarchwatch.org, also lists noninvasive milkweed-host varieties, as well as monarch nectar plants, including tithonia, cosmos, and echinacea. Butterfly gardeners can register their waystations online and even order a weatherproof sign identifying their habitats as official Monarch Waystations.

Since the program was introduced in 2005, more than four thousand Monarch Waystations have been registered.

"Loss of habitat is pinching all species," says Taylor. "It's hard to figure out how to help the larger species, but for the butterflies, there is something we can do. The individual citizen can do a lot."

PETITION

She rallied the schoolchildren—that's what Ro Vacarro did. She went into the schools and told the children about Mrs. Dively and the houses she wanted to build on the monarchs' land. She handed out petitions and urged the children to take them door to door and get signatures. The Friends of the Monarchs also canvassed the town. They needed six thousand signatures to get it—a resolution to stop the development, buy the land, and grant permanent sanctuary to the monarchs—on the ballot.

And sure enough, one day, Ro Vaccaro strode into the town hall, bearing her pages of signatures. Next, she had to write a ballot bond and convince Pacific Grove's voters to pass it.

So the Friends of the Monarchs marched in that year's annual Butterfly Parade, handing out "Vote Yes" flyers. Scholastic Review got wind of the butterflies' plight and published a cover story about it, and students from all over the country sent letters in support of the monarchs. The story ran on the "CBS Evening News" and in *The Wall Street Journal* and *The New York Times*.

In the end, the citizens of Pacific Grove voted to raise their own taxes. For what amounted to about $30 per person, per year, they purchased the $1.2 million plot of land.

Years later, Ro's sister said, "The monarchs saved her. She was just returning the favor."

CONVALESCENT

Her last two years as a docent at the sanctuary, the Butterfly Lady used a walker.

Finally, her body could no longer hold her. On top of lupus, diabetes, fibromyalgia, and emphysema, Ro had contracted lymphoma. She had no choice but to move into a convalescent home.

That is where she was living when I first made contact with her friend Sharon Blaziek, head docent at the monarch sanctuary. Sharon told me Ro was in good spirits and would probably be delighted to do an interview once I got to Pacific Grove. I wrote Ro a letter, sent it by U.S. mail, told her I was on my way.

"LUPUS ERYTHEMATOSUS"

The first part of the name, "lupus," derives from the Latin for "wolf"; the second part, "erythematosus," refers to the red rash that is a frequent symptom of the illness. This is also known as the "butterfly rash," so called because it spreads across the bridge of the nose and over the cheeks in the shape of a butterfly's open wings. For obvious reasons, Ro Vaccaro preferred the latter designation.

One day, at the convalescent home, she rolled up her sleeve and showed her sister a bruise. It was 2 inches wide and in the shape of a butterfly. "I'm so gung ho," she said, "even my bruises come out like butterflies."

MONARCH MADNESS

Nothing could stop Ro from joining the festivities at the annual "Monarch Madness" family fun day. That November, she secured an all-day pass from the nursing home. She refused to miss a moment of the fun—the butterfly storyteller, the 5 M's band ("Mostly Mediocre Musical Monarch Mariposas") singing butterfly lyrics to the songs of the '60s and '70s, the craft table and face painting, the monarch caterpillars and chrysalides on display, the milkweed seeds for sale.

She refused a chair. She stood all day—happy, talking butterflies.

E-MAIL

Four days before I was to meet Ro Vaccaro, I got an e-mail from her friend Sharon Blaziek. Ro had died.

I slumped in my chair. The Butterfly Lady was gone.

TAGGING MONARCHS

To tag a butterfly, you must first grasp it between your fingers, making sure you have a snug hold of the closed forewings as well as the hindwings. You hold the butterfly in your left hand, with the abdomen toward you. Your partner hands you a tiny, round sticker preprinted with a phone number and an ID. You place the tag on the underside of the right hindwing. You look for the small black dot of the scent gland that is in the vein of only the male's hindwing, and you report the sex to your partner, who writes it down on the log. You note any damage to the wing, and she jots that down, too. Then you put the tagged butterfly in a paper bag and wait for the sun to rise above the trees.

I have arranged with Jessica Griffiths, wildlife biologist for California's Ventana Wildlife Society—a nonprofit whose mission is to conserve native wildlife and their habitats—to spend the morning after my arrival with a handful of other volunteers who will count and tag monarchs in the Pacific Grove Monarch Sanctuary. As a kid, I had dreamed of tagging my monarchs and releasing them so that when they fluttered around the house, I would know they were mine, and when they flew away for good, I would maybe someday know where they had gone.

At 8:00 a.m., I open the door to my room and step out into the cold, damp air. It is 48 degrees. It feels colder. I walk around the corner to the sanctuary walkway and hang a right. Most of the trees in the grove are eucalyptus trees, and their scent hangs heavy and rich in the air. I look up into the trees, searching for clusters. I have been told it is a bad year for monarchs. I see one cluster, two. There they are, way up in the highest branches, hanging quietly, waiting for the warmth to come.

A small knot of people stands watching as Jessica and an intern reach high up into the trees, using an unwieldy eighht-meter telescoping pole with an attached net, collecting the torpid butterflies. Jessica is bundled up in a knit hat, a scarf and black mittens with pink butterflies on them. I introduce myself, and she pairs me up with Irene—a sanctuary docent for the past eleven years—and puts me to work. Irene and I are sitting on lawn chairs, and there is a paper bag between us. Inside are the sleepy butterflies.

When the thermometer hits the magical 55 degrees, some of the monarchs high up in the trees liberate themselves from their clusters and flutter around against the blue palette of the sky. Jessica gathers the bags of tagged butterflies and steps off the walkway. One by one, she picks the monarchs up by the wings and tosses them into the sky.

SANCTUARY

On Feb. 10, 2008, in a private nook of the monarch sanctuary, in the place that Ro Vaccaro had always described as a cathedral, a small cluster of people, about thirty in all, gathered to pay their last respects to the Butterfly Lady. It was a warm, sunny day, and the monarchs, just heading into their breeding season, were preparing to take off and head north to Canada and east to Idaho, Nevada, Utah, Arizona.

As Sharon Blaziek read the memorial tribute to her friend, orange and black monarchs lit from the surrounding trees and fluttered and soared behind her for everyone to see.

Ro Vaccaro was a good Christian woman, but she had confided to her sister that she hoped to be reincarnated as a monarch.

"I told her to make sure it's in September," said Beverly, "so she can come here and tell these monarchs about the people."

FRESH PAINT

My bags are checked, and I'm waiting for my flight home when a sharp taint suddenly permeates my consciousness. I turn around. Forty feet away, the maintenance man is painting, in vivid royal blue, the doorway to the jet-bridge. The headache starts behind my eyes. My brain fogs in.

I pick up my bags and lug them as far from the paint as I can get. But the fumes are everywhere. I stand up, look for somewhere to go. A little Japanese girl toddles up to me and grabs my legs in a bear hug. I can't get away. There is nowhere to go.

SUSURRUS

It is magic, this orange fluttering, this quiet fluttering. It is peaceful. Free. Surely, even the most cynical can't help but feel it, watching. One finds oneself breathing deeply, from the belly, in the presence of it.

"A soft whispering or rustling sound: a murmur or whisper"—that is the dictionary definition of *susurrus*. It is the word used by entomologists to describe the sound of hundreds, thousands, millions of butterfly wings, suddenly bursting into flight.

JENNIFER LUNDEN is a mental health counselor and the founder and executive director of The Center for Creative Healing in Portland, Maine. Her creative nonfiction has been published in *Orion* and *The Yale Journal for Humanities in Medicine*. A piece of short "fiction" appears in *Wigleaf*. Twice a Maine Literary Awards finalist and once Maine's Social Worker of the Year, she is at work on a book that goes by the same title as her blog: *One Canary Sings: Notes from an Industrialized Body*. She and her husband, the artist Frank Turek, live in a little house in the city, where they keep six chickens, three cats, and a Great Dane named Mabel.

Jennifer Lunden on "The Butterfly Effect"

When I was in college in the late 1980s, every attempt I made at fiction was really memoir in disguise. At the time, there were only two tracks a writing student could pursue: fiction or poetry. I want to say that creative nonfiction hadn't even been invented yet, but of course that's not really true. As far as I knew, though, no such genre existed, and I kept writing "fiction" and failing. I failed for another reason, too: Each story I wrote had a problem with narrative flow. I just couldn't seem to write anything but sequences of episodes strung together in a way that, to me, seemed herky-jerky. The stories just didn't hold together.

And then in 1989 I fell ill and didn't write much at all until I picked up the pen a decade later to start telling the story of my illness. I was like the Rip Van Winkle of writers, asleep for many years—and when I awoke, the entire literary landscape had changed. Suddenly, in this new genre called "creative nonfiction," there was a place for the kind of writing I had never been able to stop myself from doing. I could write the truth of my own experience, I could write in fragments, and I didn't have to make it flow. Although I wasn't aware of it at the time I wrote "The Butterfly Effect," this approach even had a name: the lyric essay.

I didn't know at first that my winter escape to California would become an essay about butterflies. But as I planned for my trip, it dawned on me that I would be there at the same time as the overwintering monarchs. I had learned of their phenomenal migration as a girl, and had always yearned to witness thousands of them all in one place. I Googled some configuration of "monarchs" and "California" and "overwintering," and my heart leapt at the bounty. That is how I came to know of Butterfly Town, USA, and that is how I came to hear the Butterfly Lady on NPR.

John Muir, the naturalist who founded the Sierra Club, said, "When we tug at a single thing in nature, we find it attached to the rest of the world." As I sat there at my computer clicking link after link, I learned that the monarchs were in decline, that they faced a mysterious threat. I decided to write about them. Intuitively, their story and mine seemed linked.

I see my body as an ecosystem, and as a microcosm of the larger ecosystem of our planet. I thought people might be tempted to flip past an essay about multiple chemical sensitivity and its dreary implications . . . but who wouldn't want to read about butterflies? I believed the beauty and lyricism of the monarchs would make my message more palatable.

In order to get readers to pay attention to difficult information, we writers have to give them beauty, or something else their hearts can latch on to.

"The Butterfly Effect" was rejected by several journals before winning the *Creative Nonfiction* Robert Fragasso Animal Advocate Award in 2011, and then going on to win a Pushcart Prize. It was my first major publication.

CHARGING LIONS

Chester F. Phillips

*To the rancher, I wish you could respect
the cat a bit more. Your habitats are the same.
You could seek extinction together.*

—Harley Shaw, "Soul Among Lions"

NIGHT CORRAL

"Wake up," Debbie shouted. "I think a lion's got Dutchess's calf."

I bolted awake, sitting up in bed, disoriented. On warm nights, we slept with the windows open, and I heard the shrill bellowing that was Dutchess's most distinctive characteristic, just as it was her mother's. When you spend every day for years getting to know any creatures, human or otherwise, you come to know such things: the differences of vocal inflection; calm or skittish or aggressive temperaments; degrees of adventurousness versus maternal instinct; intelligence and guile; the willingness to walk a long way. . . .

From the corral, the calls sounded again and again—loud, deranged by worry, a desperate mother's cries of distress.

UNINVITED GUESTS

When they first showed up in the spring of 1998, the raccoons were cute, a mother and three young ones that discovered the dry cat food I left on the upstairs porch of the single-room second story we used as a bedroom during the cooler months of the year. I put the cat food out for Ramble, a feral cat who'd been hanging around for a while, sleeping in a tree near our bedroom window. I'd decided to adopt him and was gradually winning him over.

When the raccoons arrived, after dark, they would climb a mesquite tree on the other side of the house, the mother first, followed by a line of three adolescents. They would scratch and skitter across the tin roof and climb down onto the upstairs porch to the cat food dish. Debbie and I would hear them on the roof and creep upstairs, crawling slowly across the wood floor until we crouched below the eastern window. Then we peered out at the four raccoons as they stood around the cat dishes, picking out single kibbles of food and dipping them in the cat's water bowl before eating. They reminded us of people standing around a tray of chips and dip at a party. Except for the clattering noise they made on the roof at night while we tried to sleep, we didn't object. They kept coming, their visits growing more and more frequent until they were a nightly occurrence.

COWS ARE PEOPLE, TOO

The first year we lived in Cascabel, our ranching mentors, Jim and Pat Corbett, had a saying they taught us—two middle-class, young-20s dropouts from strip-mall society, who showed up, with big dreams and no money, to live in a dirt-road rural community on the San Pedro River in southern Arizona. "Cows are people, too," they said. It was meant to be a little funny, but not a joke. Jim explained to us his belief that many people act autistic when relating to animals, especially to livestock in production agricultural systems, behaving as though there is no "other" there, no one observing and responding. I had read Jewish philosopher Martin Buber's *I and Thou* and found Jim's conceptualization similar but more expansive. Buber believed that healthy relations with the rest of the world come through dialogical engagements: "I" engages with any other creature as a "thou," who acts and reacts dynamically with "I," rather than merely being an object "I" manipulates according to his will. Any authentic I-Thou relationship, according to Buber, is also a portal into a relationship with God, the spirit or force that runs through all beings. Jim extended Buber's language-based philosophy to include all forms of communication, which for humans and cows means mostly body language—subtle angles of approach and gestures learned from watching the cows interact with each other.

Jim was not anyone's image of a classic Western cowboy: He had a floppy white canvas hat; solid-colored, sweat-stained shirts, partly unbuttoned and hanging loosely over his jeans and gaunt frame; a trimmed gray "Man of La Mancha" goatee; and black Teva sandals because no other shoes fit his feet. His fingers and toes were like claws, curled over one another by rheumatoid arthritis, a condition that bent and gnarled his body but could not touch his ironwood will.

I remember first watching Jim approach cows on the range back when Debbie and I, who had not grown up ranching, still felt cautious about relating to such large and powerful creatures. He would speak softly when he got within hearing distance. He made a soft, guttural sound in greeting and approached from the side, not head-on, because cows' eyes are on the sides of their heads and they regard a head-on approach as an aggressive challenge that invites a butting of heads. Jim would approach from the side and raise his hand to the cow's muzzle when he reached her, letting her take in his scent and recognize him. Often, the cows stretched out their necks so he could scratch their dewlaps, the sensitive skin below their necks. He moved among them with ease and obvious pleasure, as though they were his people and he was theirs.

I remember when Jim introduced us to his red and white, half-Jersey milk cow, Red, and showed us how to milk by hand. He used no milking stall, neither rope nor hobbles on Red's feet to keep her from kicking. He just led us into the pasture where he had a small pen in which he could put Red to exclude other cows. He gave her a bucket of alfalfa pellets, squatted on the ground with a large stainless steel pot to catch the milk and went to it, his twisted hands stroking Red's teats from the base to the tip, pulling out the milk with pressure applied between his thumb and forefinger, the only way his hands could grasp.

He crouched, tilting forward so that his head rested against Red's udder just in front of her hind leg.

"She has to accept you as one of her calves," Jim said, without looking up. It was simple and obvious to him.

To us, it was revelatory, and Jim was beautiful. Debbie and I quickly came to love Jim for living out the practices that others might have seen as only disembodied words.

Cows were people—sentient beings in a sentient world. Even good stewardship was not enough. To Jim, stewardship still implied domination, however benign. In northern Louisiana, I had watched my maternal grandfather work cattle by scaring them into a corral or a trailer. They were no more real beings to him than the tractors he rode—just obstinate, frustrating tools that resisted his will. I observed the same thing when helping to vaccinate a few hundred cattle on a more mainstream ranch in Cascabel in exchange for pregnancy-checking lessons.

I believe Jim had it right. Much of the nightmare of animal factory-farming stems from a systematic refusal to treat animals like feeling, thinking creatures, a refusal essential to the system's continuation. To find sentience in them would make clear what battery cages and jam-packed feedlots really are: sites of carefully organized mass enslavement. I objected not to ranching itself, nor even to the slaughter, but to the process of subjection: the subjection of land, of animals and of the people who came up from Mexico to work long hours as hirelings building fence or bullying cattle, not only alienated from the products of their labor but also cut off from membership in the greater community. Jim replaced subjection with what he called "land redemption" and the "symbiotic integration" of humans into the desert ecosystem. The cow became both companion and source of nutrition. Desert bunch grasses and forbs could not directly become part of human tissues. Intermediating between us and the desert, cows were alchemists transmuting grasses and forbs into milk and meat, and the alienated man and woman into participants in a vast communion.

MELON THIEVES

For a few months, the raccoon family seemed happy with cat food, and I decided it wasn't a bad trade in exchange for keeping the hens alive. Since Ramble usually left quite a bit of food in his bowl at night, I decreased the amount I put out each morning so that Ramble ate most of it during the day and only a little remained for the raccoons to clean up at night. But one night in early summer, they took a chicken anyway. A few weeks later, they took another. The second time, Debbie and I rushed outside when we heard the chicken's death squawk—an eerie, sharp cry that sounds like no other noise chickens make. We got there in time to see two of the younger raccoons, not yet full grown, escaping into the mesquite bosque. One of them clutched a red hen in its mouth.

In April, we planted cantaloupes and watermelons in two of our sunken bed gardens. By July, the plants were fruiting, and we watched the small melons grow with great anticipation. Cool, sweet melon slices from the refrigerator were a favorite summer snack after hours spent working in the grueling heat. We harvested one cantaloupe too soon, paying for our impatience by eating it even though it wasn't much sweeter than a cucumber. So we waited and let them ripen.

One morning, Debbie walked into the kitchen, holding a small, dark green watermelon. It was perfect, except that a large hole had been gnawed into it and small ants swarmed in the hole.

"Hurry up and look before the ants get all over my hands," Debbie said with a frustrated grimace. "There's another one outside just like it."

A few nights later, I spied one of the young raccoons as it slipped into the melon patch, and I charged out the door, yelling as the raccoon ran away, though it had already ruined another melon.

EARLY LESSONS IN LIVESTOCK HUSBANDRY

Our practice with heifers, young cows that have never

delivered a calf, was to corral them so we could check on them throughout the day and night as they got close to calving. It was the way Saguaro Juniper Corporation, the collectively owned ranch and integrative living project that Jim cofounded, approached everything, placing ultimate value on the welfare of the animals and the land, however labor-intensive the methods.

Calving problems could occur with any animal, but heifers experienced them by far the most frequently. We'd learned this the hard way. In 1997, during our first year tending cattle, we lost the first calf we delivered. It had one front leg curled under it, and we couldn't get the other one out before the calf suffocated in the birth canal. Following Jim's instructions after a short, urgent phone call, I stuck my hand inside the heifer to try to unfold the leg. I could not. The following year, the mother, named Henna for the dark red highlights in her mostly black hair, came up infertile. She would come into heat, be bred and then come into heat again several weeks later. Vibriosis, an infectious bacterial disease that causes spontaneous abortion and infertility, was the likeliest cause, but I always wondered whether I'd done something wrong or whether the calf's twisted body itself injured something inside her. She was one of the first three animals we'd bought from Jim and Pat and raised to maturity. She was gentle and trusting and loaded easily into the trailer to be taken to slaughter.

NAKED IN THE NUMINOUS WORLD I

When Dutchess started bawling, it was 2 a.m. on a hot, humid night in late August 2000. The cries came from the barbed-wire corral twenty-five yards from our back door. Dutchess was there because she'd had her first calf a few days earlier. Mother Poll, our oldest cow, was in the corral to keep Dutchess company. The fact that Mother Poll had also sounded the alarm woke up Debbie and assured her that the threat was immediate and very real.

When she woke me, Debbie had already been outside. She stood over me, holding a flashlight and urging me to hurry.

I'd slept in only a T-shirt and started grasping around for the jeans I'd taken off earlier.

"There's no time for that. The lion's got the calf now," Debbie said.

I stopped looking for my jeans and put on the sandals I kept by the bed in case of an emergency.

"How do you know?"

"Something was thrashing around in the graythorn outside the corral. What else could it be?"

My sandals were buckled, and we raced outside. Debbie pointed the flashlight beam toward a clump of graythorn in the mesquite bosque on the south side of the corral. But nothing moved. We walked quickly but cautiously toward the spot where Debbie thought she'd seen something. Nothing again. It was dark, a night with little moonlight, and a quick search of the area around the graythorn clump revealed no clues. There was no calf, no blood, and no lion. Dutchess and Mother Poll still stood bawling and staring out into the black mesquite woodland, and Dutchess's calf was gone. Perhaps I should have gone inside then to throw on more clothes and grab the shotgun.

Instead, we kept looking.

HIRING A HIT MAN

"I don't like to eat anyone I haven't known," Jim would say with a grin when asked to summarize his views on meat-eating. From our long conversations, I knew the age-old pastoralist's dilemma still troubled him, as it troubled me and Debbie: How do you kill and eat creatures you've raised and cared for? I'd heard the story about Jim and Pat deciding to put down the longtime S-J herd bull. Chris had been in the herd for eight or nine years. As he'd aged, he'd grown unpredictable: hard to find and move on the range without endangering the herders, and not always staying close enough to the cows to detect their heats and keep them bred. He'd been brought to Jim and Pat's pasture for the solemn occasion.

Jim wanted to do the killing himself and then participate in the butchering. Chris lowered his huge black head into a black rubber bucket full of alfalfa pellets. As he ate, Jim stood twenty feet away, steeled himself and raised his .22 rifle, the only gun he and Pat owned. Jim took careful aim at the point on the head where one shot is supposed to drop even a bull. If you drew a line from each eye to the opposite ear, the two lines would intersect at the spot. Jim fired.

His aim was close, but the bullet struck Chris's thick skull only hard enough to sting and draw blood. Chris stamped and shook his head back and forth, as if bitten by a horsefly. Then he dipped his head again and continued eating. Jim stood there, visibly shaking. After a long moment, he turned and asked Charlie Thomas, an S-J member and Vietnam vet turned pacifist, to drive several miles back to his house and bring back a high-powered rifle. Jim and the small group of people who'd come to help with the slaughter stood around, shocked and waiting, until Charlie returned.

When the killing was done, Jim, Charlie and the others labored the rest of the day to skin and disembowel the carcass, divide it into manageable pieces, and wrap them in freezer paper. This was one of the stories that deepened my admiration for Jim even further. He did not waver from his principles, however painful they were to carry out. I viewed Chris's slaughter as a bloody but profound ceremony of responsibility and thanksgiving.

Saguaro Juniper rejected entirely the agribusiness model of farming and ranching as an extractive industry, with cows as little bioreactors concentrating range plants into protein, and protein into concentrated wealth. I admired Jim's refusal to become calloused about slaughter. It wasn't supposed to be easy. He called buying meat from the store "hiring a hit man."

TO SEE BY FLASHLIGHT, DARKLY

While Debbie and I searched the outer perimeter of the corral in widening circles, the night erupted again in bellows and dust. The rest of the cattle responded to Dutchess's distress cries by charging in from parts unknown, snorting and calling, with the calves kicking up their heels in excitement. For ten minutes or so, there was no point in looking further. We could hear nothing but cow sounds, and their commotion raised a thick cloud of dust that hung between the mesquite trees, further limiting visibility.

"Any lion that was here is probably long gone," I said, discouraged.

"Yeah, but where's the calf?" Debbie answered. "Did the lion really drag it that fast?"

We stood watching as the cattle milled around the corral for a while and then began trickling back down a cattle trail that wound through a few hundred acres of bosque to the south, where they were eating the newly fallen mesquite bean crop.

"Nothing to see here," I said as they headed out. But Dutchess, panicked and distraught, kept pacing the edge of the corral, calling for her calf.

Maybe twenty minutes had elapsed since we'd left the house. After the herd left camp, the night's quiet was punctuated only by Dutchess, her calls less frequent now as they got no answer.

And then they did.

From somewhere far out in the mesquites came a bleating sound, the calf answering its mother. Once, twice, then no more. I grabbed the flashlight from Debbie's hand and took off running, still naked except for my sandals and maroon T-shirt.

Living a latter-day homesteader's life in Cascabel, I often contemplated the dilemma of being what deep ecologist and philosopher Paul Shepard called "the tender carnivore," one who both cares for and preys upon domestic animals. In addition to taking solace in Jim's philosophy of symbiosis, I sometimes took Barry Lopez's book *Arctic Dreams* from the shelf to find solace in this passage:

No culture has yet solved the dilemma each has faced with the growth of a conscious mind: how to live a moral and compassionate existence when one is fully aware of the blood, the horror inherent in all life; when one finds darkness not only in one's own culture, but within oneself . . . There are simply no answers to some of the great pressing questions. You continue to live them out, making your life a worthy expression of a leaning into the light.

Worthy or not, I was often given opportunities to confront the paradoxes inherent in my relationships with animals. I leaned into and out of the light, my questioning mind dappled by the contradictions of trying to live on and take sustenance from the desert. Debbie and I lived as both guardians and executioners, sometimes on the same day.

NAKED IN THE NUMINOUS WORLD II

Given the thickness of the thorn-scrub understory beneath the mesquites, my run soon slowed to a creep with intermittent pauses to listen for the calf. Debbie had stayed behind. I'm not sure how far away from her I was, but I could not see her. After a few minutes of walking and stopping, I heard it again, a muffled *mmmmhh*. It wasn't far away. I quickened my pace, moving toward the sound. Moments later, I came around a graythorn bush, and my flashlight's beam caught the lion full in the face, its eyes glowing gold in the light. I was far too close.

The lion stood no more than thirty feet away, facing me. It held its head closer to the ground than its shoulders, crouching over its prey. Just beneath the lion's head lay the calf, its throat almost touching the lion's lower jaw. My adrenaline surged with the fear in my throat. Too close, too close. The thought kept ringing in my head.

From the Colorado Department of Natural Resources, Division of Wildlife Web site:

- **When you walk or hike in mountain lion country, go in groups and make plenty of noise** to reduce your chances of surprising a lion. A sturdy walking stick is a good idea; it can be used to ward off a lion.

- **Do not approach a lion**, especially one that is feeding or with kittens. Most mountain lions will try to avoid a confrontation.
- **Stay calm** when you come upon a lion. Talk calmly yet firmly to it. Move slowly.
- **Stop or back away slowly**, if you can do it safely. Running may stimulate a lion's instinct to chase and attack. Face the lion and stand upright.
- **Do all you can to appear larger.** Raise your arms. Open your jacket if you're wearing one.

I had read most of this before. But I had no shotgun or even a walking stick this time. Not only was I not wearing a jacket, I wasn't wearing pants or boxers. I'd assumed that the lion was already far away, scared off by us and the arriving herd. I had already both surprised and approached a feeding lion. In fact, I was blatantly challenging it for its prey. I knew well that my mistake might be fatal, but I didn't have time to contemplate being such a moron. I had to act.

I started screaming, my voice growing louder and louder. Visceral, terrified, furious screaming. I flailed my arms at the graythorn and mesquite branches near me, tearing off small mesquite branches and flinging them at the lion, the thorns leaving scratches up and down my arms, though I didn't feel them. I stamped my feet on the ground, my body surging with the flood of adrenaline and fear of imminent death.

From a couple of hundred yards away, maybe less, Debbie heard what she described as my bloodcurdling screams. She knew there was only one possible cause. She started running.

My eyes never left the lion, and at first, the lion remained still, with its eyes on me. I don't know how long it was—maybe not more than a minute. The lion crouched there, sizing me up, a moment of pure encounter between two predators, only one of them capable of killing the other, a reversal of my accustomed role.

"Go," I screamed, the only word I said amid mostly wordless screaming. But the lion did not move. And then it did. It pivoted and moved, rippling thirty feet across the clearing, as if molten platinum flowed beneath its skin. I thought it was leaving. Maybe it was, but then some other thought, possibly lethal, crossed the lion's mind. It turned and faced me again. I knew what that meant. I charged.

My approach lasted maybe twenty seconds or less, and "charging" may not really be the best description. I stepped toward the lion, not fast but slow and steady, raising my knees high and pounding my legs to the ground, my arms raised above my head, my panicked heart thundering my ribcage. And like a phantom, the lion turned and slid, faster than my flashlight could track him, back into the hanging darkness: a flicker of tail and then gone.

I stood gasping, staring into the blackness where the lion had vanished. I heard Debbie calling out and gathered my wits enough to answer. Debbie reached me seconds later.

"Oh, my god," she said. "You're all right."

"The lion was right here," I said.

"I figured that out. I thought it had you."

"Almost did," I said. A few seconds passed, but I didn't say more, still struggling to recover my equilibrium.

"Is the calf dead?"

"Don't know. Probably."

We walked over to the prostrate calf. Debbie took the light from my hand and knelt beside it, scanning the flashlight beam up and down its body. The calf had not been disemboweled or bitten at all. There were teeth marks in its neck, but they hadn't gone deep. Its breath came so shallow that Debbie had to put her hand over the calf's nose to tell if it was breathing at all.

"He's alive," she said.

I knelt, too, and placed my own hand where Debbie's had been, in wonder, just to make sure. After a long moment, we rose to our feet, me with the calf in my arms, both of us in shock. I carried it back to the corral with Debbie leading the way by flashlight. It did not squirm, and I wondered whether it

might have received some less perceptible mortal wound.

In the morning, the calf's throat was swollen, so we gave it a shot of penicillin against infection. For months, you could look close and see a few small scars where the lion's teeth had marked it. Eighteen months later, the calf I'd saved from a lion went to slaughter. We shared the meat with our friends.

LEARNING HOW TO DIE

If you move into a very wild area as we did, and you put chickens and calves where they weren't before, you usually get a short grace period before the predators arrive. Then, at some point, you get on the food map, and they just keep coming. One half-dark morning, I saw a coyote snap a white hen right out of the air as she fluttered up toward a fence rail, trying to escape. We learned how much raccoons like chicken by losing a few, so we reinforced the bottoms of the pens with an extra layer of chicken wire.

Daily chores included refilling any small holes that ambitious coyotes dug into the soil around the pens and restapling chicken wire to posts where nimble raccoon hands had tugged it loose. Usually, the little forays were unsuccessful. Occasionally, a chicken got snatched, and then the attacks became more frequent for a while. They decreased again if we did a good job with fortifications. From time to time, Debbie and I would discuss how the raccoons and coyotes were after the same thing we were so we couldn't really blame them for trying.

I didn't blame the lion for its sharp reminder that most of the world remains beyond our corrals, that even our most intentional relationships exist within vast open systems that cannot be entirely predicted or controlled. In those moments when the lion and I stood facing each other, with the calf between us, I felt the animal vulnerability and primal terror of being torn open and apart, of being consumed—and the fear pulsing through my body was the kind that complicates the idea of communion through eating.

I survived—or, at least, saved the calf—by bluffing, by pretending to be a creature with physical powers I did not possess— my last adaptive card laid on the table. Had the lion leapt

toward me and my struggle been futile, I hope there would
have come a moment of acquiescence when I, like the calf,
no longer resisted, acknowledging an unforeseen twist in the
cosmos, dualities collapsing, "I" becoming "thou," self, other,
our bodies the truest offerings we have to make.

With the raccoons, I failed my own principles. I let myself
blame them for taking more than I wanted them to have,
though they could not have understood my limits. To keep the
raccoons from eating our melons, we tried covering the plants
with sheets weighted down with rocks. The raccoons got under
them. Though the yard was already fenced and the chain link
kept deer out of the garden, we began to consider whether we
needed to set up internal electric fencing around the melon
beds, an unsightly and expensive proposition. Then they took
another chicken. It became clear that the four of them had
come to regard our yard as one-stop shopping, a raccoon
quick-mart. We got angrier at them every day. When there was
one intact watermelon left in the bed, I made a decision to try
something more drastic.

"As long as you do it," Debbie said, but I could tell she
didn't like it from the way she looked at me and pressed her
lips together.

"What else are we supposed to do?"

"I don't know. I think I'd rather just not grow melons."

I said nothing. This was not an answer I was willing to hear.

When two of the young raccoons reached the yard two nights
later, I burst through the back door and chased them around
the house and across the driveway. One of them leapt onto the
fence, topped it, dropped to the other side and kept going. The
other one climbed a mesquite tree in front of the tack shed
by the gate. It sat on a branch, peering down at me. I raised
the shotgun, loaded with buckshot, intending to kill. I stood
looking along the barrel at the young raccoon for a very long
moment. Some part of me knew what was coming. I'd been the
boy who'd asked for a BB gun because his friends had them,

only to give weepy burials to a few feathered victims before putting the gun away.

When I fired, the raccoon dropped from a low mesquite branch onto the ground and crawled toward the fence, making it ten or twelve feet before going still. I walked toward it. Blood poured out of its head, its entire lower jaw blown off by the exploding shell. I stood over it as it died, feeling cold, sick, and helpless. I recalled watching them play and eat on the upstairs porch. They had gotten used to us watching through the window pretty fast. If we made no quick movements, they went about their business undisturbed.

It was the work and care that gave us first right to the fruits of our labors, I told myself, wondering all along if there was any such right to be had. I never told Jim and Pat about the raccoon. In Cascabel, I killed and ate rattlesnakes that took up residence in a corral or near my doorstep. I shot at a trespassing, lion-hunting hound with no second thought, preferring the lion in its place to the dog out of bounds. I slaughtered chickens. I shot cows I loved that were suffering and could not be cured. If I'd had a gun, would I have fired at the lion, as well? The image of the young raccoon falling from the tree, its last heaving strides toward impossible freedom, has never left me.

CHESTER F. PHILLIPS has worked as a rancher, fire look-out, delivery driver, Montessori assistant teacher, rainwater harvester, research assistant, environmental conflict-resolution intern, and freshman English instructor, among other things. He received his MFA in nonfiction from the University of Arizona in 2009 and is currently working on a PhD in arid lands resource sciences.

END OF THE LINE

Jim Kennedy

I was born in Baltimore on Sept. 11, 1955. I am white, a male, and a lapsed Irish Catholic. I love my family, immediate and extended, but keep my feelings too much of a secret. My father is gone. He lived a full life and left behind five children and a dozen grandchildren. One of my sons was snatched by the sea on a day when the water seemed calm. How things happen sometimes does not make sense.

I did all my growing up in Baltimore and then married Boston. For a living, as I used to tell my sons when they were very young, I crunch and juggle numbers. Then I would demonstrate this by writing giant numbers with a Magic Marker on several blank pieces of paper, crumpling each page and juggling them. I spend most of my free time writing, reading and walking. The subway stop nearest my home is Forest Hills Station, the end of the Orange Line in Boston.

The Orange Line—at least, the portion from Back Bay to the southern terminus at Forest Hills—was reconstructed during the 1980s. I now commute every workday on the Orange Line. I know it well. I am intimate with the texture of the seats on the cars. I am familiar with the looks on the faces of the passengers when one more person insists on squeezing onto a packed train, when those standing—all strangers—have already used every cavity of space in order not to press closer together than they would if they had just joined together for a slow dance.

I once became so involved in conversation with someone whom I barely knew that neither of us noticed the train had stopped at Forest Hills, that more than the usual number of passengers had departed, that the train had lingered longer than it had at prior stations. Locked in our conversation, we did not even notice, after the doors had closed and for eight more stops afterward, that the train was then moving in the opposite direction.

But my stomach noticed the moment we reversed directions. I can no longer remember any of the words we spoke, but I remember very well the queasy feeling in my stomach, as if I had violated a law of nature by not getting off at the end of the line.

I remember, too, how my two younger boys, Thomas and Max, preferred to stand when they rode with me on the Orange Line. And I knew exactly why. They gravitated to that visceral feeling of imbalance, that stimulating inner tickle. Like kids spinning themselves dizzy, always laughing. They could feel so keenly the physical momentum that pushed them backward as the train sped forward and that thrust them forward as the train came to a stop. They could maintain their balance without holding onto anything. Thomas, as he did this, would cast a smile my way. He and his brother were surfing the Orange Line.

I was delighted by their delight, even as I hovered cautiously nearby, ready to put some part of myself—an arm, a leg, my whole body if necessary—between their heads and a metal pole or a hard seat, if either of them began to fall.

On March 17, 2005, I went in to work briefly. I met with two higher-ups about an important issue, and then I headed out of my office to Haymarket, the nearest Orange Line station. It was 10:30 a.m., and I was heading home to enjoy the rest of my Saint Patrick's holiday.

If I actually stood down on the tracks (not a good idea), the subway station platforms would be at my shoulder-height. This was something I had never thought about before that day.

In Haymarket Station, you can see portions of one side of the station from the other side through openings in a partial wall that runs between the two sets of tracks. During my many waits in Haymarket Station, I had stared vacantly through these openings at people standing on the other side.

That morning, I looked through the opening and saw on the other side a large young man standing down on the tracks and desperately trying to pull himself up to the platform. A train would be coming through on those tracks any minute. I briefly considered jumping down and crossing over to the other side, but my eyes fixed on the live third rail and the terse warning sign above: a red lightning bolt. The thought of calling 9-1-1 on my cell phone or of running up to tell the station attendant flashed though my mind. Others would do those things. And all of that would be too slow.

I dashed up the stairs, ran across the station lobby and then quick-stepped down the stairs on the other side. When I got there, a scrawny young man who did not understand English and a wisp of a young teenage girl, together, were attempting to pull the guy up. They were unable to lift him even an inch off the tracks. He was a very big, very large, very heavy guy. As they kept trying to pull him up, I lay down and stretched out over the platform's edge. With both my hands, I grabbed tightly onto the back of his blue jeans. I pulled upward for all I was worth. The three of us somehow managed to hoist him onto the platform.

The big guy looked Irish American, and he seemed inebriated. I assumed he had simply begun his Saint Patrick's Day celebrating very early this year, but he must have been high on some more serious intoxicant.

I had to use all my wits to keep him from falling back onto the tracks. He kept imagining a phantom train arriving. He kept moving forward to get onto this imagined train. Finally, I convinced him to sit down on a set of steps about ten feet back. To distract him, I told him bits of stories in rapid-fire succession.

But he kept looking past me to the tracks. He stood up, and I stood in his way and pointed to an advertisement on the wall and shouted, "Did you notice—?" He kept mumbling, "Here's the train."

At that point, I was prepared to tackle him if he headed toward his phantom train. I was sure I would not have the strength to pull him up if he fell again. Eventually, the police arrived in response to someone's 9-1-1 call and escorted him out of the station.

A few months later, I found myself sitting directly across from the same guy on an Orange Line train. I did not immediately recognize him. Sitting there, sober and quiet, he seemed like a different person. It took a minute for me to feel sure it was him. He did not recognize me. I did not expect him to. I thought he might remember the event. I tried to think up a conversation starter, something like, "A few months ago, you were down on the tracks at Haymarket," but I was sure such an attempt would be met with a blank stare. I sank back into my seat and waited for the train to make it to the end of the line.

At the end of the Orange Line is a cemetery, Forest Hills Cemetery. Eugene O'Neill is buried there. I have stood at his grave and pondered his long day's journey into night.

I feel at home in a cemetery. Cemeteries are usually devoid of vertical people, chatty people, people concerned with trivial matters. They are full of horizontal people, profoundly quiet people, many of whom lived long lives and now have plenty of time to digest the full meaning of a life that had a beginning, a middle, an end.

Well, not exactly, of course. But that is the feeling I experience as I wander randomly through Forest Hills Cemetery. Though I bear a superficial resemblance to the vertical people, I have so much more in common with the horizontals. Sometimes I walk among them for hours.

In 2008, I dreamed about my father for the first time in a long time. He died in 1993. The day before the dream, I had talked on the phone with my sister, and she described herself and Mom having trouble finding Dad's grave. The image of them wandering in the cemetery stirred my memories and surely stimulated my dream.

It was a happy dream, a happy version of my father, as if he were making a personal visit. He was fresh out of college—his handsomest, happiest, most alive and aware self. After college, he served in the Navy on the aircraft carrier USS Block Island, which was torpedoed by a German sub, but he and nearly all his shipmates were rescued. After the service, almost by happenstance, he landed in the FBI, where he spent much of his career investigating bank robberies. He was a good father, a good husband, a good friend to many. In this dream, he said nothing. He simply showed himself to me, as if to say, "This is how to remember me," or, "This is who I am." The dream gave me a feeling of immense relief. It replaced the memory that had dominated my thoughts: my father, in his last years, physically shrinking away.

After the drowning in August 1995, the police began to search the ocean for my ten-year-old son's body. I was too distraught to be of much help. I have since written about every remembered moment Thomas and I spent together his last day, a day we joyfully spent together, until these last minutes:

The beach is no longer life-guarded and is relatively deserted. We are at an unusual stretch where the surf has carved a large, deep pocket into the beach, creating a surprisingly deep pool of water between the breakers and the tideline. It is an invitation to the kids, calmer on the surface than the stretches of beach to its left and right.

I stand at the water's edge, watching the kids closely. Max is finally going into the water a little bit rather than only digging in the sand or collecting shells. I decide it is better to be in the water with the kids. I go near the beach chairs to take off and toss my shirt. I speak briefly to my sister and then join the kids in the water.

I go in the water close to Max. I am there for only a moment when I hear Thomas and look over. He has been suddenly pulled off his feet and swept up in an undercurrent, his arms raised straight up as he lets out a yelp. I run as much as I can in the shallow water and then dive in and quickly swim up to him.

My sister makes sure Max and her son make it back to shore. They have been in water shallow enough to be outside the undercurrent.

I make it quickly out to Thomas and am holding him. I assume we will soon make our way back to the beach. Instead, together, we are losing control and being pulled out in the strong undercurrent, and the ocean floor is quickly beyond the reach of our feet. Just then, a series of harsh and high waves break on us with unusual frequency. I make an attempt to lift Thomas over these waves as they break, but this fails as the waves crest over his head. Exhaustion is now beginning to undermine my rescue efforts. Thomas is clinging hard to me; I can feel the fingers of one hand digging into my shoulder and those on his other hand tightly grasping the hair on my head. His weight is now on my shoulders. I cannot keep my head above the surface, and I breathe in water.

I experience the helpless feeling of heavily falling into empty space. We are drowning. Then, in one profoundly strong motion, I separate myself from Thomas's weight upon me by grasping him and throwing him off. It is a strong heave. He is facing me as he sails into the air. I see his look of bewildered surprise as briefly and as clearly as one sees lightning flash in the sky.

I soon see Thomas fifteen or twenty yards away and floating on the water's surface with his face turned down into the water. We are still being pulled out by the current. Because the waves are high and we are now far from shore, I can no longer see my sister and the kids on the beach. When I first spot Thomas face down in the water, I am paralyzed by exhaustion. Then I feel the return of energy. Because we are well beyond where the waves are breaking, I am able to swim out to Thomas and grab hold of him. He is unconscious.

The water is deep, and the only thing my instinct tells me to do is tug him in by the upper arm toward the shore; so I do, for a good distance. I am too much in shock to do any clear thinking. I am hoping Thomas can be revived once we reach shore; I am dreading that I am pulling in my dead son's body.

Then we reach where the waves are breaking. I look back and get a brief glance at a large wave just before it breaks on us. We *are roiled by this powerful wave. My last grasp on his arm slides right off; my last attempt to grasp any of him is futile amid the underwater surge of the wave. I get tossed and turned under the water, and my back bounces hard against the ocean floor. I come back up, and Thomas is gone. He has been pulled into the underwater current and is not seen again that day.*

I assumed an ocean burial. I took little interest in the search for the body and began instead, almost immediately, to search the ocean of my mind for what of Thomas's life was still in my possession and to commit that to paper, with the intent of sharing it with whoever would read it, as a poor substitute for the impact his life might have had on others.

The small police department had plenty of experience with drownings, apparently. Regarding the immediate grim task of recovering the body, they were familiar with the ocean's patterns. I was told that the bodies often disappeared for a few days but then washed ashore on Assateague Island, a few miles to the south, driven there by the near shore currents. They wanted to know what color of bathing suit Thomas was wearing. They thought that might help them spot the body from their helicopter.

I knew only one major fact about Assateague Island: Some unique breed of small horses—called ponies, I think, because of their size—lives there. The younger of my two sisters had described to me an experience that occurred years ago when she camped overnight on the island. She was having a dream, and in the dream, the thing that never happens in dreams happened: She died. She did not dream of herself almost dying and then wake up. She dreamed that she died. Imagine her surprise when she lifted her eyelids: She was alive, and one of these small island horses had its head stuck inside her open tent. Startled by her waking, the horse quickly galloped off down the beach.

Once, Thomas, a little boy then, was heading down our stairs, from the second to the first floor. I was in front of him. He was moving a little too fast and, halfway down, misplaced his next footstep. His forward momentum propelled him into a head-diving motion, but before his head hit the step, I was able to pivot and catch him upside down, my arms around his midsection.

My father, who was visiting and at that moment was just below us in the front hallway, witnessed it all. Just as I grabbed Thomas upside down in my arms, just inches from hitting his head on the steps, my father and I looked into each other's eyes and experienced the moment as one.

JIM KENNEDY grew up in Baltimore and graduated from Johns Hopkins University in 1978. He became a husband and father in Boston and works in Boston City Hall. In 2011, he received an MFA in Creative Writing from the Solstice Program. His work has appeared in *Prism International* and *Creative Nonfiction*.

Jim Kennedy on "End of the Line"

"End of the Line" was not initially an attempt to squeeze my life into a nutshell. It arrived there as one Orange Line strategy overtook another Orange Line strategy.

My original idea was Orange-Line-as-landscape. For many years I took the subway almost every day and witnessed many vivid scenes. I envisioned a lengthy nonfiction piece that covered a lot of surface in documentary-narrative style but would go deep at key points.

As I wrote, however, something happened, and Orange-Line-as-landscape became Orange-Line-as-metaphor. I did not deliberately create this *life as a ride on the subway* metaphor. I was pulled into it. It happened like this: I had simply put off for too long—fourteen years—describing with precision (even to myself) my son's last conscious minute.

As "End of the Line" grew in intensity, I realized recording scenes observed was not enough. The only Orange Line scenes I retained were ones in which I was inside the narrative. As the word count plummeted, the scope of the piece broadened and created surprises. For instance, the possibility (suggested to me by the local police) of my son's body washing up on Assateague Island in the days immediately following the drowning triggered the memory of my sister's death dream on that island (described to me decades earlier). Meanwhile, my father's presence in the piece became more important.

In the end, I realized the essay gained more from the absence than from the presence of some Orange Line stories I loved. Narrative bulk was transformed into brief landings between leaps—leaps of association linking moments that mattered. "End of the Line" became my game of narrative hopscotch, my crossing madly a shallow river's rapids on loose stones, each landing nearly weightless, each next leap almost immediate.

THE WISHBONE

Harrison Scott Key

My father did many things, but he did not cheat. Cheating required skills that Pop did not have, like the ability to whisper and make at least one good friend. Pop didn't have friends, which he believed were things meant for women and children, as were holidays and happiness—and cheating. A real man didn't need all that. All a man needed was a gun and a woodstove and maybe, if things got bad, some Vicks VapoRub. The man put it on everything: heads, chests, sore muscles, flank steak. But he did not cheat.

He followed all laws, rules, commandments, and codes, and when that didn't work, he did the gentlemanly thing and started abusing people. In fishing tournaments, where fraud was almost too easy and the purse was big, Pop did not stockpile big fish from earlier that week or shove lead weights down the large mouths of the largemouths, as others did. Instead, when he trolled up to a rich stretch of backwater and found another fisherman had beaten him there, he simply threatened to shoot the man.

"You're crazy," I heard more than one fisherman say.

"I might be," Pop would say. But he was no cheater.

Except for this one time.

It happened one cool November evening, with the hiss of fried pork chops and the pedantry of *Jeopardy*'s Alex Trebek wafting down the hall to my room, where I was staring into the mirror at my changing body. It was a glorious thing, this body, and I admired it, its pubescent blubber melting away and hair arriving in secret places with disturbing speed.

"You're a man now," I said to the thing in the mirror.

I flexed. What power!

There was a knock at the door. I jumped onto the bed, covered myself in a pillow, turned my book over, feigned reading. "Come in."

It was Pop.

There had been a great rift between us for months, ever since I'd stabbed the dagger of treason into his back. I'd quit the football team, and now I was no longer a son to him, but a turncoat. Pop had been a football hero, then a coach, then *my* coach. My quitting the team was a tragedy, a royal abdication. I might as well have tried to marry a Jew. I was dead to him.

Then came this knock at the door.

"What you doing under that pillow, boy?"

"Reading."

"What about?"

It was a slightly lusty Dean Koontz novel about a hermaphrodite whose sons possess the ability to telekinetically transport themselves through space and time, and so I said, "It's about science."

"Neato Cheeto," he said.

Something was wrong. Pop never acted positive about science.

"I need you to do something," he said. He was also not a big asker of things. Still, I was honored to be the subject of his petition, whatever it was. "Fetch them old cleats you got and get dressed. We going to Pearl."

There was only one thing in Pearl worth going to on a Thursday night: a complex of dirt football fields as flat and red as a Mars plateau.

"Why?" I said.

"I need you to suit up." He walked out.

That was odd. Not because I preferred hermaphroditic literature to football, but because I was in high school. Pop coached a peewee team. Let me say that again: He coached a team full of ten- and eleven-year-old fatlings, whose soft little necks had trouble holding up a helmet. My neck, along with the rest of me, was fully formed. I was fourteen.

Was this a joke? Ah, yes, perhaps it was. Perhaps the old

man was being funny. And then I remembered: Pop did not tell jokes. The horn on the Dodge bellowed. I grabbed my cleats, ran toward the sound.

Pop, they said, was a beast on the grass, a true wonder in athletic contest, despite being as round and thick as a mastodon. They could say this because it was back when they had mastodons. The man had a head like a medicine ball, legs like Doric columns, shoulders like two HoneyBaked hams on either side of a very wide room. It was generally agreed that he would eventually play ball for Coach Vaught at Ole Miss or, at the very least, wrestle bears for a living. Then, during a fateful high school game versus Hernando, he broke one of the more necessary bones in his leg, and—just like that—the dream died. And so, since he would not be making any game-saving sacks or game-winning scores, he set himself to making something even better: a little man, just like him, who might fill those cleats and carry the mantle, live the unlived dream. No son of his would have a choice in the matter. The gravity and density of his DNA were too much to ignore.

It took him three marriages, but finally, he got him a boy.

"Hot damn!" Pop said in a hospital just up the road from Graceland. "I do believe that's a pecker." He devoted the next eighteen years of his life to making a man of the little thing attached to the pecker. Of course, the little thing was me.

"It'll make a man out of you," he was always saying. Take the time he told me to saw a deer in half. He handed me a rusty bone saw old enough to have been used by Grant's siege engineers at Vicksburg and told me to run it through the dead thing's pelvis.

"It'll make a man out of you, boy!" he said, handing me the saw. "And don't be sawing through his nuts, neither."

This is advice I've taken everywhere with me: don't be sawing through an animal's nuts. Speaking of nuts, that's what Pop was about football. It had everything required to make a boy into a man: brutality, blood, a nearby concession stand.

On the way to Pearl, we spoke little. I had so many questions, like "Do you really expect me to hit all those children?" and "Have you lost your mind?" We powered up Highway 18 in the Dodge, not even a radio station to break the tension. He stared ahead, as he always did, with the frozen gaze one typically associates with Arctic muskoxen.

I was worried. I was not a big rulebreaker. I did not like the idea of flouting what was clearly league policy about age limits. Some of the boys who played up in Pearl, they were big. I might not stand out too much. But still. What if I was caught?

"So—" I said.

"I got you at fullback," he said, looking straight ahead into the black.

"Oh."

"We running the Wishbone."

"Good."

I had no idea what the Wishbone was. Some kind of formation. Also, a salad dressing. I suppose he could sense my wondering, because he soon explained that he was expecting only ten players to show and needed one more or else he'd have to forfeit. I suggested there'd be dozens of teams at the park and that he shouldn't have a problem finding an eleventh from another squad, some boy of some eager father who wanted his boy to get more reps in.

"It's you what knows the plays," he said.

"True, true."

I remembered none of the plays. Pop was always doing this, assuming I knew more than I knew about whatever game it was he'd ordered me to play. Overestimating my talent. Believing his DNA had won the battle with my mother's and that I was like him in every athletic way, even though history had shown us both otherwise.

When I was five, he put me on a soccer team, believing the angularity and velocity of the sport would at least teach me to run, even though he considered soccer a game for boys with vaginas. I found it disorienting, a marriage of kickball and prison riot. My only physical virtue was this enormous head, bequeathed to me through the miracle of genetics, and so I resorted to hitting people with it. The other parents became worried, but not Pop.

"My boy's got a powerful head, don't he?" Pop would say.

Next, he put me on a baseball team with boys three years older than me, hoping I'd rise to the challenge. Mercifully, they put me in right field, a clear signal to all that I was mentally disabled. On the rare occasion when a ball limped my way, I'd hurl it toward the infield and would be as shocked as everyone else to see it flying in the wrong direction, toward the heads of children on other fields. The parents shrieked, sought medical help, but not Pop.

"The boy's got a powerful arm!" he would say, sirens in the distance.

As I got older, I filled out a little, foreshadowing my future girth and power, but still lacked hand-eye coordination, as well as eye-foot, foot-foot, and head-wall coordination. In games of Smear the Queer or Two Hand Touch, I struck people and objects with great frequency. Once, after scoring a touchdown, I broadsided my grandfather's barn and knocked two planks loose. Cousins ran inside for something to soak up the blood, but not Pop.

"I swunny if he don't have him some powerful legs, too," he said, while relatives pried me from the me-shaped hole.

When I turned ten, Pop announced that I would play football. The time had come. Glory. It was an August afternoon when he took me outside, pulled from his trunk enough football equipment to make a house payment, and told me to put it on so he could hit me: shoulder pads, Puma cleats, a jockstrap large enough for a Viking warlord. I put it on. He got down opposite me.

"Say, *Hut, hut*," he said.

"Why?"

"Just say it."

Nothing's quite as horrifying as watching your extra-large father—for all practical purposes the Incredible Hulk with a heart condition and comb-over—squat down, look you in the eyes, and ask you to ask him to hit you.

"Hut, hut," I said, and I soon found myself blessed with the gift of backward flight.

"What are you doing to my baby?" Mom said, as I lay there, my nose bleeding, my life-force pooling into the dry, sandy ground.

"That's how a man hits," he said.

Pop had never been my coach before. He was safer in the bleachers, telling himself harmless lies about his boy. But coaching. Someone could get hurt. Me, for example.

Pop poured everything into my teams, building squads which might array themselves around me and help carry me to some future exaltation. He did this by trolling the playgrounds and trailer parks of our community, filling the roster with previously unknown athletes, boys whose time in juvenile detention had precluded their involvement in youth sports. He made the acquaintance of other large men, who might have large offspring, and many did. He reached across racial lines and signed up poor black children, whose parents could not afford the registration fee, or the equipment, or the gas money to get to games, and he paid from his own pocket. Which is to say, we had a roster full of lawless, large, fast, and very grateful athletes. Also, we had no savings.

"You spend too much on football," Mom said.

"It's his future we talking about," Pop said. "He'll play college ball one day."

"I sure would like to take a vacation one day."

"I sure would like you to shut up."

That was their marriage.

And it worked. She shut up, and we won bowl trophies and whipped many teams across the county. Pop soon became a vaunted member of the fraternity of coaches, a real bootstraps kind of hero. And I am grateful for what he did. It was fun, all the healthy camaraderie, the sleepovers after games, the time spent with family in the hospital while suffering from concussions.

I toughed it out, fought through phalanxes of giant cornfed children, tried my hardest to do something right. I could barely understand the cryptic metaphors Pop used in his coaching.

"Eat his lunch!" Pop would shout from the sidelines.

"Eat his *what*?"

"His lunch."

"What are you talking about?"

"Let me hear some leather pop!"

"Leather?" I would say. It sounded like something he'd pried out of a dictionary of nineteenth century hobo slang.

"You know," he'd say, clapping.

None of us were wearing leather, as far as I could tell. Should we be? Did he want me to carry some kind of a whip?

"Take a two-by-four to him, Junior!"

"To who?" I'd say. "There's eleven of them."

"Yo deddy crazy," my teammates would say. "He ack that-away atcho house?"

"Sometimes," I'd say.

If pictures are worth a thousand words, the look on my face in team photos of this era says something like, "I am uncomfortable and hot." My face is strained and stiff, the countenance of a fatalist who is suffering from a high-fiber diet. I seem to be making private signals to the camera, suggesting my location and how a well-trained team of SEALs might extract me.

Over the next four years, I tried to quit football approximately 842 times. There was one rough game where a fullback, who seemed way too old for junior high, had abused me. His age, of course, was an assumption of mine, based entirely on his lush and rather full mustache.

"I think he collapsed one of my lungs," I said.

Pop, as ever, pretended not to hear. "You shoulda eat his lunch."

"I don't even *like* lunch. I don't like football, either."

"I sho am hungry," he said. "I could eat me a turkey leg."

I dreamt of being in a terrible car accident and losing my legs. Having no feet, I believed, would make it easier to quit. During a physical in Jackson, I got the brilliant idea to have a physician sanction my unfitness to play.

"I have a heart murmur," I said. "I could die."

"You won't die."

"But I might die."

"Not from that."

"But one day."

"One day, yes," he said. Then he put his credentialed hand around my vitals and made me cough.

Back at home, I kept trying. "It's just . . . there are so many extracurricular activities I could do," I said.

"We got to get you a multivitamin, firm you up."

"Like maybe the quiz bowl team."

"Make a muscle," he said, groping my bicep.

With my other arm, I extended an envelope. "Did you see this invitation I got to join Mensa?" I asked.

"Men's who?"

"It's for geniuses," Mom said from the kitchen. "My baby is a genius."

Pop looked toward the sound of dishwater, confused. "Your momma's gone crazy," he said.

"It just seems like maybe I should focus on things besides football," I said.

"You mean, like baseball?"

"Like maybe the chess team."

Something inside him died. You could see it. He stared into the middle distance, as though reaching back through memory for some tenuous relationship between chess and balls.

I soon spiraled into a whorl of decadence with the chess and science clubs, learning very different kinds of offensive moves and establishing control groups and reveling in the empirically verifiable company of other disappointing children. Pop and I didn't speak for weeks.

Until that night when he came knocking and told me to find my cleats.

We arrived at the Center City Complex of Pearl, Mississippi, and I remembered that I did not like Pearl very much—a community best known for its excellent marching bands, violent dogs, and high rates of venereal disease. Their peewee teams were notoriously nasty, unmannered, and good. We didn't know why they had always been so much better and stronger and faster than us, but we suspected it had something to do with having stepfathers who abused them. The only consolation, for those of us from outlying rural communities, was that they would all soon be in prison.

Pop opened his door, got out. It was night. The halogen glow formed a dome around the park, over which moved low gunmetal clouds. A gust of wind blew off Pop's baseball cap, and his hairflap came unmoored, rose to attention.

"I got your pads in back," he said and walked toward the lights.

I found all my old gear, including a jockstrap that smelled of spring meadows. I undressed right there in the grassy glen, preparing to don equipment that I had first worn four years earlier, when I was not yet the size of a Viking warlord as I was now, owing to a strict regimen of Little Debbie Fudge Rounds and Cool Ranch Doritos. I had grown as big as Pop, but not in the right way. Not with the muscles.

A quart of sweat later, I made a jarring lurch onto the field, like Dr. Frankenstein's hopeful monster duct-taped inside a protective barrier of sofa cushions. My knees refused to flex, and my shoulders had grown too large for the shoulder pads, which now perched atop my clavicles rather than astride them, giving the effect of small and functionless wings sprouting from my neck.

I joined my team, a squad of cushioned munchkins.

"Who are you?" a small uniformed boy asked, looking up.

"I'm Coach Key's son," I said.

"You're big," he said, poking a finger deep into the fatty tissues around my exposed gut. More of the younglings gathered around me, as children are wont to do with Jesus and clowns.

"How old are you?" they said.

"He's tall as my uncle."

"What grade is he in? Hey, what grade are you in?"

"He ain't got no grade," Pop said, strutting over. "He's homeschooled."

It was strange to hear my father lie so imaginatively.

"I'm in high school, and I have a driver's permit," I wanted to say. But it would blow Pop's cover, so I didn't.

Then, during warm-ups, the taunts began.

"Ain't he a big one?" I heard, off to my right, from the Pearl side.

"The big ones is always stupid," another said.

"Hey, boy!" they said. "I bet you too big even to fit in the short bus!" They howled.

The Pearl parents appeared to believe I was slow of speech and had something of a gland problem.

"Good luck tonight, hon!" a tattooed mother said. "You about to bust outta that uniform, ain't you!"

I said nothing, just stared dumbly, which only strengthened their belief in my retardation. I ignored them, tried to be the bigger man. I *was* the bigger man. Bigger than some of the parents, even.

"Grab a knee," Pop said.

It was almost time. My teammates looked up to me, and I looked up to Pop, and Pop looked at a point approximately thirty degrees above the horizon, as though he'd sighted a large formation of ducks he wished to shoot. It started to rain.

"Lead us in a prayer," Pop said to me, and I did as I was told.

I was disoriented, at first, by the giant-headed children raging around below me in the rain. Then, four plays into the game, I got steamrolled by a child I hadn't seen coming and landed sideways in orange mud that was the consistency and color of an unfinished carrot cake. My teammates gathered around me, their dripping helmets wreathing the dark sky. One of them kicked me.

"I think Coach Key's son is dead."

I elbowed myself to a sitting position. My small attacker was the size of a ferret but appeared to be feeding on amino acids and gunpowder.

"I tole you he was dumb, Rusty!" his teammates said to him, high-fiving. It was embarrassing, getting whipped by a fifth-grader named Rusty.

What happened next would become the stuff of peewee football lore.

And what happened was, I sort of became an enraged gorilla. At fullback, I folded up children like bad origami, including Rusty, who soon took to running in the opposite direction, screaming. I chased down the largest players, knocked them into a new day of the week. I started calling the plays, took the handoff, ran over as many athletes as possible, which required several awkward turns and parabolic vectors, before entering the endzone. On my second—or was it my third?—touchdown, I dragged at least four defenders across the plane, along with one of my own pocket-sized teammates, who had become excited and was riding me like a homecoming float.

"It feels so good!" he said.

"It does," I said.

I ran around children, over them, under them, and, at one point, fulfilled a childhood fantasy by throwing and then catching the very same pass. I made their running backs drop balls merely by barking at them.

"He's got the rabies," they said. "He's a animal."

And I was. I played with abandon, both because I knew it would be my last football game ever and also because, owing to puberty and the shrinking properties of cotton, my jockstrap finally fit. My cup, literally, runneth over, and onward, for many touchdowns.

"Thatta way, boy!" Pop said. "Stack 'em like cordwood!"

Ah, yes! The metaphors—they all made sense now. I started inventing my own.

"I just ate a tree!" I said to a fallen Pearl athlete. Or, "I'm about to grow a new head!"

"That don't even make sense," Rusty said, from across the line.

People were starting to talk. I saw them pointing, whispering. I knew there might be inquiries made about the depth of my voice and the hair on my arms and the date on my birth certificate. From what I could tell and hear, it was believed that I was either in high school or the greatest athlete in the history of youth football.

By the time the game was over, the field was littered with bodies. Children cried in pain or wept in joy, depending, rolling around celebrating or lamenting in the soupy carnage. Parents and coaches were on the field to tend the wounded. Referees shook their heads. The score was 63-0, and every point was mine.

It was lovely, really.

Pop put his hand on my shoulder, and we beheld the spectacle of the battlefield together, where an alternate history played itself out, unraveling backward like reversed game-tape, a glorious past where I had not quit, where I had inherited the best qualities of this beast on the grass that was my father.

"We whipped 'em good," he said.

I couldn't help thinking that he'd wanted me to play, to feel what it was like to be him, at least for one game. To him, it wasn't cheating. It was fathering.

Pop was smart, and we got out of there quick, while children tried to get my autograph or a lock of my hair, and league officials loitered to get a look at the young Sasquatch. On the way home, we spoke little. My ears rang like they always did after games, but now it was from all the cheering. To my knowledge, nobody ever pressed the matter. Pop was allowed to continue coaching and did so for many years.

There in the truck, in the dark, plowing through fat gems of rain, Pop spoke first. "I sho would like you to play again," he said. "In high school at least."

"Pop," I said, "I hate football."

"A man likes to see his boy play."

"I played tonight."

I had terrorized many young children on that field, had eaten many lunches, had perhaps ruptured important organs and caused internal hemorrhaging. It felt great. Somehow, even then, I knew that this sort of triumphant feeling could never be achieved at our nation's many science fairs.

"It's fun to whip a little ass, ain't it?" he said.

"Yes, sir," I said. "It kind of is."

And for once, it was no lie.

HARRISON SCOTT KEY's humor and essays have appeared in the *Oxford American, Orion, The Pinch, Swink, Defenestration, The Chronicle of Higher Education*, and elsewhere. He lives with his family in Savannah, Georgia, and teaches writing at the Savannah College of Art and Design.

Harrison Scott Key on "The Wishbone"

When I set myself to writing a memoir about my life in the South, I knew there had to be a football story—mostly because so many memories of my father are connected to football—but it took a while before I found the right story to tell. When I started making notes, it was all montage: What Playing Was Like, What Hitting Was Like, What Running Screaming From Giant Hillbilly Mutants With Mood Disorders Was Like. I had characters, settings, descriptions, moods, passions . . . but no real setting or scene. No Big Moment.

I knew I could write a lyrical, funny, descriptive, nostalgic piece about my father and football and the fun and horror of it all. That's what John Updike would have done. Those sorts of memoir essays are like long sonatas, building up emotion and ideas with layers of description and not-quite-aimless meandering through the mind. I call it *wanderlit*. It doesn't rely so much on scene. But it's also boring, unless you're John Updike or Vladimir Nabokov or reading while chewing mescaline.

And then I thought, maybe I could write a historical, chronological, play-by-play account. What it was like to watch football with my father as a young boy, and then getting my first helmet, and then my first game, my first concussion, my first spinal fracture. It would be factual, accurate . . . and about as fun to read as getting slowly digested by a sturgeon. Too literal.

And then I remembered The Game. That experience had been inside my memory chamber, hiding. It did not want to be remembered; it was embarrassed, and afraid, and had not showered in many years. So I was nice to it. I gave it soup. And then more solid foods. And then a bath. I taught it new words. I bought it new clothes. I let it sleep in my house.

This was the moment that I could build my story around.

Initially, the essay was just the story of that night—but that, too, was boring. No stakes. You played a peewee game when you were in high school. You helped your father cheat. So what? But once I started asking *why*, it got interesting. Why did my father ask me to play? Why did I agree to do it? Why did wearing a jockstrap feel so good all of a sudden? The Why, that's the What.

Finally, I had the game—that was my big moment, my action.
And I had the right questions—that was my theme, my Why.
And so I had my story.

BREASTFEEDING DICK CHENEY

Sonya Huber

I.

It's difficult to describe my relationship with Dick Cheney—
even now, after all this time. We share a birthday, Jan. 30,
and I was born thirty years after he was. Both the eldest of
three children, we were talkative kids and avid readers. We
rode in the back seats of our parents' cars on long, low-budget
road trips. He was raised by Democrat parents and turned,
as I turned against my Republican parents. Our trips to elite
private colleges led to panic and homesickness. We have each
struggled with codependence—the feeling of our identities
being subsumed into another person—but have dealt with our
anxiety issues in opposite ways. I've tried to get over mine.
Dick has made his a way of life.

I will not assume you share my feelings toward Dick
Cheney, but I will assume there is a person on the globe who
raises your hackles, whose misuse of power troubles your
heart. Please believe me: This is not directly about politics. It is
about that fearsome wave of hate. The only strangers here are
those who would deny having such feelings.

II.

I am a Midwesterner with a Middle Eastern shadow. I belong
to the generation bookended and contained by the conflict in
the Middle East. My childhood carries the echo of the word
shah, the hostage crisis and all the others, then the Gulf War
in college, the 576,000 dead Iraqi children in the economic

embargo, then another war. In the dark, I cast my mind across the oceans to Iraq, to Persia, to Babylon. Heat rises in the pink of my eyelids and my esophagus. My mom was born in Germany after World War II and says she owes her life to the Marshall Plan, which funded the reconstruction, so I have a bias in favor of rebuilding after bombing and ousting dictators. I Google "rebuild Iraq" but don't know whom to donate to. Iraq has probably had just about enough of people like me wanting to help.

Cheney shares my fixation: "We're always going to have to be involved [in the Middle East]. Maybe it's part of our national character: You know, we like to have these problems nice and neatly wrapped up, put a ribbon around it . . . [I]t doesn't work that way in the Middle East. It never has and isn't likely to in my lifetime."

III.

I got pregnant about a month after President George W. Bush uttered the fateful "Sixteen Words" in his Jan. 28, 2003, State of the Union address: "The British Government has learned that Saddam Hussein recently sought significant quantities of uranium from Africa." Cheney pushed the connection between 9/11 and Iraq, and personally brought evidence to the CIA. I spent the couch-days of morning sickness watching the war unfold, watching this man who duck-talked through a mouth slotted like a crooked piggy bank.

I made chocolate cake for my son's first birthday in 2004. He's had six war birthdays since then, and now he doesn't like chocolate. In the grocery aisle, I stop in front of the icings and cake mixes. I reach for a box of Duncan Hines and wonder if maybe this year he will turn back to chocolate.

I can't make myself buy yellow cake. In the shadows of my mind, the sunshine substance is linked to yellowcake uranium. Cheney claimed Saddam Hussein had purchased yellowcake to enrich and use in weapons. One time, my son insisted on yellow, and the lumpy, toxic look of it in the bowl made me sick. I usually buy white cake mix with multi-colored confetti sprinkles.

IV.

Overwhelmed with bitterness, I visited a Buddhist temple
in Columbus, Ohio, for the first time in the spring of 2004. I
had read about a meditation practice to cultivate *bodhichitta*,
the love for all beings. Another practice, *tonglen*, asks you to
imagine another person and then breathe in all pain while
breathing out peace and happiness for them.

I imagined a map of the country and the world, but with burn
marks like cigarette scars to fit neatly around certain people. All
beings: This is the part that makes you crazy. If you haven't tried
it, feeling love for Cheney creates heartburn and a headache. Your
brain has to grow four-wheel drive to handle the terrain, and even
then, this is all you notice: neurons busting out of their tracks.

I clutch my Cheney-hatred like a teddy bear. I worry that
if I don't hate him, somehow someone will forget what he's
done. In dropping Cheney-hatred for one minute, I free-fall. I
don't know who I am without hating Cheney. He is the star I
navigate against. But I have to learn to trust the world. It's all
written down; we bear it together.

Cheney had his first of five heart attacks in 1978. With every new mention of Cheney's heart difficulties, I pause. Driven
by my rage at a wasteful war waged as a business, I imagine
being able to reach into Cheney's chest and jostle that heart.
Others share the horrifying, delicious thought. Readers of a
Wonkette blog post, "Waiting for Dick Cheney to Die? Get
a Chair," expressed their own murderous thoughts and even
wondered—in both prose and poetry—whether the proper
resting place for Cheney's body might be "in the dumpsters
behind the Hague prison" or transfigured into urinal cakes.
I want to lift off my sternum to examine my hate, pick it out,
and force myself to understand it. This murder thought is the
dream of terrorists, assassins, and children. My Cheney problem is a child's story. Dehumanization is the quickest way to
turn bodies into fuel. Maybe we know we will have to use these
simple ideas to keep us warm when the oil runs out.

Heat any substance to around 525 degrees Celsius, and it
will start to glow. This is known as incandescence: Light and

heat are released, along with gases that combine with the oxygen and carbon dioxide in the atmosphere. The heat keeps the fuel hot, which releases more gases and makes more fire. The word *incandescent* also means "wound up to a sustained white heat of anger." My Cheney problem is an incandescent light bulb of hatred.

Do I have a right to be angry? I am an American, and it takes so much oil to fuel my anger. I hear the heater roaring in the background. I have a load of clothes in the washing machine. I will take a hot-water shower. I type on a glowing monitor. The Internet blazes with the secondary incandescence of trapped energy.

Whenever I see electricity in motion, I think of Iraq. What is the byproduct? What work is being done in the light of this fire? What is the size of Dick Cheney's carbon footprint?

V.

Iraq leaked into my writing classes in rural southeast Georgia. I told my hunting, camo-wearing, mostly Baptist country students this wasn't about politics. It was about the Middle East in our heads, about the arguments at the bars and frat parties. Nobody complained; no irate parents called. I handed out a blank hand-drawn map of the Middle East. "Name the countries," I said. The students failed, mouths agape. "This isn't going to count toward our grades, is it?" I told them no; I had taken the quiz and failed, too. We learned that Middle Eastern cities had downtowns and McDonald's, that kids there wore jeans and wanted to dance. We aimed for humanization, so I had to look back at my brain.

VI.

Advanced Buddhist monks sometimes hang out in graveyards or stare at dead bodies or think of themselves decaying, all to confront the brain with its own lack of control.

I found a new meditation teacher, Dzigar Kongtrul Rinpoche, at the end of 2009 and began a year of preparation to become his formal student. He assigned four basic scenarios, expressions of Buddhist visualizations that have been used for millennia to generate compassion and love for all beings. The point isn't to walk around feeling special like a mini-monk—"Oh I'm so nice; I'm a Buddhist." The point is to see our hate and attachment, how we use and consume each other.

I listened to a recorded talk of a guided meditation and followed the instructions: I am to imagine myself with my own parents. We are all being threatened by a dangerous enemy. The enemy should be someone I fear or have great difficulty with, someone who arouses fear and hatred. I have used bosses and exes in the role of the dangerous enemy, but Cheney? My brain made excuses: Haven't I had a crappy enough year? Hasn't he done enough?

Then, feeling curious or bold, I chose him for a day's meditation project. I saw the cloud of his cool, collected calculation threatening to seep in, to poison the world and dissolve us.

After the scenario became a vivid bubble in my mind, my teacher's voice told me to change my mental picture. I was now to imagine breastfeeding a newborn and also trying to eat bits of fish for lunch. A dog nags for scraps of the fish. I feed it, but then become impatient and kick it away. This moment, too, became a bubble vivid with senses and details.

"Snap," said my teacher: Imagine a moment of awakening. I was suddenly to overlay the image with a deeper truth, to realize that the dangerous enemy has been reincarnated as my infant. My father has been reincarnated as the fish—my lunch. My mother has returned as the dog I kicked. I'm sorry, Mom. Thank you, Dad. And Cheney, my child . . . We Buddhists struggle with that one.

As it turns out, many Buddhists use versions of the enemy-as-child meditation, and the question of how to generate compassion for Cheney-as-enemy is not uncommon in Buddhist circles. Buddhist advice blogger Auntie Suvanna provides a specific visualization:

Firstly, firmly establish in your mind the image of Richard sound asleep in giraffe pajamas. Richard is the name you

*gave him. You also gave him the pajamas. Notice the device
inside his chest, poised to deliver a shock to restore the beat of
his worn out, sad and violent heart . . . [E]ven though he has
made many terrible mistakes, you can't help but love him . . .
[Y]ou are always honest with him and encouraging him to do
the right thing.*

Cheney in giraffe jammies was too much. I kept seeing his old,
bald head on a baby body, so I stuck with an anonymous baby.
Alone with the glow of candles, the image of Cheney's lips
approaching my breast brought the visceral chill of the parent's
worst nightmare.

Try it: your baby Cheney. You have given birth to Hercu-
lean levels of world damage. Nothing in your life matters more
than raising this child to be a good person. The point is to love
him. Love: Dip your heart in lava. Do you think you are too
good for this baby? But then I fall out of it, wheeling backward,
feeling dirty and haunted and empty.

VII.

I started looking for Cheney's childhood to get beyond the
images of Damien or Rosemary's baby. Google found his football photo: He wore number sixteen for Natrona County High
School in Casper, Wyoming. He's long-nosed and striking,
yet approachable, with a shaggy crew cut and a shy half-smile
pulled up at the left-hand side of his innocent face. His left
hand is taped up loosely, and his helmet rests in his lap. In his
gangliness, he reminds me of my own son, who looks frozen
in photos because his natural state is motion. Cheney enjoys
fishing and still does, like my own son.

Cheney and his girlfriend Lynne Vincent met when they
were fourteen; she was a cardigan-wearing blonde with a large,
ruthless forehead and ice-blue eyes. She worked during the
summers for Thomas Stroock, an oilman with deep connections to Yale University, where he became close friends with
classmate George H.W. Bush. She impressed Stroock. Cheney
was in—though, of course, he didn't know it yet.

VIII.

I had no Tom Stroock to help with private school, but cash
came together. If I had been sent to Yale under the watch-
ful eye of a benefactor, I believe I, too, would have imploded.
At Carleton College in Minnesota, someone told me I had
markers of the working class; the way I talked with my hand
in front of my mouth and hid behind my hair. "I'm not! I'm
here!" I protested weakly. But that was the culture I came
from. I graduated convinced I was stupid. After college, I
blundered on the East Coast, working low-paying jobs, to get
away from the Midwest, which I identified as the problem
inside me.

Cheney has a chip on his shoulder, too, or maybe the large
chip has a small dangling Cheney. Maybe his ax to grind
against the liberal elite was born at Yale. Cheney missed home,
drank and partied, and lost his scholarship in 1960. He left for
home and climbed light poles as a card-carrying member of
the International Brotherhood of Electrical Workers. He later
got an internship with a Republican representative almost by
accident.

Then came the DUIs in 1962 and '63. I wonder if he and
Lynne fought over his drinking, or if it scared her. One theory
posits that Lynne calls the shots and gives him structure, as
often happens in codependent relationships.

A posed photo from his junior year at the University of
Wyoming—1964, the year he married Lynne—shows no hint
of a smile. The left eye looks gentle. The right one stares out
coldly. I want to write that I see anger and a desire for revenge.
Yet, on second look, I see only a young man, filled out from
his lanky high school days, staring. His lips are full; you would
have to describe this man as good-looking.

IX.

After college, we began to mystify our parents. My Republican father tried to connect with his anarchist daughter, and
I sprawled on my mom's bed as she patiently listened to me
describe anarcho-syndicalism. Before Gulf War protests, the

planning committee asked volunteers to get arrested. I wanted to, but I didn't. I couldn't ask my parents to pay bail when they didn't agree with me.

In 1991, *The Washington Post* profiled Cheney's parents. Cheney's father reported "mixed feelings" about the invasion of Kuwait, but they saw time collapse: "'Be sure to put in there that he was senior class president,' added his mother. 'And that he played football,' said her husband." They cast back to what they knew, their boy.

X.

I like looking at some Cheney photos. The earlier ones show the polyester-blends, longish haircuts, and boxy eyeglasses that marked my childhood in the 1970s and '80s. Cheney served as President Gerald Ford's assistant, and my mom always loved Gerald Ford because he fell down so much. As a three-year-old, I fell down a lot, too, so we were half-bald kindred spirits. I half-think that what my mom really loved was Chevy Chase's impression of Gerald Ford falling down. She was a Republican because my father was. In the 1980s, you could even say my father and Cheney looked alike, with their suits and aquiline noses. But my dad ran a small business in Illinois while Cheney reached for the reins of the country.

I linger on the photos that show Cheney forgetting his posture, the photos in which none of his limbs are suffused with cruelty. He is a man doing his job. He isn't yet hunched, and his hair isn't white. Hunching and white hair don't equal meanness; something else will change.

In a 1980 photo, Cheney and his wife chase his kids in the family yard in McLean, Virginia. He was a U.S. representative from Wyoming. His daughters, Elizabeth and Mary, were eleven and thirteen; I was nine. In the photo, the sides of his mouth turn up in happy symmetry, but he holds his torso and arms tightly, which makes the photo seem somewhat posed. He's no longer a man you would describe as attractive. He's rounded and balding, with a rim of hair around the back of his head.

XI.

Cheney's heart betrays him, and my bones hatch rheumatoid arthritis. Meditation helps with the pain, so I light candles and close my eyes. I dive into the fish scenario: eating lunch, breastfeeding, feeding then kicking the dog. Yes, the baby is Cheney with his lips wet with milk.

One of my favorite photos of my son shows him sitting in his high chair, head half-covered with pureed sweet potato, even in his wisps of blond hair. I'd sculpted his hair into a Mohawk. He leans with one arm reaching over the tray as if he's James Dean leaning out of a dragster. And he's got that smile, the same one, cocked up at the left. The smile of a charmer.

Breastfeeding, for me, was never a mystical, sleepy union. My wiry son was like a crazed ferret, and I had to lock him under my arm in what the lactation consultant called the "football hold," which must explain his passion for the NFL. His face slammed at me, desperate for milk, but his arms and legs flailed, and I could barely hold onto him. I was covered in sweat at the end of each wrestling match. I imagine this is how it would be with Dick. There would be taking and giving, but no merging.

I weaned my son very quickly after he tried his new teeth on my nipple one day. I pulled out to break the wet suction and yelled, "Owww!" I checked for blood and clenched my jaw. He grinned cheekily, overjoyed at my reaction, as if to say, "I got you. This is me, separate, myself."

I weaned him because he was obviously done. He slobbered on my nipple, flubbered at it, irritating the skin. Or he would suck on it weakly but turn his head to look toward interesting noises while pulling my nipple with his clenched mouth. I never mourned the loss of that contact; I want him to find his own sustenance. Separation is ultimately my goal for him. Remembering this helps with the Cheney meditation: I can feed this baby, and feeding is fine. But I don't have to cross into his soul.

One analysis describes Cheney's "dependency solution": He wants "powerful patrons [to] have confidence in him.

He writes everyone else off." Another profile of Cheney says George H.W. Bush sought a guiding force for his son but "found a man who would make his son's dysfunctions worse." A third analyst calls George W. Bush the "emotional bully" in the codependent relationship. Bush said, "When you're talking to Dick Cheney, you're talking to me. When Dick Cheney's talking, it's me talking."

XII.

Cheney's stint as the Secretary of Defense matches my college years, 1989–1993. At twenty, I stood in the cold of a Minneapolis winter, surrounded by protest signs, sniffling. I did not know then that Cheney oversaw the first Gulf War. He and Rumsfeld learned from the Nixon-Vietnam era, and almost none of the demonstrations appeared on the evening news.

In 1989, he was offered a celebratory beer after winning his Pentagon post; he was rumored to have said, "Beer, hell. I'll have a double Scotch." Maybe this fascinates me because I have a history with substance abusers. The struggle in their darkened eyes is pain that can look and act like evil. Cheney supposedly carries a marked sense of "inner dread, gloom and fear."

My first rounds of compassion meditation were spurred by the pain of loving addicts. That was my immediate reason for becoming a Buddhist. My meditation teacher told me not to envision absorbing the addiction. I wished happiness for all beings; for the addicts, I hoped for the clarity to see their own agony.

People with substance abuse issues tend toward control, secrecy and lies. Or maybe it's that people with control issues sometimes drink. Cheney's hair turned white, his posture stooped, and his eyes squinted. By the time he got to the White House via the intoxicating wealth, power, and lack of oversight at Halliburton, he seemed to equate power with the ability to do whatever he wanted. Cheney stamped his daily correspondence *Treated As: Top Secret/SCI*, meaning "sensitive compartmented information," a designation usually used for hugely important government secrets. He had his daily calendars and visitor logs destroyed. His General Counsel argued that the Vice President was not part of any branch of government and was, therefore, bound by no rules.

A 2004 photo of Cheney, taken in his kitchen at home, shows him talking on the phone to his daughter after George W. Bush was declared the winner of the election. He leans on the counter, smiling, though his body and arms are curled together as if protecting something. The phone cord is wrapped around his body and held by his elbow. This is a touching detail: a corded phone in 2004. The kitchen is relatively small and beige, not huge and ostentatious. On the refrigerator door, magnets and maybe a spray of plastic alphabet letters hold family photos and a child's drawing. On the counter are a roll of paper towels, two bottles of wine, and a toaster oven. This is what I would call his evil period. He looks flushed; his mouth is making the slit shape of a smile. His eyes look elsewhere, as if his brain is detached. I realize I cannot know what is in his head.

XIII.

I am on a short plane ride by myself. Because the rheumatoid arthritis pain is bad again and I don't have energy to read, I go to Cheney. As I begin with the baby, I realize I have never thought about my potential power over him. In this scenario, I am huge and could crush his small body. It has never tempted me.

I must pull up my shirt and let this creature find sustenance without judgment. But wait, this is a fussy baby—of course. And so I envision patting the back of this cosmically whiny baby, doing the baby dance, singing, "Sshhhh—ssshhhh—shhh—it's gonna be all right—shhhh," waiting for the gas to die down, hoping to soothe his jangled nervous system.

We each have a will like the third rail of a subway track, and I feel this baby's hot anger. I have felt my own son's acute frustration with limits and the rules of life. We all want dominion. This baby I have borne is going to plug its ego into huge electrified tracks of the train that slammed into Iraq, as Afghanistan and Saudi Arabia slammed into us, as we slammed into the USSR, as the USSR slammed into Afghanistan. Even wishing harm on this baby Cheney won't unplug him from the generations of rage and desire he has dutifully served. I have a right to be horribly angry at him, even if he were my child. I have a right to disagree.

As I imagine holding this wiry ferret baby against my thighs, I realize I can hold his body, but it is not my business—nor am I able—to touch the live third rail of his soul. Putting your hands on someone else's third rail results in instant death. My baby is on fire with the electricity he sought, on a powerful train that has led to destruction. I know this baby-rage wants to annihilate me, too, but the one peace I see is that I can step back from that rail to see what that surging lust for power has consumed. It has devoured my son for its own heat and power.

SONYA HUBER is the author of two books of creative nonfiction, *Opa Nobody* (2008) and *Cover Me: A Health Insurance Memoir* (2010), and a textbook, *The Backwards Research Guide for Writers: Using Your Life for Reflection, Connection, and Inspiration* (2011). Her essays have appeared in *Fourth Genre, Brevity, Hotel Amerika, Puerto del Sol*, and many other literary journals. She edits *Dogwood: A Journal of Poetry and Prose* and teaches at Fairfield University and in Fairfield's Low-Residency MFA Program.

Sonya Huber on "Breastfeeding Dick Cheney"

I've been keeping track of what made me mad since I could hold a pen, but it's only since I started meditating that I began to develop a limited ability to write about anger. Meditation, for me, is less like sipping green tea and more like plunging a toilet. If there's peace it's mostly in being stunned by the Mack Trucks of my emotions barreling along my internal highways. Then I have to feel the anger all over again (and again) as I sit at my computer—a process which is kind of overwhelming at first and then turns into an invigorating wrestling match demanding precision.

I've looked hard at and learned from some of my favorite authors, who explore moments and lifetimes of anger at injustice and at the petty suffering doled out by life. These include Joy Williams, Sonali Deraniyagala, Richard Wright, Phillip Lopate, Marita Golden, Emily Rapp, Harriet Jacobs, Scott Russell Sanders, Dorothy Allison, W.E.B. DuBois, James Baldwin, Tobias Wolff, and bell hooks, and my list is ever-growing. Many of these authors, coincidentally or not, are African-American and/or women. What concerns me is that some of these authors (though not all) continue to be described as "angry" first—as if their emotions and the experiences that provoke them are peripheral and special interest rather than central to the human experience.

Those authors have also taught me to find an "objective correlative," some outside thing that is real, more than a symbol, an embodied element of the universe it's possible to look at deeply, a thing that can function as a hook for larger ideas. Dick Cheney worked as a hook in this essay because he served as a frame for the anger I had grown up in and carried around the U.S. engagement in the Persian Gulf region. Of course, what I don't touch in the essay is what else made me angry at that point in my life, and the answer is: many things, and I'm still writing to figure it all out. But Cheney was a way in. Thanks, Cheney.

Politics is a hard subject to write about, and in the face of that steep challenge, many essays decline and instead take on other matters, turning to an aesthetic or formal puzzle with a construction as delicate as a needlepoint pillow. When I read such constructions, I am forced to admire the skill displayed in their execution. It is good to have a density and range of forms in our work to inspire each other to experiment and to express everything that nonfiction has to offer the world. Yet I worry that fine-threaded constructions are coming to define "the essay," just as that form is in the process of reifying itself as an academic and literary genre. I wholeheartedly support this consolidation as nonfiction takes its rightful place as literature, but I worry that the future canon will include only those pieces in which white space and references to definitions from the Oxford English Dictionary carefully conceal all the freak-outs and deepest sadness, which will be consigned to memoir's messy basement. Those emotions, too, are equally worthy of essaying. They contain the most vulnerable points of our lives, the moments when the soul itself makes broad leaps—either backward in fear, or forward, maybe even toward justice.

TEACHING DEATH

Todd May

About a decade ago, I decided it was time to confront what seemed to me to be the most important issue a human being can face: death. I decided to do so in the way you might expect an academic philosopher to confront a difficult issue. I would teach a course about it. Along with a dozen or so willing (or unwilling) fellow travelers about half my age, I would read about and reflect upon the fact of my mortality.

It is not unusual for me to teach about issues about which I'm thinking. Often, I use teaching to reflect on issues that I don't want to approach in specialized philosophical language, issues that are important but not in my particular area of philosophical expertise, issues that deserve thought and consideration but that aren't necessarily topics about which I would write a technical article or a book. War, justice, technology. Sooner or later, I suppose, it was inevitable that death would be added to that list.

But why a course on death at that particular time? Why was it somehow ripe for me to drag myself and these students into a reflective confrontation with death then? I suppose that if I say I was in my mid-forties, many readers won't need further explanation. And, in fact, that was likely it. I was at that point where I could see the far shore of my life more clearly than the shore from which I had set out. And that had me thinking.

As I began to put together a syllabus for the course, the first thing I discovered was the difficulty of cobbling together a good list of readings for a seminar on the philosophy of death. The problem wasn't that I couldn't find any philosophical writings on death. I could. They simply weren't the kind of writings I was looking for. Philosophers of death mostly seemed to write about the technical matters that define life and death and that, perhaps, help doctors who are uncertain about whether to sustain a particular life. Not that there is anything wrong with that angle, as far as it goes. But I wasn't really interested in thinking about the question of when someone is technically dead or whether someone who dies of cancer two days before she would have been run over by a car anyway really suffers a tragedy when the cancer gets her first. I wasn't interested in the question of whether someone who dies after having Alzheimer's disease is a different person at her death from someone who dies with her mental facilities intact.

What I was interested in was the fact that I am going to die—that each of us is going to die. I wanted to confront that fact reflectively with my students. I wanted to look death in the face, have it look back at me and then figure out how, in the glare of its gaze, I was going to continue on. And when it came to philosophical writings on the fact of death, I discovered that after the ancients, it was pretty slim pickings. There was material in Plato and Aristotle, a wealth of riches in the Stoics and the Epicureans, and then only an essay or an excerpt here and there until Heidegger's famous chapter on death in *Being and Time*. And that was about it. In the end, I turned to literature for assistance. That did the trick. Tolstoy's *The Death of Ivan Illyich*, Jim Crace's *Being Dead*, Milan Kundera's *Immortality*— these and other texts helped me design a syllabus that would keep us on track in thinking about our lives and our deaths.

Then there was another hurdle I hadn't predicted. The curriculum committee in my department didn't want to allow me to teach the seminar. Why? It wasn't philosophical enough. Too much literature. In the end, I was begrudged the course mostly because there were no other seminars being offered that semester. I got it by default. And it turned out to be the best course I ever conducted, or am ever likely to conduct.

There is much about the course I still reflect upon. Among those is the dearth of philosophical writings on the fact that we will die. Why is it that so few philosophers—and, in particular, so few modern and contemporary philosophers—write on this? Contemporary philosophers who do write on the fact of death mostly seem to engage with Epicurus's and Lucretius's raft of arguments to the effect that we have nothing to fear in death: because in death we don't exist (so there is no is nobody there to mind being dead); because we didn't mourn over not existing before we were born (so there's no reason to mourn over not existing after we die); or, in a more generous vein, because we need to exit our lives gracefully to leave room for the generations that follow us. These are all interesting arguments, and they deserve attention. But, with the exception of that single chapter in *Being and Time*, is there really so little else to be said about the issue philosophically?

Maybe the problem is that each of us, as Heidegger tells us, must confront death alone. There is nobody to do it for us, no one who can stand in as our representative. If that is true—and certainly it is—then perhaps philosophy is not the place to confront death. Philosophy's coin of trade is generality, even universality. It tends to reside in the realm of what is true for all rather than in that of what each must confront singly. And so perhaps literature is, indeed, the proper place for reflection on death. In literature, humans don't die; individuals die. Each of them dies his or her own particular death. Ivan Illyich dies. Jim Crace's Joseph and Celice die—hand in hand, to be sure, murdered together on the beach. But, as Crace makes us understand, they die alone. Maybe my colleagues on the curriculum committee were not entirely wrong. Death is not a philosophical issue; it is a literary one.

And yet, if philosophy is supposed to have something to do with thinking about our lives, should it not also have something to do with thinking about a defining fact of those lives—i.e., that they end? I suspect it is not enough for philosophy to define the problem as one out of its realm. It is not enough to say, "Death? That's down the hall in the English department." I also suspect most philosophers would agree with me on this. So again: why the dearth of philosophical considerations of death?

I believe the reason is twofold. First, philosophers are human beings. Like non-philosophers, we die. And this causes us anxiety. So we think about other things in regard to living—how to act, what we can reasonably know, what justice is, how our minds relate to the world—rather than dying.

But what about the ancients, for whom death was a central issue? They died, too, and a number of them thought and wrote about it. There is something that distinguishes us from the ancients, something that encompasses all of us, not just philosophers. We live in a period where the denial of death, at least for those of us fortunate enough to live decently well in technologically advanced societies, is not merely a social temptation but instead a phenomenon approaching a collective illusion. We are no longer on intimate terms with death.

I am told that the average life span of Americans about a hundred years ago was not much more than forty years. Now people regularly live into their eighties. And when we begin to decline, we do not so much think about death as about medicine. We look for ways to prolong our lives. This, in itself, is not a bad thing; all things equal, a longer life is better than a shorter one. However, in the same gesture that we prolong our lives, we also postpone thinking about death. It is as though death becomes a misfortune, a medical or personal failure, rather than an inevitability. We might even be forgiven for thinking that one of the reasons we prolong our lives is precisely so we don't have to think about death.

If my seminar is any evidence, the thought of one's death can be more than frightening. It can be overwhelming. The first day of class, I asked my twelve students to take out a piece of paper and write on it the four things most meaningful to them about their lives. I assured them no one else would see what they wrote. Then I asked them to fold the papers up and pass them to me, again saying that I would not see what they had written. I held the pieces of paper in my hand and told my students to keep in mind what they had written there. Then I tore the papers into shreds. I thought this might impress them a bit with the stakes involved in the course.

I was not ready for the collective gasp my students let out as I ripped up the papers. It was as though something foreign, and threatening, had just entered the room. And, for those of us in the contemporary world, that is probably exactly what happens when we are forced to confront our deaths.

Philosophers—like my students, like me, like the rest of us—don't think about death because the tools of our society permit us to forgo thinking about it. And the medical and other health advances of the contemporary world—in contrast to so many other recent developments, such as advanced weaponry, environmental degradation, neoliberalism—are undoubtedly among the developments we could unreservedly call historical advances. We have extended our lifespans to lengths our recent ancestors couldn't have imagined. The cost it seems to have exacted, however, is the loss of our intimacy with the most important fact about ourselves. We live as though we are immortal, and the more we train our eyes on the immortal, the more farsighted we become and the less clearly we can see that the horizon is not laid out endlessly before us. If, instead, we cast our vision upon ourselves, we would see that we are not, in fact, immortal. Death comes to each of us. Sooner or later, it is our lot.

And this, I want to argue, is necessary if our lives are to have the meaning they do.

There have been—in literature, of course—a number of reflections on immortality. The most famous among them is probably Jonathan Swift's struldbrugs, who live forever but continue to age. They are a pathetic bunch, wizened and decrepit, shunned by their fellow creatures, who put them out to pasture with minimal provisions and support. And yet, since the promise of modern medicine is not just longevity but vitality, perhaps the struldbrugs lack relevance for contemporary audiences or immortality-seekers. Perhaps Jorge Luis Borges's short story aptly named "The Immortal" provides a better comparison. Borges's protagonist, Joseph Cartaphilus, finds himself among the immortals, whose landscape is dismal indeed. He learns that the immortals have stopped caring for themselves or others; life has lost all urgency for them since everything will happen of its own accord, sooner or later. Cartaphilus meets Homer in the City of Immortals and reflects that Homer having composed *The Odyssey* is not such a remarkable feat, for "if we postulate an infinite period of time, with infinite circumstances and changes, the impossible thing is not to compose *The Odyssey,* at least once."

Our age—and again, I emphasize this applies only to the few of us fortunate enough to live in comfortable circumstances in developed nations—is one that denies death in favor of immortal strivings. But have we really thought about what immortality might mean? Imagine that you were to live forever. Imagine that your life were to go on without cease. And, to give it the best gloss, imagine that you were to do so as a healthy human being and that everyone you cared about could join you in this immortal condition. Would this be a future worth having? Would you want it?

In order to see what is at stake, let us give this imagining some flesh. What are your favorite activities? Sports, music, reading, watching television, talking with friends, eating at interesting restaurants? Take any or all of these, and then consider doing them for five thousand years. Or ten thousand. The first ten thousand years, of course, would be only a flicker in the span of immortality. One image that captures immortality for me, one which I believe comes from earlier sages, is that of a desert the size of the Sahara. To this desert flies a bird every thousand years. The bird collects a grain of sand from this desert and flies off, only to return a thousand years later to collect another grain. When the bird has cleared all the sand from the Sahara, not even an instant of eternity will have passed. Immortality lasts, I think we can agree, a long time.

Over such an immensity of time, what happens to our projects, our relationships, the meaning and character of our lives? They become shapeless. When there is time for everything, and perhaps everything will happen over the course of one's time, then the urgency of living is sapped. The threads tying us to our lives go slack. The philosopher Martha Nussbaum explains this concept in her book on the Stoic philosophers, *The Therapy of Desire*: "[T]he intensity and dedication with which very many human activities are pursued cannot be explained without reference to the awareness that our opportunities are finite, that we cannot choose these activities indefinitely many times. In raising a child, in cherishing a lover, in performing a demanding task of work or thought or artistic creation, we are aware, at some level, of the thought that each of these efforts is structured and constrained by finite time." It is not that structure and constraint alone give our lives meaning. But without the finiteness of time, it is unclear if they could sustain us in the meaningfulness they possess for us mortals. As Homer concludes in Borges's "The Immortal," "Everything among the mortals has the values of the irretrievable and the perilous." One might argue here that there is so much to do in life, so many activities to engage in, that it would be myopic to say immortality would leave our lives shapeless or bereft. After all, there are people being born every day. There are different activities and pursuits being created all the time. Think of the video games and novels being written as you read this, the basketball games yet to be played, even the slow changing of the earth's surface.. There is always something new to do, some project to be pursued, someone else to meet. How could a person at all dedicated to life lose the intensity of living under these conditions?

This line of thought fails to appreciate the uniqueness of each of us. We cannot be just anybody. The trajectory of each life offers particular passions and interests and styles of relationships. There are certain people with whom we form deep relationships; others are just acquaintances. There are projects and engagements that stir us; others are just ways of passing time. There are places we want to see and immerse ourselves in because they resonate with something inside us, perhaps something inchoate even to us; other places are just amusing. The idea that novelty could continuously lend our lives shape misses this essential fact about us. For me, a life where what was left to do involved fishing, romance novels, racquetball, cocktail parties, and gardening would not be a life that compelled me. I would not be living; I would just be soldiering on.

In order for our lives to have a sense, we must die. We may try to avoid thinking about this, but it remains a cornerstone for our living.

And yet, we cannot conclude from the fact that immortality would be bad for us that we should embrace the fact of our dying. Death is not good for us, except perhaps for those among us in extreme pain or suffering.

This is the paradox of human mortality. We need death to give us meaning, and yet the meaningfulness of our lives is precisely what makes death so frightening. Without death, our lives would be shapeless. Since we do, in fact, die, our lives often take on a shape, but once they have a shape, a meaning, who wants to die?

As a philosopher, I am supposed to have a solution to this paradox. I am supposed to guide people on the narrow straits between death and immortality, to navigate us through this Scylla and Charybdis into the tranquil waters of a consistent and non-paradoxical relationship to mortality.

I cannot do so.

Death and its other, immortality, present us with the paradox our lives must grasp. We must simultaneously recognize the evil to each of us that death inescapably is and yet also not pine for a future that would bleed us of the reasons to fear death. We must embrace the fragility that lends our lives beauty and, at the same time, withdraws beauty from us. There is no straight path, nor a crooked one, that will lead us beyond all this. Our home lies here, we might say.

There are those in philosophical circles who seek a bid for immortality through the back door of this paradox. They argue that however many days I am granted, if I were asked at the end of that time whether I wanted another day, would I not say yes? And if, at the end of the next day, I were asked again, would I not continue to say yes? And in the end, would this not be the embrace of immortality that I have just denied?

This is clever, but ultimately it requires the mortality it

seeks to overcome. If I am asked on a given day whether I would like another one, the background of the asking is the fact of my death. I live that day, in the hours before I am asked, as a mortal creature. I am not granted immortality; I am granted another day within mortality. And, then, another and, perhaps, another. The framework of my life remains a mortal one. I remain someone who faces death but with an indefinite reprieve. How long this cycle can go on without, one day, my saying I have had enough of these extra days is a question for which I have no answer. However, the frame of the question presupposes the extension of a mortal life, not the granting of an immortal one.

In any case, this offer is not a choice we are given. We are only given one choice, which is to die. And this, of course, is no choice at all.

Near the end of the fifteen-week seminar I taught a decade ago, during the discussion of Crace's *Being Dead*, one of my students became noticeably silent. She wouldn't make eye contact with anyone and just stared in front of her as each class unfolded. After a week of this, I asked her after class whether she was OK. Yes, she replied, she was OK. But, she added, she didn't want to talk. She couldn't talk. For the first time in her life, I realized, she was looking right at death. And, although she didn't say this, it was looking right back at her. I knew what she meant and knew that there was nothing I could do to take away what she saw. After all, there were moments in class when I had to stop speaking because the hitch in my voice was beginning to overtake me. After all, I myself was waking up from nightmares, covered in sweat, knowing only that all of this would one day end. And after all, wasn't all this why we had embarked upon this journey? She sat in class in those moments, staring straight ahead because she knew that when death appears before you, when it really appears, there is nowhere else to look.

In the end, then, the philosophers whose reflections on death I could not find because they were not there were half right in their avoidance, in their refusal to have death really appear. There is much to fear from death, just as there would be from immortality. In seeking to come to terms with death through the course I taught, I was treading on ground that rightfully stirs the deepest anxieties among all of us who consider our lives from outside the immediacy of what they ask of us. I was lucky to have had that particular group of people, young but game to confront the most intractable problem most humans ever face; several of them, long since graduated, still keep in touch and write to tell me about how the course affected them, how they think differently about their lives knowing that they will die.

I would like to say that since teaching the course, I have risen above the silence this fear of death often induces, in order to place it before myself and others. But this, too, would only be half right. I have written on death, and have been asked to speak on death. But I have not taught the seminar on death again and have no plans to do so in the future.

TODD MAY is Class of 1941 Memorial Professor of the Humanities at Clemson University. He is the author of eleven books of philosophy. Many of these books concern issues in contemporary French thought; however, he has also written on friendship, politics, and, of course, death. When he is not pondering these issues himself, he teaches them to others in the United States and Europe, listens to music, and exercises just hard enough to keep death temporarily at bay.

SELF-INTERVIEW

Gordon Lish

Editors' note: According to the author, a reporter from Interview
Magazine *initially interviewed Gordon Lish for an article.
Evidently,* Interview *was unsatisfied; it subsequently sent Lish
a list of questions, asking him to make the interview "more
accessible"; this "Self-Interview" was the result.*

This is a setup, right? It's all a setup, right? I mean, I am
not sitting somewhere shooting my mouth off to somebody sitting the same somewhere with me. There is no
tape-recording going on. There is no note-taking going on.
What the deal is instead is that I, Lish, am sitting by my
lonesome with a list, which list is the product not of my
contrivance but of *Interview*'s. (How else have the composure
to manage the acoustical divertissement of *list* and *Lish* whilst
evincing seeming indifference to an exhibition of an absence of
humility?) I mean, the entries that constitute it, this list,
Interview entered them. Fine. I'm ready. Got pencil and paper.
Actually, it's a lie—got felt-tip and paper. Anyway, here is the
list as *Interview* made it—Death and Immortality, the Most
Overrated Writers in America, Harold Brodkey, Harold
Bloom, My Being Called the Antichrist, Knopf, What Writing
Means to Me, What My Enemies Mean to Me, and, finally, Me,
Gordon Lish. Hey, that's me again—Lish again! Swell. Here
goes. *Death*? Scared shitless of it. Not of dying—which I elect
to accuse of being sexy and dramatic and an occasion for
rapturous opportunism and for a certain ultimacy in narcis-
sism—but of being dead. Which state of non-being, reported

allure of consciouslessness notwithstanding, I would do
anything to get out of. Even art. Like remarking, for example,
the hallucination written into the gerund just used: because
you're not going to, I'm not going to, no one's going to, be
anything. So to say *being dead* is to get it wrong because you
are saying it wrong. And ditto, less tellingly but tellingly
enough, goes for saying *non-being*, fair enough? So by my
saying speech says it wrong, I can believe myself to be in charge
of the conditions, which is indeed an illusion, but, I claim, a
not unprofitable one. Skip it, it goes without saying I am not in
charge of anything by saying. But I give myself to believe that I
sort of maybe tragically magically pretty pathetically pitiably a
little am—by placing into motion a spoken token of myself, a
meagerness, yes, but one whose dialectical action I can pretend
transmutes me, its origin, into a muchness by reason (irratio-
nal reason) of my being the father of it, okay? Doing art is not a
way of saying it right but of saying it as wrong as you can say
it—namely, an act of saying under the sign of your hallucination, not under anyone else's. Which is why the other famous
faith system we devised for ourselves doesn't do a job for me.
Likelier for me to get myself to think I can overcome, or can
march myself to a distance from, Beckett's sign than God's.
God's sign—the event of my end, that unimpeachable dissolu-
tion—is very dense and specific. Whereas Beckett's transgres-
sion against me, his text, is nowhere near as material and
aggressive. I wake up innocent but hours nearer my undoing.
This is an offense God delivers to me—Jesus, Jesus!—in
irrepressibly vivacious and precise detail. Everything else in
experience (we can take Beckett again, or take *pease porridge
hot, pease porridge cold*, or take the mortification of the flesh)
is comparatively soft and insubstantial and thus more or less
resistible, yes? God—God's agent nature—is the one object
whose incommensurate power nothing I can do can subdue.
Oh, fiddlesticks. Give me Beckett—and the other mighty
dead—that I may vie to be among them or even to trick myself
to believe that I am over them. Give me—guess I am quoting
Frost—any chance bit that I might manipulate it—am done

with the quoting—that I might make of the labor a deforma-
tion in my name—the controlled conjunctions, continuities,
turbulences, morbid deviations, and so forth. False, false, false,
to be sure, but here's a deception I can let myself succumb to
because my name is Gordon, is Lish, is language, is not God, is
not the clock, is not the rock. Vanity, vanity, vanity—you bet.
So, therefore, why not—next-entry-wise—notions of *immortality*? Which all it is is vanity imagining for itself a future, no?
Well, immortality, yes, such a notion is right up there with the
other enabling fictions—those of no fear, no severance,
unbreachable sovereignty, anxiety-free freedom, perfection,
completion. It couldn't hurt. It could only help. Glad to go
along with it for the time being. *Most Overrated Writers in
America*? You mean writers of fiction of my generation in the
context of their fictions? Okay, how about this—how about
every writer of fiction but Lish? That's one answer to your
question—probably the only unquestionably durable answer
the person named Lish could contribute. But here's another—
every writer of fiction but the Don DeLillo who wrote any
novel Don DeLillo wrote, every writer of fiction but the
foregoing and the Cynthia Ozick who wrote "Bloodshed" and
"Usurpation: Other People's Stories," every writer of fiction but
the foregoing and the Cormac McCarthy who wrote *Outer
Dark* and *Blood Meridian*, every writer of fiction but the
foregoing and the Harold Brodkey— of course, of course!—
who wrote "His Son, in His Arms, in Light, Aloft," who wrote
"Verona: A Young Woman Speaks," who wrote "Ceil," who
wrote "S. L.," who wrote "Largely an Oral History of My
Mother," who wrote "The Boys on Their Bikes." Please, you
want for me to badmouth? I am happy to badmouth—both the
living and the dead. I could give you names and addresses till
the cows come home. But so go pick for yourself. Because
whatever proposition you come back to me with, chances are it
wouldn't be in me to rumpus around with you on account of it.
Neither, it seems reliable to assert, will it be in history for it to
do so. On the other hand, I beg you not ever to come back to
me with any of the dozens of, with any of the scores of, with

any of the hundreds of grandeurs America underpraises, dispraises, or—the fuckers!—appraises neither one way nor the other. I mean, ignores, is ignorant of, proclaims its smug ignoramusness because of. As witness your *New York Times*, your *Village Voice*, your *New York Review of Books*, to cite certain more notable igginesses in sight. Having not one word to say, the lot of them, either for or against, for instance, Dawn Raffel's *In the Year of Long Division*—or either for or against Sam Michel's *Under the Light*, for instance. Ditto Brian Evenson's *Altmann's Tongue*, ditto Victoria Redel's *Where the Road Bottoms Out*, which for-instancing I guess I could also get myself to keep up until kingdom come. *Harold Brodkey*? We used to be friends. Or we used to appear to be friends. Now we are no longer friends—neither actually nor apparently. *Harold Bloom*? We used to be friends. We used to appear to be friends. Now we are no longer friends—neither actually nor apparently. Ah, but these states of affairs hardly rule out my reading Brodkey and Bloom. You would have to watch me pack up and take myself off to jail if there were a law made that tried to make me quit reading Brodkey and Bloom. Which would just this minute go double for Donoghue and Kristeva and Deleuze and Guatarri and Levinas and Lentricchia and Langer and Nelson Goodman and Adorno and—who have I just now got laid out on the tiny table next to my toilet?—Hegel. Hey, hey—how about, what about "Gordo, why come is it that you are no longer friends with Brodkey, for one, and with Bloom, for another?" Answer? Because he's a shit, for one, and a shit, for another! Answer? Because he's a stinking rotten shit, for one, and a stinking rotten shit, for another! But who's calling names? Am I calling names? These men will be among the mighty dead one day—gods, be gods, such as anyone might come gloriously to install either or both for himself. But better revered as ghosts changelessly vaporous in the firmament than spotted as all too fleshly moral dishevelments for the children to see panhandling on the Rialto. *My Being Called the Antichrist*? No kidding. Somebody did that? Who did that? Maybe in Los Angeles maybe. Maybe in Portland. Maybe in Chicago.

Here in NYC all I am trying to do is betray, betray—but on the page, baby, on the page!—such that the ties that bind me will be let loose from me for long enough for me to get a toe or two into a hitherto untrampled domain. This means being against everything—against it!—but that means, first and foremost, being against myself. So, check, if there is good in me, then I am against it—but let us seek to keep the categories discrete. I'm all for anything, all for being Yertle the turtle, plus also all for opposing what I say I'm all for—but on the page, baby, on the page! Which happens to be the elsewhere I chose and still choose. Well, okay, I admit it—maybe also, you know, forgive me, don't get excited, but, right, right, no argument, it's true, put the cuffs on me, you got me, I give up—it all goes ditto for in the class, where I am the demon's consort, its thing, its conduit. *Knopf?* We used to be friends. We appeared to be friends. (Come on, you know the rest of the dirge by now.) But so what's the deal here, so friendless at sixty-one? Am I, at long last, wising up? Which, however, is not to say you will catch me looking one inch inattentive to the careers of any of the following Knopf undertakings—Gary Lutz's *Stories in the Worst Way*, Jason Schwartz's *A German Picturesque*, Diane Williams's *The Stupefaction*, Christine Schutt's *Nightwork*, Ben Marcus's *The Age of Wire and String*, Ken Sparling's *Dad Says He Saw You at the Mall*, Anne Carson's *Plainwater*—since it was I who, before my being Knopfed off, took them all on—not to mention, proud to mention, Denis Donoghue's *Walter Pater*. Oh, and another thing—Wayne Hogan's *Book of Life*—no, correct that, *Book of Tubes*—be smart and get in touch with me at the Q, at 212-888-4769, if you are a publisher who is not too chickenshit to stand strong for a corker. Now then, *What Writing Means to Me?* Meaning itself. Despite the meaning-lessness of it. An answer to the insult. Despite the exorbitance of it. The works, or Works, which was my dead wife's name before it was Lish. But best to say time. Because time beats meaning. Best to say writing means life lived in Lish-made time, not life spent in given time, not life suffered in death-row time, which is nature's time, dig? *What My Enemies Mean to*

Me? Everything—the works (oh, don't worry, I know all too well, I know exactly what I am saying) again—the inertia-taunting otherness in me—starting with God and with time and with Mommy and Daddy and ending with the vicious incurable ironizing instability of the sentence. Oh, heck—of the comma, of the period. On the other hand, who, what, is there anything exterior or, for that matter, interior, that is not the enemy? That is not an impediment to your existence, to your freedom? *Gordon Lish?* Hey, that's me, that's me!—my name, not the first governance but the most agreeable governance. Well, isn't it, wasn't it, a naming, the whole damned deal, an onomatologically determined act of being? Which, when you get right down to it—which is where we're all going to one day have to get to—namely, right down on your back on your deathbed to it—which would you sooner say? Give you two choices. "Oh, well, that's life." Or: "Yeah, that was me." It of course being conceded there is any say left in you.

GORDON LISH is the author of *Collected Fictions, Dear Mr. Capote, Peru, What I Know So Far, Mourner at the Door, Extravaganza, My Romance, Zimzum,* and *Epigraph.* His most recent book is a collection of stories, *Goings: In Thirteen Settings.* This body of work, together with his activities as a teacher and editor, has placed him at the forefront of the American literary scene.

RACHEL AT WORK: ENCLOSED, A MOTHER'S REPORT

Jane Bernstein

In the spring of 2002, the crocuses pushed up and the daffodils blossomed and froze, and I worried about work—not my own, which I love, but what kind of work my developmentally disabled eighteen-year-old daughter Rachel might be able to do when she is no longer in the shelter of school.

On one April morning—an average morning, in fact—after quarreling with her because she would not put her dishes in the dishwasher and threatening to take away her Uno cards if she did not brush her teeth, I asked her if she knew what *work* meant. After a few false starts—trying to make a case for computer solitaire as work, for instance—she pretty much nailed it. Work, she said, was "when you have to do stuff they ask you to do."

Did she like to work? I asked.

"Not really."

"How come?"

"'Cause the way they talk to me is really mean. They talk harsh on me, Ma. Put it this way: When they talk to me, they tell me to be quiet and all that junk."

Outside, a horn honked. I trailed behind Rachel as she reached for the banister and slowly edged her way down the porch steps, then onto the van that takes her to the Children's Institute, where, on a typical day, she will sort and deliver mail, make a bed, and wipe down a table.

After the van pulled away from the sidewalk, I stood for a moment, limp from a combination of exhaustion and relief, since my

daughter, with her long list of "special needs" is an exceedingly
difficult person, especially in the morning and evening when
I ask her to do the routines that most of us do without much
thought. Most of us—*us* meaning the population that designates
itself "normal"—don't need to be prompted to use the toilet,
don't at eighteen insist on wearing a sweat suit on a day when the
temperature might reach eighty. We don't finish breakfast with a
ring of food around our mouths—or if we do, are grateful when
someone says, "Honey, you've got food on your face." Most of us
don't mind touching our own faces to wipe it off. While often I
am reminded that Rachel is one of us, deserving of the rights and
privileges accorded to her by our constitution, on this morning—
during this whole season, while I have been thinking about how
to make her into a working girl—I have been reminded instead of
all the impediments in her way.

I always imagined that Rachel would work. Even after it became obvious that she would never read books or write a single
sentence, after I realized that she would never walk on the street
alone or live without supervision, I had a vision of her having
some sort of job, somewhere. When I saw a janitor or a person
busing tables, I would close my eyes and try to picture Rachel
doing that job, sure that despite her cognitive deficits, her poor
vision and poor fine-motor skills, she could be trained for
some job, somewhere. I speculated on the challenges of making a worker out of someone like my daughter, who is unable to
understand concepts like altruism and loyalty, who doesn't seem
to take pleasure from a job well done and would never fear being
fired. Still I went to sleep at night believing that some job would
be found and that the structure and routine it provided would
be good for her. Unlike many of "us," her capacity for happiness
was great, it seemed. All we had to do was help her find a job and
a safe place to live, and we would be on our way.

My vague dream was nourished by several factors: First,
that Rachel would be in school until she was nearly twenty-two.
Second, that she had been given an after-school job at Café J,
a snack bar staffed by people with special needs at the Jewish

Community Center near our home. Though a trained therapeutic staff-support person (TSS) was always at her side, making sure her behavior was appropriate and keeping her on task, still it was work. Third, I believed in some equally vague way that the law would protect her. In the back of my mind was the knowledge that if Rachel had been born less than a generation ago, I would have been advised—pressured, perhaps—to put her into an institution. Even if I had ample funds, I would have been hard pressed to find a nearby school she could attend. In those days a conversation with the words *work* and *Rachel* in the same sentence would not have been even vaguely feasible. The Developmental Disabilities Assistance and Bill of Rights Act of 1975 and the Education for All Handicapped Children Act of 1975 (now called Individuals with Disabilities Education Act, or IDEA) passed only eight years before Rachel's birth. These laws guaranteed her access to free education, the chance to find decent, affordable housing in her own community, the opportunity to work and play—in short, the constitutional right to choose how and where she wanted to live.

I was lulled by these laws and by the fact that thus far I had not had to fight for Rachel's right to be educated. In New Jersey, where we had lived until she was eight, she'd had excellent services, starting with an early-intervention program she attended as an infant. And when I moved to Pittsburgh, ready to fight if necessary to have her placed in an approved private school of my choosing, the school district looked at her medical and educational documents from New Jersey and cooperated fully with my desires. In 1992 she began attending the Children's Institute, and since then the school has been fulfilling the law by providing her education.

When Rachel turned fourteen, she began the "transition process" as stipulated by a 1997 revision of IDEA, the time when we—parents, educators and Rachel herself—were supposed to begin to prepare her for life beyond school. Each summer since then, I'd filled out long questionnaires with dozens of questions about her likes and dislikes. I listed the agencies that had worked with her, the stores and restaurants she liked. I wrote down her favorite foods and games, her after-school activities and some activities I wanted to see her try. Could she be trusted with money? I was asked. Did she understand the passage of time? Could she accept responsibility for her actions, make appointments, talk on the phone? I answered these questions carefully, with her best interests in mind. I prided myself on being realistic, believed that I had no illusions about my expectations for my daughter. I could see the big picture, I would have said.

Then in September 2001, I opened a manila envelope from Rachel's school, looked at her curriculum for that academic year, and saw *washing machine, dryer, setting the table*. I didn't think, *This is great*, or even, *This is the law*. I thought, full of utter despair, *They've given up*. Of course I knew that she'd been working at school—she and her class had tried out some lawn-maintenance jobs and had torn paper for the kennels at the Animal Rescue League—but her educational program in past years had included looking at pre-primers, sounding out words, learning to develop a sight vocabulary, answering verbal-comprehension questions about a story, counting by rote to thirty-five, identifying seasonal changes, the needs of a plant, the characteristics of lions, tigers, elephants. Though she continued to function well below grade level, the tone in the documents had always been full of strategies that would be employed and accommodations made for her, full of hope for what she might yet become.

The language in the document that set out her plan for the 2001–2002 academic year was blunt: "Due to neurological disabilities and extensive need for modification in all areas, Rachel is unable at this time to participate in the general regular education curriculum." She would be in the Life Skills Program instead. Her goals would be to learn the location of classrooms, sort mail by number up to twenty with sixty-percent accuracy, count five items without cues, collate four color-coded items with verbal cues. The tasks seemed so meager—so pathetically small. First I bristled. Then I thought, *She really is delayed*, though for eighteen years I had known this, believed I had accepted it fully. But there was something final about it—*is and always will be* "unable to participate."

Looking at this document, I was forced to see that progress for this school year was being measured by my eighteen-year-old daughter's ability to deliver mail independently to a two-room route in a building she had known for nine years.

In October at the meeting to discuss her IEP—Individual Educational Plan—I said I wanted her teachers to continue working with her on some basic academic skills, since I believed it was important for Rachel to know the difference between Women's Room and Men's Room, between Entrance and Exit, Cheerios and Frosted Flakes. And indeed, with just the spirit of cooperation I'd always felt at these meetings, some additional goals were drafted: that Rachel would "identify words related to shopping, community signs, menus, and recipes," that she would make change up to one dollar. I thanked her teachers and the representative from the school district for working with Rachel and left the building alone.

I was still reeling, utterly stunned. What about the progress she'd been making at the café? Her TSS had been telling me that lately she had been more cooperative about working, that she was using the cash register and closing up the café without being reminded of the sequence of tasks she had to do. Yes, I understood that the JCC café was a protected environment and that she had someone at her side prompting and cueing and redirecting. Still, two rooms without distraction—was that the most her teachers at the Children's Institute thought she could achieve?

The only way I would learn whether I was deluded or her teachers underestimated her abilities was to observe her in class. But several months would pass before I stepped into her school. And that, I think, had to do with the fourth reason I had held onto my some-job-somewhere dream and let myself imagine that those 1975 laws would be carried out flawlessly, that along with some job for Rachel, there would be some*place* for her to live, some guaranteed safety net. I was tired. Rachel is a difficult person. She gets funding for mental health services because of her "long history of behavior problems, particularly when she is with her mother." Whatever doesn't require my urgent attention goes into an okay-for-the-present category.

Her teachers and staff were there, and so had been her future out of school.

I've tried hard to understand my inscrutable daughter. I listen to her, interact with her, worry about her. I've accommodated to her deficits and championed her strengths and thought of myself as her advocate and her interpreter, the one who understood her best. That spring, after visiting Rachel's school, I realized that I had failed to integrate all I knew about Rachel. My view of my daughter was limited. So was my understanding of "work."

Here's what I learned:

1. RACHEL MUST LEARN HOW TO MAKE TOAST.

She was around five when we started working with her to put on her own shoes. An occupational therapist strung elastic laces in her shoes so that tying and untying would be unnecessary. Then we reinforced—and reinforced—the procedure, starting with "off," which was easier. First you sit in a chair. Next you bring one leg up and over the other. Cross that leg. Reach for the heel of the shoe. Pull. It was the first time I considered how complicated, and how frustrating, it might be to take off one's shoe.

I thought about teaching Rachel to put on her shoes when I observed her morning cooking class. The group had been doing a unit on breakfast, and on this particular morning, their teacher, Bob Russell, produced a bag of bread and announced that the topic for the day was toast. Learning to make toast, like putting on one's shoes, is a multi-step operation. First you had to wipe down the counter "because you might drop the toast, and germs are *gross!*" Then you had to figure out what you wanted to put on the toast. And then, after the students slowly offered suggestions for what they might put on their bread—butter, peanut butter, margarine, jam—they had to figure out where they might find these things.

For instance, "Where is butter kept?" Bob asked. What about the jelly?

So you have this purple jelly. What flavor is purple? What flavor is the red?

Sometimes you have to push hard on the toaster handle to get the bread to go down. Sometimes you don't.

How do you get the containers open? Sometime you lift the lid. Sometimes you unscrew the jar.

What do you use to get the stuff out—a spoon or a knife? Can you manage a butter knife, or will you need a broad, flexible spreader?

Safety. Germs. Hand-washing. Choice. Spreading what you've chosen to put on the toast as evenly as possible. Trying to cut the toast in half.

That night at dinner, I sat across the table from my daughter and heard myself say, "Don't shove giant chunks into your mouth. . . . Chew your food—with your mouth closed please. . . . Use a napkin. . . .Wipe your face and hands."

I thought about work not merely as a specific job or career but as "exertion" and "effort," which also are definitions. I thought of how hard Rachel worked, how for her getting dressed is work. So is clearing the breakfast table, brushing her teeth, negotiating the front steps on a sunny day. Even eating was full of lessons: You could choke. You'll gross people out. Cleanliness counts. Little is self-evident to my daughter, since she is not attuned to matters of safety or health or other people's judgment of her. And these small, necessary things—cutting her food into smaller pieces, opening the napkin, wiping her fingers—are labor for her.

At the same time, she can be astoundingly lazy, capable of standing for a half-hour in the shower and never once reaching for the soap. She tries to manipulate everyone she meets. The instant a new person is within earshot, my princess of Pittsburgh will get that person to lift, tote, fetch, serve, and attend to her every need.

Rachel must learn to make her own toast. Even if she is blessed with the most accommodating friend or aide, she must learn to choose what she wants to eat and where she wants to go. She must be responsible for basic hygiene and cleanliness. The more independent she becomes, the better chance she has for being out in the world, something my gregarious daughter craves. The domestic skills she learns will carry her beyond the kitchen into the world where things have levers, lids, and screw tops, are stored in cabinets behind wooden doors, where there are slots, stairs, escalators that go up and down, revolving doors. Learning to make toast is helping her live with dignity.

Toast is more than toast.

And Life Skills doesn't mean this is the end. These skills will help her be part of a community and part of the working world.

2. SUPPORTED EMPLOYMENT IS NOT A SURE THING.
To most people there's a single face of individuals with intellectual disabilities out there in the workplace: the supermarket bagger. It's the most visible job, the one we see most often. A bagger, like my pal Jimmy, an older man, balding, missing a few teeth, who bags groceries efficiently and carefully at the local supermarket, heavy stuff on the bottom, the eggs in a separate bag. (When Jimmy sees me, he stops, opens his arms wide, grunts with utter glee, and then *pronto* is back to work.) According to the 1990 census, about eighty-seven percent of the seven million people in the United States with intellectual disabilities are, like Jimmy, mildly affected, a little slower than average in learning new information and skills. In the workplace they have proven to be diligent and loyal; they don't job-hop or pose any additional health or safety issues.

At Rachel's school this kind of "competitive employment" is only one of three categories for students in the transition program and a possibility only for those who can become independent, learn time-management skills and how to use public transportation—all this before mastering the job itself. Other students are learning skills that will enable them to seek "supported employment," in a sheltered environment. In the third group are those with the most extreme health problems and disabilities, who will go to respite care or an adult training facility.

In April 2002 I visited a work-production class where students were learning specific skills.

When I visited Bob Russell's class, I learned that making toast was more than figuring out how brown you liked your bread. After I visited Dawn Tomlin's class, I understood that succeeding in work production meant not merely mastering specific job skills, like sorting, counting, or tallying, but also improving "time-on-task" skills, such as endurance, work rate, and speed. Good workers must be able to interact properly with each other. They have to learn to ask for supplies when they run short and seek help if there is something they don't understand.

Dawn's room was wonderfully familiar, on its walls a map of the world, a poster of baseball legend Roberto Clemente, a banner that read, *Understand the similarities. Celebrate the differences.*

The day of my visit, seven students sat around a long table. For several class periods, they'd been helping refurbish science kits for area schools for the Asset Project. The plastic pieces—thousands of them—for these kits had been separated into storage bins and stacked on the shelves of a cart. That afternoon the first job was sorting two tires into a Ziploc bag.

Two students were in wheelchairs. One had partial use of one hand. The other boy, Robin, writhed continually. On the tray of his wheelchair was a state-of-the-art language board that had been programmed to say at his command the kinds of things any student might need to say, for instance, "I need more supplies." He needed only to touch an icon on the board for it to speak. It was quite forgiving. The board "understood" Robin even when his aim was imperfect.

Five other workers were at the table—two dreamy-looking kids, and three others, including Rachel, on this day wearing her purple shirt and two strands of purple Mardi Gras beads. A teacher, two aides, and a student teacher were also helping out.

"Everyone will start with a yellow bin," Dawn said in a loud, clear voice. "Everyone will have—what do you have? A tire. You have to put two tires into one bag. This is the first step.

Okay. Does everybody have a large tire? Everybody should have a large tire. Now, what do you need?

"A bag!" someone eventually offered.

"Set two tires aside. You're going to have to put two—listen, Jake. *Two* tires into *one* bag. Okay? This is the first step."

And so they began, each with his or her spectrum of behavioral, cognitive and physical limitations. Each with issues. In this class, as in cooking, Rachel's were less apparent. My being at her school had put her into a bashful mode.

The boys in the wheelchairs first worked the tires into a plastic container. This made it easier for them to slide the tires into the Ziploc bag. If the sheer effort was obvious, so, too, was the absence of frustration, at least on this day.

The teachers prompted and coached without stop.

"*Two* in a bag."

"Good job, Jake."

"Robin, you are phenomenal!"

"Nice job!"

The language board said in its sci-fi voice, "I need a bag, please."

One boy had a hard time opening the Ziploc bag.

One girl was so slow it was as if she were floating underwater. Beside her a girl filled the bag without prompting or delay, then held up the bag, eyed it, placed it on the table, and very precisely, a fraction of an inch at a time, pressed down on the zip line until the bag was sealed. The whole process took a couple of minutes.

Meanwhile:

"One in each container!"

"You need to *ask* if you need more supplies."

"Dawn! Dawn!" This was my kid's familiar, maddening, attention-getting chime.

Dawn was busy with Jake, asking, "How many are in a bag? How *many*, Jake?"

"Two."

"And how many are in *that* bag?"

Jake looked up, fastened his huge eyes on her.

"I'm running out of bags!" Rachel said. Then catching my eye, she gestured *come here* with her fingers.

I ignored her, and she went back to her task.

And then—here's the thing—everyone was at work. Except for the teachers' enthusiastic prompts, the room was quiet. There was no sign of discord or unhappiness, no sense that this was drudgery. These students were more focused than the kids in an average public-school class. They were working! They were engaged. And they kept at it for twenty minutes, until the first sorting job was done. The next step would be for them to put smaller tires in the same bags.

But first, break time. A chance to stretch or move about, get a drink of water, chat with their friends. One of the aides put on latex gloves, filled a huge syringe with milky-colored liquid, and squirted it into Robin's mouth. He gurgled and gagged: it was a messy, difficult process.

When Rachel found me, I asked what she was doing. "They have them putting in tires for other people," she said. "They have a lot of stuff for students to sort." Then she whipped out a bottle of purple nail polish from her pocket.

Her classmate, a dark-haired girl, dreamy and angelic-looking, approached, getting right up in my face to sign. I was embarrassed that I did not understand her, reminded that I was a foreigner in this country where my daughter spent most of her time.

At last she formed a word. "Mommy?" she asked.

"Yes, I'm Rachel's Mom."

"Boots?" she asked.

I lifted up my pant cuff and showed her. "Yes," I said. "I'm wearing boots."

A boy came over to show me the mean-looking dog on the front of his T-shirt. "Kmart!" he said. I'd already heard him tell the teacher where his mom got the shirt.

When break was over, the students were back in their seats for a second, shorter session. Dawn reminded them with the same short, crisply delivered sentences that they would be putting two little tires into a bag that already had two bigger tires. And then they were back to work.

When I told Dawn that I was impressed, she agreed that the kids had been working well. "We can't keep them supplied. Their rate and speed has really improved."

I *was* impressed.

I was also stunned—by all the effort it took to put two tires into a plastic bag, by the sight of my daughter with her peers, by the range of ability and disability in that room, the sheer diversity of this population we so blithely lumped together as having "special needs." But mostly what stayed with me was the diligent way the kids worked.

On the way to see Michael Stoehr, who heads the career-education program, I thought how I felt when work goes well, when I have been so absorbed by my tasks, so "in the flow" that time vanishes. I thought about my sense of well-being at the end of a day like that, and how much I wanted that for Rachel, not because work per se would be good for her soul, not because I was pretending her life would resemble mine, but because when she was focused—playing Free Cell or solitaire on the computer, for instance—she was at peace. When we play Uno, one of the few games that fully engages her, she is fun to be with, her constant talking silenced at last.

So I was full of dreamy good cheer when I knocked on Michael Stoehr's door.

We talked about Dawn's class and some of the other work experiences Rachel has had at school—counting, sorting, housekeeping tasks. "One of her biggest difficulties is concentrating—just staying on task," he said. "She's distracted by what's going on around her." Though she was being considered for supported employment, it wasn't a sure thing.

In the world outside school—even in the world of supported employment—she would be expected to be "somewhat independent," he said. The job-coaching she would need was "pretty intense, pretty long range. And at this point, the supports just aren't out there."

Supported employment wasn't a sure thing.

Sometimes reality hits like an ax.

3. SHE TALKS SO MUCH IT'S HARD FOR EITHER OF US TO KNOW WHAT SHE WANTS.

What did Rachel want? Maybe it was ridiculous the way we were pushing her to do so many things that were so difficult for her, I thought when I left Stoehr's office. Maybe she just didn't want to work. But if she didn't have a job, what would she do all day long when she was no longer in school?

In this era of self-determination and person-centered planning, I was supposed to be asking these kinds of questions. All the literature I got explaining the transition process urged me to view my child as a "total person," and make sure her desires were "at the heart of decision making." The materials prepared by the Allegheny County Department of Human Services reminded me that self-determination is "a fundamental human right." People with intellectual disabilities should have "the freedom to choose the services and supports they want, the authority to control limited resources, and the responsibility for the decisions they make."

How can I respect Rachel's fundamental human right to choose what she will do after she is out of school without abandoning her to a world she cannot fully understand?

Well, there's conjecture: what I think she wants, based on my observations. And there are the dozens of questions about her likes and dislikes that I attempt to answer for her as honestly as I can when I fill out paperwork. And, I can't deny, there's my own will at work, since left to her own, Rachel would rather sit in front of a trough of potato chips and eat until she falls asleep than go to Special Olympics basketball. But I say, "She likes basketball" because when I spy on her from the doorway, I can see she's enjoying herself. I know I'm cheating, that I want her to play basketball and swim because it's good for her. Still, because I really do want to respect her desires, I sometimes set up my little micro-cassette tape recorder and interview her. I mentioned this to a friend once, and she was somewhat taken aback. "Why don't you just *talk* to her?" she asked.

I interview Rachel so I can hear her. In everyday life, she is so demanding, her nonstop talk so full of what I think of as sheer nothingness—endless questions about each move I make, about future plans, mostly to do with food, which I've answered dozens of times. Yes, I'll make dinner as soon as you hang up your jacket and use the bathroom. Yes, *hang up your jacket*. Yes. *Bathroom first*. Yes. *Be sure to flush*. Yes. *I said use the bathroom*. Yes. Did you wash your hands? Yes. *Wash your hands first*. Yes. *With soap*. Yes. *You didn't flush*. Her conversation is full of things that are real, overheard things that happened to someone else, things that are wrenchingly true.

If Rachel's incessant talking is both her prime means of communication and her strength—she can be funny and charming, full of personality—it is also her most profound, most unmanageable behavioral issue. She is, as one document states, "attention seeking, with a tendency to interrupt and begin talking about a non-related topic. . . . She is difficult to redirect."

Sometimes it is so noisy when I'm with her that I must expend a great amount of energy willing myself not to shriek at her to just shut up.

Sometimes I'm an earthmover, and she is the mountain. I am up there in my little cab, yelling, "Get a move on!" and ramming her.

When I interview her, I wait until she's out of the house before I replay the tape. Sometimes what I hear is how extraordinarily hard it is for her to process more than one or two simple, concrete questions before a tweeting bird or footsteps in another room set her off on a tangent. Sometimes I can sort out someone else's interests from her own. And sometimes in the silence of my room, apart from her, what I hear with great clarity is her heart's desire. Then I am close to all that makes her human. Listening to the tapes, I think about her in bed, lost beneath a huge gorilla and teddy bear and a dozen smaller stuffed animals. I think about her own, very clearly defined sense of "cool"—the hooded sweatshirt and sweatpants her sister chose for her birthday, which she sneaks out of the closet and tries to wear every day, even in summer. I think about the books she cannot read but insists upon getting at the library every Saturday and carrying everywhere, about her purple Mardi Gras beads. I think about her telling a friend that she wants to drink beer when she turns twenty-one.

I recall the day we were preparing for her first-ever sleepover guest and that, when I asked what she wanted to do with Jennie, she said, "Thnuggle." I think about the childish lisp that, given all the crucial therapies, all the urgent tasks she must master, we've never tried to correct, and this most human desire to be close to others, a desire that her incessant talking and her resistance to hygiene threatens to prevent.

I listen to the tapes and hear myself asking and asking what she wants, and I hear her say:

"I want to go on the bus."

"I want to be able to go out with a friend once in a while and do stuff."

"I want to see if I can get a cell phone, Ma."

"I want to look for an apartment."

I ask if she wants to have a job.

"Yes," she says. "Somewhere in this area."

What would she like to do?

"Look for something me and Jennie can do together."

I cue Rachel, try to get her to name some favorite jobs.

"Making dinner," she says. "Computer." "I like to look at the newspaper once in a while."

I back up to try to get her back on track. "What's my job?" I ask.

"Teaching," she says. "Writing."

"What about the JCC?" I ask. "What's your job there?"

"Working at the café."

What does she do there?

"Sell stuff to drink and eat. They have all different ice creams and all that stuff."

"What happens if a person comes and wants something?"

"They don't have any more sandwiches."

"So what happens if—"

"Listen! Listen. Just listen! They don't have any more sandwiches because they sold them all last time, and that's why we're doing this, because we don't have any more. We only have what's on the board."

Again I back up and try to redirect her. What does she do when the customers are gone?

"We clean up. The whole purpose is to clean up after we're selling candy and selling drinks and locking up machines. And we're doing that because we always have power-walking, but not today. With whatever her name is. She didn't show up, so Jennie left, and then I left."

I remind her that the confusion with power-walking was something that happened a few days ago. Maybe she can tell me about cleaning up.

"There's a big problem with the machines, usually."

What machines?

"The yellow-and-gray machines. The Popsicle machines, Ma. The ice-cream machines. They got locked up wrong yesterday by someone, and what happened was, after the fact that they had them locked up wrong was like a weird compliment, accomplishment, with like after this was going on it was fine, and then after that was—what are you writing down?"

Later I ask if she likes her job at the JCC.

"People talk to me too much, and I just can't stand it. It's hard for me to concentrate. It's better for me to do the dry cleaning, Mom. Better than the café."

Part of that statement is profoundly true. My daughter, with her relentless talking, is so terribly distractible that she cannot concentrate anywhere there is noise or conversation. But the dry cleaning, which she could nicely define ("It's where you take your clothes to the Laundromat, and you have to pay for it") is something she knows only because her friend had some with him one day. Dry cleaning is like drinking beer at twenty-one and going to college—things that others have or discuss, rather than a wish from her own heart.

A few days after my visit to Rachel's work-production class, I asked her what jobs she was doing in school.

"I'm not doing the cups anymore," she said.

"What do you do in the mornings?"

"Only the paper towels."

And what did she do with the paper towels?

"Put them in the holder. In the paper-towel bin."

"And what else do you do?"

"Plates. We fill plates. Although here's the big part, Ma—are you ready for it?—we're selling chips and stuff like that now."

And so we had moved in time and place, from school, perhaps on that day, to her job at Café J on a nameless day in a month that fell as randomly as a snowflake.

4. THERE IS NO SAFETY NET.

Though Barbara Milch's official title is division director of children, family and youth, I think of her as the person who has helped make the JCC of Greater Pittsburgh into a near-perfect world, where people with special needs are a visible part of the community. She spearheaded the current programs that make it possible for kids with special needs to be included in after-school programs and summer camps. Nor have teens and adults been forgotten: Most of what Rachel does outside of school—her chance to go to a play, see a ball game, be with friends—originates here at the JCC because of Barbara's efforts.

The café was initially a joint project Barbara initiated with Jewish Residential Services to employ people with chronic mental illness as a primary diagnosis. When funding from a startup grant ran out, she was able to put anyone in the job. Thus Rachel and her cohort (and their therapeutic staff-support people) were given shifts.

In my some-job-somewhere phase, I took great pleasure in seeing Rachel in her red apron, wearing her staff badge. The JCC is a busy community center with nearly fifteen thousand members. Lots of people I know who use the athletic facilities or have kids in child care stop at the café and are served by Rachel. It made me feel good to think of my daughter out in the world this way, not merely some mysterious, hidden-away, half-grown child I was rumored to have.

Now that I am looking beyond the gloss made up of relief, gratitude and fatigue, I am forced to ask: What will happen when Rachel has no TSS?

This is not doomsday thinking. I've already contested the proposed termination of funding for this costly behavior-management therapy, and though I was successful, still I know that these services are designed to be "faded," even though her issues may never be completely resolved. Rachel cannot work in the café without this assistance—not for the foreseeable future, at least.

She's learned a lot since she began at the café. She knows the prices of everything and that the customers should check the board to see what is being offered that day. She has memorized the sequence of tasks necessary to close down the café.

Skills are not enough. Before this spring I imagined Rachel's future based merely on her strengths (she's gregarious) and deficits (poor vision, poor fine-motor skills). But I had failed to regard the rest of her. It was as if her behavior and attention issues were things that made it hard for *me* to live with her but would not impact her ability to work. I had somehow failed to integrate what I had known all along: The greatest obstacle to her working is her distractibility.

At Café J she has "difficulty balancing appropriate socialization with her peers with the need to focus and concentrate on the demands of working in the café," I read. "She continues to ask for assistance with skills she has mastered and can successfully manipulate various JC staff to engage in 'over-helping.' Often she does not want to follow through with requests to complete her responsibilities for the café."

And didn't she herself manage to tell me exactly why she was struggling? *People talk to me too much, and I just can't stand it. It's hard for me to concentrate.*

Barbara has tried to reassure me. "She will always have a home at the JCC."

But at this time, in the spring of 2002, I am forced to wonder—*a home doing what?*

Though I cannot underestimate the importance of

community, neither can I bear to imagine Rachel wandering the corridors of the JCC, trying to engage unwitting strangers in meaningless talk—unwitting strangers because, if she stays long enough, only strangers will not know to avoid her.

Wandering, following people, trying to engage them—this is what Rachel's day will look like if she cannot be trained for supported employment. It is what she's like at home, that most unstructured place, where everyone else is off doing something—reading, paying bills, talking on the phone, walking up and down the stairs. When we are home for too long together, Rachel's calls for attention, her birdlike *Ma? Mommy? Ma?* are so insistent I choose the most distant part of the house just to escape her.

Michael Stoehr warned me that the supports Rachel gets at school are entitlements mandated by law, that after school these supports are often unavailable. At present they aren't there for millions of individuals in the United States with intellectual disabilities. Only seven to twenty-three percent of these people are employed full time, in part because of the inadequacy of vocational training. Rachel, with her greater needs, is at far greater jeopardy. At school and at the JCC, she has staff at her side nearly all the time. In the outside world, it's different.

"Some agencies will say they're going to follow her, but the reality is they'll provide support for about a month or two," Stoehr says. "After that they're looking for results and turnaround, ready to pull out. . . . It's a very unfair system. There are not a lot of easy answers or nice solutions."

I know this is true, just as I understand that distractibility is Rachel's most serious handicap. And yet I have seen her quiet down. I have watched her sit at the computer for long stretches of time. And it makes me wonder. In this era adaptations are made so people can learn and travel and work. There are language boards and gigs and orthotics, bicycles that can be pedaled by hand, computers that speak, lifts to bring wheelchairs onto buses. Must I believe that an adaptation can never be made for Rachel? Must I say that she will never be able to work? If I do that, I am left imagining my daughter wandering aimlessly, trying to engage people, unwittingly pushing them away—a lonely, marginalized person.

5. TAKE A NAP AND THEN WAKE UP.

So you're tired. So what, I need to remind myself. Take a nap, and while you're sleeping, dream some sweet dreams. And then wake up.

You know what she needs. Now search for it. If you can't find it, you'll have to make it happen.

It's exhausting, but what can I say?

She has her work, and I have mine.

JANE BERNSTEIN's most recent books include the memoirs *Bereft: A Sister's Story* and *Rachel in the World*. She is also an essayist, a lapsed screenwriter, and a member of the Creative Writing Program at Carnegie Mellon University.

Jane Bernstein on "Rachel at Work"

Rachel's first experience in a workplace after the classroom visit I wrote about in "Rachel at Work" was at a huge Goodwill warehouse on the South Side in Pittsburgh. Her task was to pick clothes from a hamper and put them on the appropriate hangers. When I visited her I could see the placement was a disaster. The site was noisy and full of distractions, and the task itself, which required the kind of fine motor control she lacked, was frustrating. Even so, I was stunned when some time later I read the evaluation of her five-month stint hanging clothes. Rachel was "attention seeking," asking others to complete work for her. She claimed she couldn't do something when it seemed she didn't want to do it. In her work-production class she didn't ask for more supplies, as her peers did. Instead she simply said, "I'm done." Explore other options, the letter said. A day program, where "basic life skills" were reinforced, would be more appropriate.

For twenty years I'd been reading evaluations and reports that left me feeling as if I'd been kicked in the gut. Sometimes I cried, sometimes I got angry, but for the most part, I knew what I read was accurate, so after a pause, I'd change my course and set out on an altered plan for my daughter. Not this time. Even after sitting in on her classes at the Children's Institute, where I'd gained a deeper understanding of what it would take for Rachel to be a worker, I knew it was important to keep pushing. In my quietest, most self-aware moments, I continued to believe that Rachel would be able to work.

Part of my conviction came from watching all the time she spent beading, and the way she quieted down when she was focused on working tiny beads onto a plastic string, her annoying behaviors gone. Trying to get a garment not to slide off a hanger was a different kind of task—nearly impossible, like making a bed. My classroom visit reminded me that beading wasn't work, that she needed all the skills that surrounded this one small ability, and still, watching her able to be engaged by a task was very powerful. I also knew that at a day program, she would not have the kind of structure she needed and would alienate everyone around her with nonstop talking. It seemed an awful fate.

When I read the evaluation letter from Goodwill, Rachel and I were in Israel; I was on a Fulbright Teaching Fellowship, and she was living in a kibbutz-like community for adults with developmental disabilities, two hours north of where I lived. The residents at Rachel's community all worked—in the kitchen or on the farm, with the chickens or at the kennels. When we'd talked about a job Rachel might do, I'd suggested having her help set tables in the kitchen. It had been a disaster. Though the staff at this community was undaunted and tried another placement at what they called the "plastics factory," getting the report from Pittsburgh frightened me and made me feel very far away from home.

I put the evaluation letter into a folder and a few days later drove to visit Rachel at the kibbutz. When I asked for directions to the plastics factory, I was led to a room above the dining hall, a large, bright space. Three people sat at a single table assembling tool bits in plastic cases. When I tiptoed close to watch, Rachel was fitting a blue Styrofoam square into a box. Then a yellow molded piece, with a notch that had to be lined up with a clasp. She did not notice me in the room because she was so focused on her job. It was everything I imagined possible.

Rachel, being Rachel, could not draw on that experience of success. When we returned to the US, and she started back to school, she was exactly the same person, with the same seemingly intractable distractibility. During her last year at the Children's Institute, no one was hopeful or enthusiastic about her chances of working in supported employment.

A young, energetic "supports coordinator," a social worker assigned to her case, urged us to visit a worksite in McKees Rocks, PA, where onsite staff trained workers for each new job. Days after Rachel began to work there, the staff, experiencing her chattiness, changed her workspace to the back of the room, with her chair facing a wall.

Eight years later, this is still where she works. Her supervisor has told me she is the best worker they have, the only one on the site capable of greasing a tiny little screw and carefully working it through a little nut.

Work is the center of Rachel's life. She has friends there, a community, a sense of purpose, and a paycheck; she's paid by the piece. When I ask, she will tell me about a particular job—assembling "flood guards," for instance. I'm amused and greatly pleased to find that much of her work is as mysterious to me as mine has been to her.

MRS. KELLY

Paul Austin

"It's not that bad." Mr. Kelly[1] smiled. "I'm not even hurting now." He was a forty-two-year-old house painter who'd been having intermittent chest pain for two days. Three wires ran from under his patient gown to the monitor in the corner, where a fine green line bounced with every beat of his heart.

His wife shifted in her chair. A disposal box for contaminated needles jutted from the wall, next to her head. She leaned away from it, as if she wanted to scoot her chair over. A stainless steel supply rack hemmed her in on the other side.

"It was just a nagging little pain." He gestured toward his chest. His fingernails were square and stubby, trimmed close. His nails glowed pink against the white paint stuck to his cuticles.

"How long did the pain last?" I asked.

"I don't know, Doc." He looked at his wife, then back to me. "About ten, fifteen minutes."

"Did you tell him about your arm hurting?" Mrs. Kelly was a thin woman. She sat with her feet tucked beneath the chair and her hands held tightly together in her lap.

"It didn't hurt that bad." He rolled his left shoulder. "I mighta pulled it at work. You know, moving ladders and all."

Mrs. Kelly shook her head.

I asked him about the cardiac risk factors: He didn't know his cholesterol, he smoked about a pack a day, and his father had had a heart attack when he was in his late fifties. I wrote orders for the standard work-up: EKG, cardiac enzymes, chest X-ray, and routine labs. "When the results come back, we'll talk." I went to see my next patient.

The EKG was done promptly. Normal. The blood-work and chest X-rays were normal too. But I had been practicing for ten

---

1. All names, except those of the author and his family members, have been changed.

years, and knew that in the evaluation of chest pain the symptoms and risk factors are more important than the tests.

During a myocardial infarction—a heart attack—heart cells die, releasing enzymes into the blood. Early on, the level might not reach the threshold of "positive." We check subsequent levels to catch any rise that may occur over time. The safest thing to do would be to admit Mr. Kelly overnight.

Mr. Kelly didn't have a physician, so I called the on-call doctor to arrange for an overnight admission and serial enzymes.

In training, interns and residents work incessantly. I remembered being on call, and to a bleary-eyed intern who was hoping to sneak off and take a nap at three in the morning, no page from the ER was good news. It didn't mean that I was getting the opportunity to help someone, or that I was getting a case I could learn from. It just meant that I was getting screwed out of the few hours of sleep I'd been hoping to steal.

When a patient needed to be admitted to the hospital where I trained, the senior resident went to the ER and checked on the patient. If an admission was unavoidable, the senior called the intern, who came down to do the history and physical and write the admission orders. If there was some doubt as to the necessity of an admission, the senior resident might put up a fight with the ER attending physician, and try to talk him into sending the patient home. Some of the senior residents never questioned the ER attending. We called them "sieves," because they let everyone in. Those who consistently argued against admissions were called "walls." "Sieves" were despised by interns. "Walls" were worshipped; they shielded their interns by thinking of fifty different reasons every patient could be discharged. And they just seemed smarter than the sieves.

This attitude is understandable when you consider the hallucinatory, sleepless fog of residency and the fact that residents are young, still in training. Most physicians gradually outgrow this attitude as they work easier hours and take on more responsibility for patient care. Some, though, even years out of training, seem to take pride in being a "wall," sending people home from the ER. George Packard was one of those guys.

He was the doctor on call for patients without a primary care physician, so I called him. He'd been in practice for years, and he was a "wall." Proud of it. Had a cocky little walk he did when he discharged a patient from the ER. When we called him about one of his own patients, he'd try to talk us into sending him or her home. When he was on call for unassigned patients, he argued even more stubbornly. I wasn't looking forward to the call.

George returned the page, and we talked.

"Sounds like he could go home."

"I don't know, George." I stared across the ER at a drunk who was leaning farther and farther across the side rail of his stretcher. Blood dripped slowly from a laceration on his forehead. I covered the phone's mouthpiece. "Someone help that guy in room eight," I yelled. "He's about to fall." One of the health care techs strolled into the room and pushed the drunk back on the stretcher.

"The guy has a strong family history and he's a smoker," I said into the phone. "Stoic guy, may be in denial. I think he's real, and he needs to come in."

"You think everyone needs to come in."

"This guy has a good story." The drunk had his head over the side rail and was looking at something on the floor.

"You're saying you think he's having a heart attack?"

"I'm saying he could have a plaque that hasn't ruptured yet."

"Didn't you just tell me he had a normal EKG and negative enzymes?"

We both knew Mr. Kelly could be having a heart attack and initially have normal studies. That's why we admit patients for serial tests. "I don't know what to tell you, George." I shook my head. "Guy's dad had an MI in his fifties, he smokes a pack a day, and his pain is typical of ischemia."

"With a normal EKG, and negative enzymes after two days of intermittent pain. If anything was going to be positive, it already would've been. You know that."

"I think he needs to be admitted." I wished we had an equation we could apply to the problem. So many points for this risk factor, so many points for the other. But there isn't one. It all comes down to a judgment call, based on a few risk factors and very subjective symptoms. Pain versus pressure, discomfort versus pain. Is the patient exaggerating or minimizing his symptoms?

"I'd be glad to squeeze him in at the office, first thing in the morning. Do an accelerated outpatient work-up."

"I don't think he should go home tonight."

"Do you know how many hundreds of patients with bullshit chest pain we admit for every patient who has real disease? Or have any idea how many billions we spend every year on these worthless admissions? How much 'covering your ass' costs?"

"I'd love to talk about that sometime, but not right now." The drunk had given up whatever he'd been trying to do, and lay with his head half off the stretcher, passed out. "And we're not talking about 'covering my ass.' We're talking about a guy who needs to be admitted to rule out MI."

"If I come in, I'm just going to send him home."

"That'll be your decision."

"You're going to make the patient wait another two hours?" George's voice scaled upwards with incredulity. "Just for me to come in and send him home? I'm offering to see him first thing in the morning. That's only fourteen hours from now."

Two paramedics stood in the hallway with an asthmatic patient on a stretcher, waiting for the charge nurse to tell them where to put him. He opened his mouth like a fish with each inspiration, the muscles in his neck tightening into cords with the effort. His skin was gray, and shiny with sweat.

"George, the guy needs to come in."

"It's up to you," George was probably shrugging on the other end. "I'll come in, but it sounds like he can go home."

We didn't have a bed for the asthmatic and he was too sick to stay in the hall. No point in tying up a bed with Mr. Kelly if George was going to send him home. "You'll see my guy first thing in the morning?"

"Glad to." George's voice warmed up.

Mr. Kelly and his wife looked at me when I walked into the cubicle. "Your EKG and labs are normal."

Mr. Kelly smiled, looked at his wife, then back to me. He waited.

"I think we can let you go home."

"Great." Mr. Kelly grinned and gave me a thumbs-up. His wife looked down at her hands.

"I've spoken with Dr. Packard, the doctor on call. He'll see you in the morning, in his office."

His wife didn't look up. I got the feeling that she wanted her husband to stay, but she didn't say anything.

"I think you'll be fine, but if you have any chest pain, come back immediately." I waited for them to respond. If either of them objected, I could call Packard back and tell him they were balking at going home. Mrs. Kelly didn't look up. Of course, I could call Packard back anyway, and tell him to get himself to the ER and see the patient. Let *him* send the guy home.

I didn't.

Joanne, the charge nurse, had pulled a different patient into the hall, to make room for the asthmatic.

Lisa, one of the nurses, was slapping the back of the asthmatic's hand to find a vein in which to start an IV. "The line EMS put in blew." She didn't look up from her task. "I went ahead and started another breathing treatment."

"Good." I nodded to the patient, then, with my stethoscope, listened to the tight, high-pitched wheezing sounds of air barely moving in and out of his lungs. "You sound tight," I said to the man.

He nodded.

"Let's give him Solumedrol," I said to Lisa.

"Got it in my pocket." She looked up. "Can you hand me some tape?"

I tore two thin strips of tape and handed them to her.

"Thanks." She taped the IV in place. "There." She looked to me. "Portable x-ray?"

"Yup." With good nurses, an ER doc can get a lot done, just by saying "yup." I saw Mr. Kelly and his wife walking toward the exit. I wanted to call out, "Wait, let's check another EKG." But a repeat EKG would probably be normal too, and

I would've felt foolish asking him to stay after I'd discharged him. And I'd arranged follow-up for the next morning. He'd be OK for fourteen hours.

"Paul," Lisa called, "this guy's looking sick."

I turned to the asthmatic, and forgot Mr. Kelly.

The next day when I started my shift, Joe, one of the other ER doctors, was sitting in the dictation room. He was a runner, and looked like it. Tall, bony guy with broad shoulders and a skinny butt. He looked up from the chart he was working on. "Paul, you remember a guy named Kelly?"

My stomach felt queasy. "Guy with chest pain?"

"Yeah." Joe looked up from the chart he was holding. "He came back, about four thirty in the morning. Cardiac arrest."

I sat.

"You OK?"

"Yeah." I felt prickles in my scalp and down the back of my neck. I glanced at the trash can, afraid I might vomit. "He'd been having chest pain off and on. Didn't have any while he was here."

"I worked the code for at least thirty minutes before I called it."

Mr. Kelly was dead.

Joe adjusted the stethoscope draped around his neck. "I looked over his EKG and labs from when you'd seen him. They were normal."

"I know." I'd sent Mr. Kelly home, and now he was dead.

"It's gonna happen." Joe shook his head. "We can't admit every single chest pain that comes in. I would've done the same thing."

I still wanted to puke. "I had a bad feeling about him when I let him go."

Joe shrugged. "I sent home a guy last year. Came back a couple of hours later with ST segments like Mount Everest." He was describing a classic EKG pattern of a heart attack.

"Did your guy make it?"

"Yeah," Joe said, "but that's not the point. I'd sent him home. I was just lucky."

He was trying to help me feel better. Every doctor has had

a patient die as the result of a wrong judgment call, or a brief lapse of attention. It's inevitable when fallible people make mortal decisions. There are people who'll say, "This should never happen." And they're absolutely right. It shouldn't.

I struggled through the shift, oppressed by the knowledge that I'd sent Mr. Kelly home, and that he'd died. Maybe if I'd paid attention to his wife, her unease would've prompted me to ask more questions. Maybe I would have learned something to make me insist on his admission. But I'd looked Mr. Kelly in the eye and told him I thought he'd be OK, even though I had misgivings. I'd not paid enough attention to an intuition, an uneasy feeling, and there hadn't been enough hard data to convince George Packard to come in. I'd trusted his judgment over mine.

In lectures, seminars, and magazine articles, malpractice lawyers tell you never, never, never to discuss a potential malpractice case. With anyone. The other side will ask if you discussed it, and ask for a list of names. Then they'll interview people until they find one who remembers your admitting a mistake. In one class I listened to on cassette tape, the speaker told about a doctor who'd confided in his wife about a mistake he'd made. Before the case went to court, the doctor and his wife went through an acrimonious divorce. In the malpractice trial, the ex-wife took the stand against him with a vengeance. The class had roared with laughter at the poor schmuck's bad luck. You don't discuss the case, and you never, ever, apologize. To the malpractice lawyers, "I'm sorry" is just another way to say "I'm guilty."

The shift moved slowly, like a bad dream. Finally, it was over. Before I left, I copied Mr. Kelly's phone number down on a scrap of paper.

When I got home, everyone was asleep. I wanted to talk with my wife, Sally. But she was sleeping soundly, so I went downstairs and turned on the TV. A tall, handsome attorney with a very good toupee was on the screen. His voice was deep, and caring. "If you, or anyone in your family, has been injured by a doctor or a hospital, call me." A 1-800 number flashed on the screen.

"We'll get the money you deserve." He somehow managed to mix enthusiasm with sadness in his voice. I vaguely wondered if Mrs. Kelly was at home alone, watching the same ad.

"What if she is?" I asked out loud. I clicked off the TV. "She may want to give dip-shit a call." I went to the kitchen, got a beer, and went out on the front porch and sat on the steps. Two large magnolia trees shaded me from the streetlight. Mrs. Kelly was probably awake too. Maybe sitting on her front porch looking out into the night, stunned by the emptiness she faced.

The next morning I was off duty. After the kids were in school, I told Sally. She listened to the whole story.

"Paul, there's no way you could've known he was going to die."

"His story was good enough to buy an admission."

"No one's perfect." She shook her head. "I know it makes your job scary, but everyone is going to make mistakes."

"Yeah, but not like this." I rinsed my coffee cup. "Missing a fracture, or a UTI, stuff like that, sure, you're going to miss a few of them. But sending a guy home to die?" I felt the pain continue to build, of all places, in my chest. Maybe if I cried, I'd feel better.

"You didn't send anyone home to die." Sally sounded a little irritated. "You evaluated him, and made a decision." Simple as that. "No one expects you to be perfect." She hadn't seen the ad last night on TV.

"Even if I'd admitted him, he probably would have died."

"That's true." Sally nodded.

I leaned against the kitchen counter, my back to the sun coming through the kitchen window. "Must've been a huge MI, to have killed him so quickly." I needed to believe Mr. Kelly would've died even if I'd admitted him, because nothing in my experience had prepared me for feeling so guilty. Up to the moment I'd heard about Mr. Kelly, the possibility I could make an error of that magnitude had remained an abstraction, a theoretical possibility with no grounding in personal experience. I'd been trained well and I was careful. I thought that if I was vigilant enough, I could practice indefinitely without seriously hurting anyone.

I sat at the kitchen table, replaying the scene of Mr. Kelly and his wife shuffling down the hall in the ER, wishing I could rewind it all and call out to tell them that I'd changed my mind, that I'd admit him to the hospital.

The phone rang. It was Ken, one of the guys in our group. He's been an ER doc for twenty years. He has graying hair, a calm voice, and never seems to hurry. Even when the ER is rocking, Ken looks like he just strolled off the golf course. I don't know how he does it: each month we get a report on how many patients we see each hour, and Ken's numbers are consistently good, but he rarely seems perturbed, and I've never seen him look rushed.

"Paul," he said, "I was going to drop by if you're around."

"Sure," I said. "You know our address?"

"Yeah," he said, "I'm about a block away." Car phone.

"OK." I hung up. "That was Ken," I said to Sally. "He's coming over."

"It'll be good to talk with him," she said. "Why don't I go work in the yard some, give you guys some space." She stepped forward for a quick hug, then walked out the back door.

I went to the bathroom, then looked at my face in the mirror, hoping I didn't look as vulnerable as I felt. I also hoped I wasn't in trouble with the hospital, or the group of ER docs I worked with. I felt vaguely nauseated again.

Ken knocked on the door, and I let him in. He followed me back to the kitchen.

"I was just about to make a pot of coffee," I said.

"Sounds good." He sat in the chair at the end of the kitchen table.

"Are you here about Mr. Kelly?" I rinsed the basket of the coffee maker, and put in a clean filter.

"Yeah."

I turned to look at Ken. "I feel terrible."

"You should," he said. "The man died."

I turned back around, hoping I hadn't outwardly flinched. Neither of us spoke as I silently counted the scoops of coffee. I dropped the scoop back into the coffee jar, and closed it.

"And good doctors," Ken continued, "are bothered when one of their patients dies."

Ken still thought I was a good doctor? I felt a wave of gratitude and relief. I put the coffee pot under the basket and punched the button to start the brewing. "I feel like I killed the guy."

"Whoa," Ken said. "Back up a minute. You didn't kill anybody. You're not even sure of the cause of death."

"Guy comes in with chest pain, comes back dead?" I turned to face Ken. "Not exactly rocket science."

"OK, say the man died of a heart attack. No matter how careful, how smart, or how compulsive you are, eventually you're going to make a mistake."

"Yeah, I know." I sat in the chair at the other end of the table. "Missing something really obscure, or something so rare no one else would've picked it up either," I shrugged. "To me, that wouldn't be so hard to live with. But sending home a patient who is having a heart attack?"

"Paul, we can't admit every single patient who comes in with chest pain." Ken shook his head. "It's impossible. The hospital wouldn't hold them all." Ken looked over his shoulder at the coffee pot. "I think it's ready."

I got up and poured us each a cup.

"I'm just glad it was you, and not me."

"Thanks, pal." I tried to chuckle.

"What can I say?" He sipped his coffee. "Luck of the draw who picks up what chart."

"Ken, have you ever sent someone home and they came back dead?"

He carefully set his cup down, and gently rapped the table with his knuckles. "Knock on wood."

I wrapped my hands around the mug of coffee to feel the warmth.

"But Paul," he said. "It's going to happen. It's like driving a car. No matter how careful you are, someday you're going to glance down at the radio to change stations, look up, and there's a car right in front of you. You've had a clean driving record for thirty years, you're a model citizen, and boom. You've plowed into some little old lady's Cadillac." He shook his head. "I'm not saying you made a mistake with this guy, but even good drivers have accidents."

"How do you do it?"

"Do what?"

"Keep on making life-and-death decisions, knowing that you're fallible."

"Paul, I don't make life-and-death decisions." He carefully put his coffee cup on the table. "I make medical decisions." He gave a slight shrug. "I work as carefully as I can, but it's not up to me, who lives and who dies."

I stared at Ken's face.

"That's God's department."

OK.

"Do you know what happens when a patient dies?"

"Yeah," I said. "The doc feels like shit."

"That's not what I mean." Ken looked away, then looked back. "We can describe, down at the molecular level, what happens when a cell dies: membranes break down, oxidative phosphorylation fails, hydrogen ions accumulate in the cytoplasm, all that stuff. But do we really know why people die?"

I couldn't see what he was getting at.

"Say someone comes in with a pulmonary embolism. We understand the pathophysiology: hypoxia, hypotension, acidosis, etcetera." He paused. "And we know how to intervene."

I nodded.

"But when a patient dies, what happens?" He raised his eyebrows. "I mean, one moment they're alive, and the next, they're not. You've felt it. We all have. Something's happened, and we don't know what it is. Sure, we can trace out the failures of the circulatory system, and we can get EEGs for brain activity." Ken shook his head. "But the fundamental thing of death itself is something we still don't understand."

"So?" I said.

"So, I look at each EKG as carefully as I can, and interview each patient as carefully as I can, and I make decisions as carefully as I can. Then I do my job and I let God do his." Ken held his hands out, palm up. "How can we possibly claim the credit for success, or take the blame for failure, in a process we don't really understand?"

I shrugged.

"Paul, you and I both know you did your best for that man." Ken shook his head. "That's all any of us can do."

When I'd first started working in Durham, I'd been surprised by how much I liked talking with Ken. In so many ways, we're polar opposites: He's a conservative Republican. He wears knit shirts and khaki pants on his days off. He belongs to two country clubs: one here in Durham, one at his beach house. He thinks Rush Limbaugh is smart. I'd always thought of Ken as someone with useful answers to questions about buying stocks or avoiding taxes, but I hadn't thought he'd be the one to say something that would help me deal with the unexpected death of a patient.

Ken stood, and took his coffee mug to the kitchen counter. "Give my love to Sally."

"I will. Tell Barbara I said hey."

Ken rinsed his cup, and left it in the sink. "You're going to feel bad for a while," Ken said. "That's OK. Just keep feeling bad. You'll eventually feel better."

We walked to the front door.

"When do you work again?"

"Day after tomorrow."

"See you then." He stuck out his hand. "Paul, you're a good doctor."

"Thanks." We shook hands and he left. I felt my eyes fill, and hoped Ken hadn't noticed. It must've been awkward for him to come by and talk with me, and I didn't want to go all gushy on him. I felt as though being a good father, or a good husband, or a good man was a hollow success if I wasn't a good doctor as well. Sure, he's a great guy, just don't go to him if you have an emergency. I was relieved that Ken thought I was a good doctor. I just wished I could agree with him.

After Ken drove away, I walked outside. It was a bright, sunny day, but Mr. Kelly was still dead. I sat in a wicker chair, and

When I knocked on her office door, Karen said, "Come in." She walked from behind her desk, and gestured to an upholstered chair. Another chair faced mine. She pulled it toward mine a little, and sat. "Are you OK?"

"Yeah, basically." I told her the story. "I feel so bad. So guilty." I looked at the floor, then back to Karen. "You know, in the Bible, it says if we want God to forgive us for something we did to someone else, we should first ask that person's forgiveness? Something about leaving the gift on the altar, straightening out the problem, then coming back."

Karen nodded.

"I want to call Mrs. Kelly, and tell her I'm sorry."

"It'll be a tough call to make," Karen was looking me in the eyes.

"Not as hard as walking around feeling as bad as I do now."

"Maybe."

"I don't know if I'm wanting to call Mrs. Kelly to make her feel better, or to make myself feel better."

"And?" Karen's face seemed to say that either reason would be OK.

"It's probably a little of both."

Karen waited.

"Do I have the right to call Mrs. Kelly, just to make myself feel better?"

"Paul," Karen's voice scaled down several tones. "It's all right for you to want forgiveness." She shook her head. "God doesn't want you to carry guilt and pain every step of your life."

I didn't feel anything in my chest loosen up, or feel any burden lighten. But I caught a glimmer of the possibility. I thanked her.

When I got home, I looked at the phone number on the scrap of paper.

Sally walked into the kitchen. She was sweaty from mowing the yard. "How did it go with Karen?'

"I'd hoped I would feel better."

Sally smiled. "You look a little better."

"I think I'll call Mrs. Kelly." I walked to the sink and got a glass of water. "Tell her I'm sorry."

wondered if I could get some relief by praying. A Quaker
upbringing had taught me to pray silently. I started that way,
but felt a need for something more physical and real than
closing my eyes and thinking about God. "Lord, you know I'm
not much of a Christian. I doubt. I curse. And I think about
sex all the time. You know that. And you know I'm too quick
to laugh at tragic stuff if it's funny." I took a deep breath. "You
know all that. And you know I sent Mr. Kelly home. And he
died." I blew my nose into my fingers. "I don't know if it counts
as an honest mistake or a sin." I wiped my hand on my jeans,
and looked out at the street. The sun was still bright, the porch
was still in the shade. A woman walked past, a dog tugging on
a leash. I closed my eyes. "God, forgive me. And be with Mrs.
Kelly, and their kids, if they have any." I took a deep breath.
"Comfort them. And let them know I did the best I could, and
I'm sorry." I opened my eyes. No change.

Maybe I should talk with Karen, or James, I thought. They're
our pastors, at the Pilgrim United Church of Christ. When
Sally and I had kids, we started going to the Pilgrim UCC in
Durham. The folks there seem like Unitarians, only less embarrassed to be called Christians. We went to Sunday school and
church almost every Sunday I was off duty. Matthew, my Sunday school teacher, was a constitutional law professor at Duke.
Worked with Janet Reno and Al Gore on some legal issues. I felt
lucky to discuss Christianity with such smart people, because
so much of Christianity in the South seems anti-intellectual—
TV preachers sputtering about sin and pleading for money,
telephone numbers flashing on the screen. I've always felt like
a second-rate Christian, insufficiently saved, with inadequate
fervor. At the same time, I feel the Bible drawing me back,
particularly the four Gospels. I believe there are answers there.
And a model of grace. A model of how I can live.

I wiped my hand on my pants again, then went inside and
called Karen. She said I could come over right then. I changed
jeans, splashed my face, and drove to our church, a brick building that's mostly roofline, tucked in among a thick stand of
trees that shields it from the traffic on the street.

Sally hugged me from behind. I could feel the damp of her shirt.

I sat the water on the counter, and turned to return the hug. Mrs. Kelly didn't have a husband to hug any more. Damn.

"If I call her, and it goes to court, they'll make a big deal about me calling her to apologize."

Sally shrugged.

"If the award goes past my malpractice coverage, it could come out of our pockets."

"So what. It'll probably never happen." She shrugged again. "And if it does: Fuck 'em."

If nothing else, I'd married well.

Sally pulled back to look at me. "Call her. You may feel better." She hugged me again. "I'll be on the front porch."

Mrs. Kelly picked up the phone on the third ring.

"This is Paul Austin. I'm the doctor who took care of your husband the first time he came to the emergency room."

"Oh."

"I'm calling to say I'm sorry." I paused. "I'm sorry your husband died."

She didn't answer.

"Mrs. Kelly?"

"I'm here."

I waited. "If you have any questions, or concerns..."

There was another pause. "Why did you send my husband home?"

The question thumbed me in the chest. "I thought he would be OK." I took a breath. "I was wrong. And I'm sorry."

She didn't answer.

I waited.

She didn't say anything.

I looked down at the crumbs on the floor. "If there's anything you want to say to me..." I winced at the accusations she might unleash, but held a glimmer of hope she'd say she forgave me.

"I've got nothing to say to you right now."

I gave her my home phone number, and told her if she ever had anything to say, or any other questions, I'd be glad to talk with her.

We hung up.

I didn't feel any better. And it seemed that Mrs. Kelly didn't feel any better either.

I walked out to the front porch.

Sally looked up from her novel. "How did it go?"

I sat in the chair next to her. "She didn't have anything to say to me."

Sally closed her novel, keeping her place with her finger.

"I didn't really expect her to flat-out forgive me, but I'd hoped for something." Glints of sunlight reflected off the hard, waxy leaves of the magnolia tree in front of the porch. I could barely make out the pitted gray bark of the trunk through the dark openings between the leaves. "Some human contact."

"It's early." Sally patted my knee.

"Did I call too soon?" I felt my dismay grow heavier, like a rain-soaked coat. Had I added to Mrs. Kelly's pain, just to ease my own? Every place I turned, I was screwing up.

"Probably not." Sally shook her head. "But who knows when you should've called? She might've been sitting at her kitchen table just now, wondering why the ER doctor hadn't even bothered to call." Sally turned in her chair to face me. "At least now she knows her husband was important to the doctor."

"Yeah, I guess."

"You guess? Paul, you've done everything you could—you saw the guy, did all the tests, thought about it, and told him to come back if he had more pain." She held up a finger with each point. "Nobody's perfect."

"I know." Every single thing she'd said was true.

But Mr. Kelly was still dead.

PAUL AUSTIN's first book, *Something For the Pain: Compassion and Burnout in the Emergency Room*, was published in 2008. His second book, *Beautiful Eyes: Down Syndrome, Fatherhood, and What it Means to Be Human*, is due out in October 2014. His essays have appeared in *Creative Nonfiction, Gettysburg Review, Southeast Review, Ascent*, and *Turnrow*.

Paul Austin on "Mrs. Kelly"

In 2006, for the first time in my writing career, I was invited to submit a piece of writing. It got even better: the invitation was from *Creative Nonfiction*. The bad news? The theme of the issue was *Silence Kills: Speaking Out and Saving Lives*. As it was explained to me, the issue—it was also published as a book—was to expose the code of silence about medical errors. It sounded as if the project would be a literary assault on doctors and nurses.

I'm an ER doc. For the past twenty-five years, I've been working rotating shifts—days, evenings and nights. I've worked every other Christmas and Thanksgiving. My co-workers —other docs, nurses, paramedics, cops, firefighters—are some of the most caring, pragmatic, and funny people I've ever known, and if it wasn't for them, I don't think I could keep doing this job.

But when I'm off-duty—after I'm home and safe, and after I've stripped off my scrubs and put on a pair of jeans—I write. The invitation was a dilemma. I had a chance to take a giant step forward in my writing career, but I'd have to backstab my friends to do it. At least that's how it felt at the time.

I knew I was capable of writing a suitable essay. I could trot out the pervasive fear of lawsuits and point out that admitting mistakes is difficult for most people, no matter their line of work. I could suggest that in medicine, a mistake doesn't feel like a mistake. It feels like a moral failing. *If I'd only been more careful, or more knowledgeable, I would not have caused this person to suffer.*

Apologizing for an error that has caused someone harm is a difficult conversation to start. People ask, "Don't the medical schools *teach* you how to have difficult conversations?" Well, yes, they do. But like any skill, it has to be practiced. Riding a bicycle, playing the violin, telling a woman you're sorry for a mistake that caused her husband's death . . . these are all hard to do. And it's hard to trust that a patient or a family may forgive an error.

For me, trusting the editors of *Creative Nonfiction* was almost as difficult. As it turned out, I decided to trust the power of nonfiction narrative—the power of a true story. I sent them "Mrs. Kelly," a chapter from *Something For the Pain: Compassion and Burnout in the Emergency Room*, a memoir about the way my job almost wrecked my family.

It had been a difficult chapter to write, but once I had a rough draft of "Mrs. Kelly," the story became a thing, an object, like a canvas with paint on it. Writing it wasn't therapeutic. Wasn't cathartic. But it gave me the chance to safely spend time in that moment of being wrong. Unlike working in the ER, there was no time pressure as I wrote; I could take as long as I needed. It is only now, as I write this short piece, that it occurs to me: I spent hours and hours on the story, but only minutes in Mr. Kelly's room.

Writing the story was painful, though not nearly as painful as the event itself. The book, *Something For the Pain*, is a source of quiet pride, but the memory of Mr. and Mrs. Kelly is a source of sadness, still—a mild, dull ache in my chest. It feels like an echo, as if from a distance.

THE WORLD WITHOUT US:
A MEDITATION

Carolyn Forché

Yesterday, everything changed. Lightheartedly—unthink-
ingly—I went to the clinic to have "additional films taken,"
and after three hours, walked into the sunlight with the
image of two black marbles floating in the snow and fog of
what had been an ultrasound image of my right breast. *Do you
see them?* Dr. Johns asked, helpfully providing tiny computer
arrows to guide me to the pronounced blackness of the "densi-
ties," as he called them, and then he said, *I don't know what
they are.* Dr. Johns ordered more films and told me he would
share all the films and images with Dr. Ott and telephone me
in the morning with Dr. Ott's recommendations.

After a fitful night, I woke without remembering this news
and then remembered it. When Dr. Johns phoned, he told me
they recommended ultrasound guided-needle biopsies, and he
told me to call my own doctor, get the order, and then to make
an appointment with Jessica at the clinic. I talked to my doctor,
who took notes and reassured me that these biopsies are often
negative, and then I spoke with Jessica, who arranged my procedure for the morning of July 28, which was then only days away.

As I cannot write anything else, I will write about how I feel,
hour by hour.

Israel is bombing Lebanon again—the beautiful city, Beirut: the airport, the port, all avenues of escape. City of our

courtship. These images of rubble cannot but bring me back to winter, twenty-two years ago, in the earliest months of what would become a long marriage. Our wedding rings were made by a jeweler in Beirut, who worked through nights of shellfire from the Christian east and brought the rings to my husband in a velvet box just days after I evacuated with the Sixth Fleet. His jewelry shop had been destroyed, as had most of our quarter, and to come to our darkened hotel, he had to walk streets slick with the shattered glass of shop windows. Never mind, he said, we are all alive, and you are getting married.

America is unbearably, stiflingly hot at this moment. All states are in deep red on the weather maps. Here, it is thirty-eight degrees Celsius or about one hundred degrees Fahrenheit. The dogs won't go out. I won't go out. It is a droning heat, as if the trees are crying out and the grass hissing.

Unpacking our library, which has been packed up since our house was flooded three years ago, I notice certain titles: Simone de Beauvoir's *A Very Easy Death* and Jacques Derrida's *The Gift of Death*. I consider taking them up to my bedside table but instead shelve them. I have been unpacking and reshelving for months, a few volumes at a time. I thought our life was beginning again and that all I had to do was put things in place. Things. When, on a winter night, water gushed into the house from a broken main, much was destroyed, and we were stunned into ruin, but now we are back, and the carpets that were left to stiffen in the snow are again spread on our floors. I have only to return everything to where it was—or so I had imagined. *The Gift of Death* will not come upstairs, but I am not surprised that it is among the titles lifted out of the box I open this morning. It has always been so for me: strange correspondences between my thoughts and the outer world. The world has always sent messages, whether from God or an intelligent universe, whether self-issued or bequeathed, and I was ignorant only of how many messages I had missed.

Nothing has changed since yesterday, except the fear that I am running out of time. This alphabetization of my book collection—why?—this careful unpacking and the delight at finding certain things again: a letter on blue foolscap from Graham Greene that I thought might have swirled into the debris that night, but, no, I'm holding it in my hands and reading as if I am someone else reading the papers of a dead poet.

And just now, the clouds above the darkened poplars opened to a late light.

I feel terror, pending loss, isolation and also a strange elation, a floating sense of the present moment, a weightlessness as if I have entered a state of mind leading all the way out of the world. On a clear day, cloudless, to the low hum of beetle and cricket, I tell myself to make a list of everything I remember. The details of my life from the earliest year.

This morning, I think to write a poem titled "The Dove Keeper," arising from the memory of the old man in Beirut who had a dove cote on his rooftop and whose doves alighted on his head and along his outstretched arms; in an earlier poem titled "Curfew," I wrote that he was "cloaked in doves." As he released his flock for me, he tossed his head back and laughed into the rising of their wings, an applause of light before the shooting began again in the streets—*tut tut tut tut tut* answered by *tut tut tut tut tut*, as other old men folded up their backgammon tables and market sellers ran behind their carts of tumbling lemons and dates. Then there was only dust, gunfire, glass in an emptied street and, later, utter darkness, with only candles here and there, guttering in the stairwells.

The darkness into which we sail at death, I am thinking, as I open John Berger's correspondence with John Christie, *I Send You This Cadmium Red*, to a letter written by Berger: "We have no word for this darkness. It is not night and it is not ignorance. Maybe from time to time we all cross this darkness, seeing everything, so much everything that we can distinguish nothing. Maybe it is the interior from which everything came."

These cannot be crickets because it is not night.

The flowers that tiger swallowtails feed upon are in bloom again in the garden, but there are not yet any tiger swallowtails. That is how I remember my last conversations with J, my childhood friend, before he went mad again for a time and again sought refuge in monasteries—first, with the Trappists and, then, the Benedictines. As I talked on the telephone with him several summers ago, I watched, through my study window, the butterflies he and I used to catch in the Michigan fields as they descended to feed on those flowers, and I saw him again, too, running through the fields with his white net held above the chicory and Queen Anne's lace.

This is shock: a floating, oddly disembodied mindfulness, dread without respite, but experienced at a remove.
    Write everything, I tell myself. Hour by waking hour. This is my first such clarity.

I spend some of the morning in the study, unpacking, and find, among other things, a photograph of myself amid the ruins of Beirut in 1984 and a list of the items in my friend Ashley's "musée hypothétique," along with a narrative of the museum's history, and I think I might write a poem for him entitled "A Hypothetical Museum" which will include objects from his collection: sand from the Sahara, a bottle of Gauloise smoke, a glove used in renovating the Louvre, a Roman sword dug from an English garden, a shovel from Verdun, the Great War. How much world he has assembled! How much time would I need to write this poem for him? Enough.

This morning, I found two black silk Chinese jackets in a trunk, among rags that should have long ago been discarded, and I took them to the Mongolian women, who examined them very carefully, as if they were seeing before them the ghost jackets of another epoch.

An afternoon of sudden downpours from a sky by turns pearl and pumice. I found a sweater I bought in former Yugoslavia in 1978, summer. I washed it and was hoping it would dry on the rail outside and it almost did, but now it is soaking from the rain. I talked to Jane, who phoned in having heard the news, and it took some time to convince her that I am calm and that I am not trapped in the darkest thoughts. I also talked to other friends—dear sisters, these women who circle me in my hour of gravest uncertainty and fill me with gratitude.

The sweater will smell of rain and sunlight. I think it is from Zlatibor, and I find myself wondering what happened there during the recent war years. I'm sure that Vasko is no longer alive, among the many people I have known who went before me in death.

In my thoughts, I'm heading into the open sea.

A cloudless day. So we have the dove keeper poem to be written and, also, the "musée hypothétique," but they must be written by a hand guided by a mind that cannot alight. Like the birds over the fires of Beirut. Unpacking the library is a labor of unpacking a life: the scattered interests in philoso-phy, religion, poetry, literature, languages and the history of languages, art, photography, ideas, ecology, cosmology and, particularly, books about crimes against humanity. There are many books among them that I have not yet read, that I may have no time to read, and there is also all that I have not writ-ten, and the little time left, even if it is measured in years. We are asleep, we are dreaming, we are flickering between two darknesses.

The shed door was open, so I went out to close it, thinking also to turn on the sprinkler for the lawn, and as I approached the shed, I heard a creaking above me, as if a door were opening, and a long-dead branch fell almost upon me and I watched it fall, as if slowly, and then I moved it toward the fence.

There is the first tiger swallowtail, flying above the fan of water.

There are two days of waiting left, then another week of waiting. I am submerged in quiet fear, a giddy courage that is a form of daring, a peculiarly futureless dread. In two days' time, the testing will be over, and then something else will happen that I cannot foresee, that I have yet to experience, but I know that it will be as unfamiliar as what I am feeling now and that what I am learning cannot be learned any other way, nor can it be described or lessened or lifted or altered to any degree, nor is there escape except fleetingly and only through distraction, which is not true forgetfulness, and always the "feeling" returns as strongly, and if this is fifty years ago, then I am a monarch butterfly not yet dead, but nevertheless pinned through the thorax to a poster board, futilely opening and closing its wings.

The feelings wash over and through me. They must be endured then let go. I try to let them come and go without interfering. I try on scarves in the mirror. I pull my hair back to study the shape of my skull. I will get to see my head for the first time without hair.

SOME MONTHS LATER:

Dear M,

Forgive me for not writing sooner, but the hours have been taken up with all manner of medical procedures as, alas, my veins proved insufficient to the task of conducting chemotherapy throughout my system, so I have had a little titanium pillbox sort of object implanted in my chest, and conveniently, it can remain there up to ten years, if I should wish, and is used to make withdrawals and deposits. A bloodstream teller-window. It is covered by my own skin (conveniently) and appears as a lump (currently a red and sore lump) on my chest near the shoulder. As it happens, I am to lose my hair on Sept. 27 precisely, so I am having it all cut off on the 25th, deliberately and so as not to endure the sight of hair in the basin. My first chemotherapy will be Tuesday, and then every three weeks for a total of four treatments. Near Thanksgiving, I will most gratefully begin daily radiation, and by Christmas, perhaps I will have "ground cover" on my bald head and a tree in the living room with nothing beneath it but medical bills tied up in ribbons and, as I used to receive in my childhood, a Christmas navel orange. (I remember Sean telling me that this—the thought of his mother excited to receive an orange—was sad. And I assured him that it wasn't sad at all, it was delightful, and the trick was to get the orange cold in the fridge without a sibling making off with it.)

I have been thinking about the lake house, and we must think about naming it before it becomes by default The Lake House. But your idea to extend the porch to the second story is delightful, I think, and will very economically enhance the house. As the view is so very fine, perhaps this addition could be many-windowed, almost a glass porch, like the glass church on the raft in "The Illuminations." I miss you and remember often driving along the long and mysterious body of water that was the Hudson River. ...

Much love and slightly panicked,
Carolyn

FROM INSOMNIA:

Writing to keep awake, to find my way back with words, to follow phrases back into a lived life, to remember something by way of syllables, to "music" the meaning, stitch the soul to its making, it's impossible not to feel that this poetry by which I have lived is an accident, as it also seems my life has been: the significant events—all coincidence and happenstance, near misses. Only my son was chosen, deliberately, was seen and beheld and welcomed. The rest, all the rest, seemed to happen of its own accord, and only in hindsight may it be assembled into a meaningful whole: this led to that, that led to the next this. In our sojourn on Earth, we are presented a curriculum for the education of a human soul, comprised of lessons that seem mysteriously to repeat themselves as if not properly learned the first time, or as if they were lessons failed, but this curriculum moves in a spiral rather than a circle, never returning quite to the same instruction, and the fortunate few experience, I think, epiphanies in their late years, so that even failure is embraced and welcomed. It is as Samuel Beckett wrote: "No matter. Try again. Fail again. Fail better." The final realization might be that we ourselves wrote this curriculum within the depths of our being.

Along my particular path, I have been taught a little of the experience of "near death": in a car blown across an icy road on a mountain pass, caught by a grove of trees; several times under shellfire and sniper fire in countries at war; and in El Salvador, in the time of the death squads, when "near death" bestowed its lesson as I escaped the fate of the others three times in a month.

In these encounters, death was outside, glimpsed fleetingly, harrowingly. There was no time to learn the lesson of death, only the lesson of heightened terror. This time, death appeared from within, so invisibly that it could be perceived only through radio imaging and magnetic resonance, and could be held back only through surgery, radiation and chemical therapy. The beginning of death could be cut out, excised, and the surrounding territory bombarded and poisoned, and still it would not abandon me ever—as has always been true for all of us, but I didn't know this. I didn't live my life with this realization constantly before me, teaching me to be in awe of every drawn breath. But is it possible to live without ever forgetting death? Could we endure such turbulent radiance? Isn't it necessary to forget so as to get on with remembering the past and planning the future? Death holds us in the present, a moment that spirals outward, a moment revered and treasured beyond comprehension: the last moment, the moment before we go out. In this moment, it is possible to love having lived, to hold one's life sacred and to be filled with gratitude for the gift bestowed at the explosion of our conception. If the "I" were immortal, the self continuous, unthreatened, in this body or another, from time immemorial to infinity, without interruption, if this "I" could remain conscious forever, without limit, in the prison of selfhood—what? There would be "time" for everything and everyone, for all permutations of experience, and thus all urgency would be removed, all longing and wonder, all disappointment and, with it, expectation, leaving us suspended not in an eternal present but an eternal nothingness, without the immense spiritual satisfaction of having schooled a soul.

The quest for immortality has always mystified me, whether pursued through cyborg research or medical advancement; it seems that, as with other supposed "good ideas," the consequences of success, however tenuous, have not been well-imagined nor entirely thought-out. The prospect of immortality, for me, is as horrifying as certain heavens: endless and unrelieved, whether forever singing in the spheres near an old, bearded God or dwelling in one of the heavenly mansions promised by the Christ. The scientifically bestowed immortal life would keep us here, no longer making room for others, no longer allowing the world to be refreshed and re-envisioned, the soil to be replenished with our remains and our works to be beheld independent of us and for their inherent value.

There is another immortality, however, that has always been available to humankind, and it is this immortality that I hope to achieve: the possibility of living on in the hearts of others, of having touched lives that will touch other lives, of having made something, a poem or garden, that will somehow be read and visited beyond one's death. The twenty-one-gram soul may depart the body, and the energy within it also—so palpable that it is impossible to mistake a corpse for a sleeping human—and this almost weightless force may be, as with all energy, indestructible, and so we might in some measure survive death.

I hope to remember this—the lesson of "near death," terrifyingly luminous—if and when I leave the tunnel of illness.

MORE MONTHS LATER:
I'm no longer bald. Just as I was becoming accustomed to the
woman in the mirror, so pale she shone in the dark, those
nights of frequent waking, startling myself at every glimpse,
my ghost-self cupping her hands to her face or coming closer
so she could see that, no, there were no eyebrows or eyelashes,
not a single fine hair anywhere. Without hair, my eyes seemed
strangely large, and they were filled with fuller measures of
light, grief, terror, and solemnity. *Come back,* I pled with
myself. And more than once, I stood before myself in the glass
and whispered, *Who are you? Tell me who you are. Who have
you ever been?*

I have been going through my things, bearing in mind that
nothing should be kept that someone else wouldn't want, that I
must prepare everything "just in case," I tell myself, that I must
clean and sort and clear away the debris of my life. No two
of anything. No duplicates. A friend thinks I should pack up
the books having to do with the century's horrors because she
wants to fill my room "with peace and light." *You're finished
with that,* she said. *It's time for something else.* For something
else, room must be made. Emptiness must be created.

AND A LITTLE LATER:
Now the sun comes through the fir branches, and in the
window's reflection, the fire I have made is burning in midair
above the field, and dew whitens the field, or silvers it, and
I'm here in utter silence except for the sound of the flames.
Somehow, it seems to me, all of this has been arranged. This
is my heaven. I am alone here, yes, and I have always feared
being alone, especially in houses, especially at night, but in
recent years, I seem to have overcome that. I'm not afraid. And,
of course, we go alone in the end, by ourselves, our souls go
into the light that is death, and our bodies go into the darkness of the grave or the ash of a cremation. So it is as if I've
been brought here, to a cottage on an island in Puget Sound,

so that I might experience the heaven I imagined in childhood. My heart is full, as it was then, with love and gratitude for everyone in my life, for all who made me possible, for the light over the Sound, for the owl in the firs, the egrets standing in the thin lagoon. The moment of the present is still radiant, still precious, and this is why I think it's possible that I have come near the end of my life and, perhaps, with luck, veered off again into living.

So this is what I have to say about immortality: we live as radiant beings between two realms of darkness. We die so that the world may go on without us, so as to enable us to give ourselves back.

Hedgebrook, December 2009
With thanks to Dr. Johns.

CAROLYN FORCHÉ is a poet, translator, and editor of the groundbreaking anthology *Against Forgetting: Twentieth Century Poetry of Witness*. She has received fellowships from The John Simon Guggenheim Foundation, The Lannan Foundation, and The National Endowment for the Arts, and has taught poetry and literature for 35 years. She is the Lannan Visiting Professor of Poetry and Professor of English at Georgetown University.

SCRAMBLED EGGS

Marilyn A. Gelman

L ife goes on after brain injury. Not like before. Not like you would have imagined, even if you could imagine it happening to you. Not in a clean, safe, nourishing environment. Not with your needs met. Not with the same tastes, smells, thoughts. Not with time out for a family wedding or cancer.

You inhabit a body you do not recognize, driven by someone else's mind that limps down the highway of life with three tires on four wheels. Your scar-free chassis mocks your shattered working parts. No road map shows the way.

Because you desperately wish to conjure the familiar from the usual, against the laws of common sense, you keep trying to cook. Until tasting, you think you have combined the same ingredients.

The final product lacks your spice of life.

Pot Roast
October 12, 1997

PRE-PREPARATION
Three years before you want to prepare Pot Roast The Way It Used To Be, you incur a brain injury on the way home from work when another person makes a foolish left turn into your car.

INGREDIENTS
Chopped onions—a small plastic storage bagful that Mary, the chore-service worker, cut up two days before. Mary spends three hours one week with you and two hours the next, and so you must plan how much chopping to assign her in one visit.

You must leave the kitchen while she works because the sound disables you.

Lean top of the rib—from the butcher, delivered two days ago, on the day he delivers to your town, and souring, but you cannot resupply at will. You do not get out to shop, so you have lost the seasons. Are peaches plentiful now, or apples? Are matzohs on display, or candy canes?

Crisco brand shortening

Boiling water—not really at a rolling, vigorous boil the way you would like, but at the best you can manage safely under the circumstances.

Potatoes—the plastic bagful that Mary peeled and cubed two days before, now multicolored. You would have preferred to cook when the potatoes were white, the onions crisp, and the meat not on the cusp of spoiled, but just having Mary softly walking about and doing chores is too much stimulation for you.

You had worked all evening and all morning preparing lists for her. There are supermarket items, bank chores, post office instructions, and bags for the dry-cleaner and the library. But there is no second chance. Whatever you omit must wait until next week. When she leaves, you must rest or risk injury by falling or crashing into the walls or dropping things on your foot. You've already made two emergency-room visits for fingers smashed under similar circumstances of overload and exhaustion.

PROCEDURE
1. Place a heaping tablespoon of Crisco shortening in a big pot. It is good finally to use the pot again. Because you cannot manage to get the pot to and from its storage place, it has been sitting on top of the stove, collecting dust, for months. Pick up

the shortening can after you drop it upside down. Try to discount the buzzing in your ears and the slight feeling of dizziness and nausea produced by the sight and sound of the flying, crashing can. You jumped away well.

2. Turn on stove.

3. Bend down to retrieve the bag of diced onions from the bottom shelf of the refrigerator. The onions cost you a great deal of money because Mary gets a fair hourly wage for her labors; she is a very good, precise worker. Most of the onions are the same size and thickness, and she diced all three as you had requested. But you forgot that you stuffed the bottom shelf with food that arrived at a later date, and the onion bag had been shoved to the rear.

You were uncertain about the amount of food you would receive from a charitable organization the day between the dicing and the cooking. The new food is in a large paper bag, enclosed in a larger plastic bag; only the bottom shelf would meet its "easy-to-find-later" positional requirement. The bag of charity food is heavy; when you stooped to store it in the refrigerator, your neck cramped, your arm felt numb, and you became dizzy and nauseated. So you rushed the task, and the plastic bag of onions lost its place.

A plastic tab slides across the top of the onion bag to seal it securely, and the bag itself is expensive. No onions will spread throughout the refrigerator in a wild dash for freedom or drop to the floor while the bag is in transit to the stove. It will be a shame to toss the bag out after only one use, but the noise and sight of the running water required to rinse it out will contribute to your general sensory overload at food-preparation time. The mental effort to remember to wash it out later would cost more than the financial gain accrued in saving the bag.

Now, foraging around the bottom shelf of the refrigerator consumes a great deal of your internal resources and pushes you closer to mishaps.

4. Brown the onions on medium heat. The noise of the sizzling onions will increase your dizziness and disorient you.

You will lose your ability to distinguish distance and so burn the inside of your right forearm on the side of the hot pot.

You must stand close to the pot of onions because you cannot smell them burning; you cannot take your hearing problems away from the fire. You try to distract yourself by unloading the dishwasher. Since you are addled already, a little more bending and stretching should not make a difference.

As soon as you open a cabinet door, a flying box of coffee filters grazes your head. Even though you have not used the pile of pink china dishes on the right side of the most accessible cabinet since the BMW hit your Chevrolet, you have been unable to move them to a quieter spot in the kitchen. The dishes take up one of the few places you could store things you use every day, and the coffee-filter box was balanced so precariously on top of the soup plates that it assaulted you at the first opportunity.

Unfortunately, you cannot delay the pot roast. You are at risk because Tuesday's meat and potatoes are becoming the worse for wear. Unexpected fresh produce rots in a box on the kitchen floor, over the furnace as it happens, because there is no room in the refrigerator until the meat and plastic bag of potatoes are removed.

5. Wash the meat and season it with garlic powder and onion powder.

6. Stand far back from the stove. Position yourself so that the pot of burning onions will not reach you if the meat lands in the wrong place; lob the meat into the pot; sear it over a high flame.

Remember to remain in the kitchen at all times, so the noise of the cooking meat can feel like little electric shocks. You are safe until you have to turn the meat. You will have to figure out how to hold the pot, and you must enforce your decision with deliberate and exacting thinking.

Even though you are in the kitchen and can hear the meat sizzling, you cannot smell progress. Periodically evaluate the color of the smoke rising from the pot to determine when to flip the slab of meat. Safe again, until it is time to add water.

While the meat cooks, receive two telephone calls from a man who wrote you a letter and seems to be masturbating. Call the police and hit *57 to trace future calls. Call friend to discuss anxiety and guilt over guy masturbating over phone. Rehash a form that has been haunting you for weeks. The form is for Meals on Wheels; if you could make phone calls and leave messages, it would have been off your plate after one or two chews. But it persists, tough to swallow and often reheated.

You must not get distracted. Back to the pot roast.

The secret to this recipe is the temperature of the water that you will add to the pot once the meat is browned all over and cooked through. The water must be boiling.

You have not boiled water in a whistling kettle on top of the stove since you wrapped your right hand around the body of the kettle to move it off a burner when it was very hot. You have been boiling water in the microwave oven. It never quite gets to that vigorous rolling boil you remember from before, and steam does not rise up as you pour the water out. But now, you are lucky. The two-cup Pyrex measuring cup is clean and ready, and you put tap water in this and put the cup into the microwave. Fortunately the microwave rings a bell when the appointed time has been spent, and shuts itself off, because you have forgotten that you have put the water in the microwave.

7. Carry the cup of boiling water from the microwave, and pour it into the pot containing the hot onions and the sizzling meat. If you manage this task safely, and remember to lower the light on the pot, you must try your very best to stay awake for an hour or so. The effort and the sensory stimulation of the flying Crisco can and coffee-filter box, the sizzling onions, and the scary boiling water march exhaust you. You worry that you will fall asleep, or that you will be in another room and forget the stove is on.

You try to stay in the kitchen, but there is not much you can do. You are in no shape to wash the grime off the refrigerator, or water the little plants on the windowsill that look so thirsty, or polish anything you have missed touching for so long.

Sometimes cleaning things is like making love to them, and you haven't been able to dust, polish, or shine since the crash.

It is difficult to tell if the pot roast is the same as the one your mother, then you, used to make. Nothing tastes quite right since the collision, on the lawn of the Maywood, New Jersey, Bon Buffet restaurant three years ago, scrambled everything you knew to be true.

Making a Meat Loaf
1998

PRE-PREPARATION
As a passenger in a car that gets hit, exacerbate injuries from four years ago, add new ones; wait six months; try to cook again.

PART ONE: SALIVATE
1. Do not make any telephone calls or write anything demanding of mental attention, or bend or stretch, in order to maintain optimal functioning.
2. Have ready in advance: 2 lbs. chopped meat, 1 chopped onion, already-opened jar of marinara sauce.

PART TWO: MACHINATE
1. Move stuff away from oven door; reach up to get matches; reach down to light oven.
2. Move portable dishwasher away from pantry door because first glance on shelf did not reveal meat-loaf pan that was in clear, easily accessible location.
3. Bend for pan; reach for oatmeal; replace dishwasher.
4. Bend for marinara sauce in refrigerator; reach for chopped onions; swivel for marinara sauce.
5. Reach for bowl in Hoosier cabinet.
6. The world is spinning already.

PART THREE: ACTIVATE
1. Break and mix up egg; add oatmeal and marinara sauce. Mix. Get dizzy and nauseous.

2. Add chopped meat; mix with other ingredients; find another, larger fork because there is too much action for so little mixing.

3. Close eyes while working; right shoulder feels funny and center of back of neck hurts. Keep mixing.

4. Pour meat loaf into pan and shape with two forks. Pour some marinara sauce over top from jar that is now only one-third full. But it feels very heavy. Smooth sauce over top of meat loaf carefully because fork is hard to keep a grip on; muscles lack coordination.

5. Reach into bottom of refrigerator for sweet potatoes since they are known to be in refrigerator, having been placed there last night in a convenient location for today, now completely forgotten. Difficult to focus on task at hand; wash sweet potatoes. If phone were to ring now, answering machine would do all the work because you do not think your lips would work the words correctly.

6. Carry oh-so-heavy meat-loaf pan to oven and sweet potatoes. Shelf is up a rung too high. You are too uncoordinated now to move it; you would only get hurt or drop something or react poorly to an emergency.

PART FOUR: RUMINATE

You are astonished at how much functionality you have lost. You have pain across the shoulder blades and in the back of the neck; your vision has become less . . . cooperative (? you can't think of the word); your head is spinning; feels like your fingers are swollen; your tongue feels swollen; your left ear feels funny on the outside (like it is swelling). Even sitting still with your eyes closed, you are overwhelmed by sensory overload. It is a terrible struggle to type this; you have made and corrected many typos; you have changed many words because you *ca not* think of the right ones; and you fear falling off the chair. You don't want to lie down now, but you had better. And you bet the room will spin while you are lying in bed, and you will see light flashing on and off within your closed eyelids, and you hope no one you need to speak to telephones you today because you will not be able to do whatever it is you would have had to do if they called (this whole phrase is unnecessary, but you are unable to find a word to follow "able to"). Your back and your arms hurt, and you are yawning.

So much for today. It is over as far as you are concerned, and all the rest of the day will be an ate

MARILYN A. GELMAN lives in northern New Jersey with her beloved dog, Buffy. Her work has appeared in newspapers, magazines, and anthologies, including *The New York Times*, *The Paterson Literary Review*, *Modern Romances*, and *A Cup of Comfort* books. She is a copy editor for *Easy English News*. Mild traumatic brain injury colors every part of her life.

Marilyn A. Gelman on "Scrambled Eggs"

THE TIMES

I read the call for submissions for a special brain issue of *Creative Nonfiction* while struggling with the effects of mild traumatic brain injuries sustained in car crashes on June 13, 1994 and April 11, 1998. Then, mild traumatic brain injury (mTBI) was thought to be as temporary and harmless as a mild cold. People like me were misdiagnosed, uncounted, misunderstood, and underserved.

MY INTENT

I reviewed my old 1994 *Creative Nonfiction* guidelines (still in my files) and wondered whether it would be foolhardy for a writer with my impairments to submit material to a magazine with such high standards. But I was determined that the editors receive at least one submission from a person living with an injured brain. I feared that only scientists and professionals would contribute and we, in the trenches, would remain invisible and silent. Still reeling from the effects of the second crash, with far diminished organizational and writing skills, I felt lucky to find material I could use.

PRE-PREPARATION

Because I did not look disabled, and had surprising abilities and disabilities, I was treated as a fraud by government officials and insurance company doctors. I kept copious notes to compensate for my memory problems. When I realized lawyers would ask how the injury had changed my life, I began to detail my frustrations and struggles with the activities of daily living in Day-Timer 2-Page-Per-Day Reference Planners.

PREPARATION

The first part of "Scrambled Eggs" was composed in fury and with passion, not lovingly crafted with care. The body came from notes I made while cooking pot roast on October 12, 1997, and meat loaf almost exactly a year later, on October 9, 1998. I compiled the essay on January 21, 1999, revised it on the 23rd, and mailed it on February 6.

The parts are not equal to me. "Pot Roast" has more detail, flavor, rage. "Meat Loaf" shows the effect of the second crash. It is simpler, yet was more difficult to prepare.

I remember Lee's excitement during the acceptance call. I was surprised; an essay submitted to make a point had won publication. My notes show an easy work relationship, and I was pleased the journal ended the essay as I had submitted it. I wanted the last word to trail off, to show there was no ending, that a period at the end of a sentence did not reflect the truth of the matter.

AFTERWARDS

"Scrambled Eggs" reached the general public, members of Congress, and physical and occupational therapists and helped develop awareness about the daily struggles of people who do not look disabled.

In the past fifteen years, people living with mTBI have become visible to the government and academia. The Centers for Disease Control and Prevention estimate that at least 75% of the 1.7 million traumatic brain injuries sustained each year are mTBIs. We are being counted and studied. I have been told that my writing, including "Scrambled Eggs," helped bring these changes about.

As one for whom mTBI's effects never went away, I continue to be embarrassed because I failed to get better. When refusing opportunities just beyond my abilities, I usually remain mute about the reason. Managing medical care and daily living activities is like cooking now.

Since that BMW crashed into my Chevrolet, I have had few sources of pride. The publication of "Scrambled Eggs" in *Creative Nonfiction*'s Issue 13, "The Brain: A Nonfiction Mystery," is one of them.

REGENERATION

Brenda Miller

It looks like a ghost heart. And it feels a little like Jell-O.

—Doris Taylor, bioengineer, on the cellular scaffold
she creates to regenerate a human heart.

I.

On the radio show *Speaking of Faith*, researcher Doris Taylor is
telling us how to build a new heart. They take a cadaver heart, she
says, and wash away all the dead cells with shampoo until only a
"ghost heart" remains. This ghost heart will provide the scaffold
for stem cells that will create the new heart on their own.

I look at pictures of the ghost heart online. It looks a little bit
like halibut: white fleshed, resilient, translucent. It's almost all
water, with just enough structure to hold it in the shape of a heart.
Taylor will implant stem blood cells on this medium and wait for
the heart to start beating. The cells know what to do: she just has
to create the environment for everything to happen at once.

"We're regenerating the heart on many different levels," Taylor
says. "Physically, emotionally, spiritually. If you put a new heart
back in the same environment, it's going to get damaged again."

II.

In her installation "The Sound of Cells Dividing," Geraldine
Ondrizek invites us into cells: small rooms made of translucent
paper, cellular, where we're allowed an auditory glimpse of the
inner body's hum. "Visitors entering the luminous sculptures
can hear the sounds of healthy cells dividing and damaged
cells dying—" the gallery brochure tells us, "sounds taken
from an atomic force microscope, which uses a needle to feel
and record the actual vibration of a cell." We walk amid this
fractured music, our living cells pricked alert. Our bodies emit
music, something the mathematicians have known all along.
The artist weaves other cellular sounds into the mix: monks

chanting in their cells, families laughing and arguing, voices just short of decipherable.

In another room we encounter a Torah, its binder embroidered with the chromosomes of Ondrizek's dead son. She tattooed his genetic makeup on the cloth. His body has evaporated—gone—but the ghost body remains.

As I look, the dead son's chromosomes morph into the shape of a tree of life. The background: a flurry of stains, amniotic, smudged fluids of birth. She has stitched a recording, a threaded calligraphy. I imagine her at this work, bent over the needle and thread for years, toiling to inscribe her son on the surface of the world.

III.

My friend tells me it's called "neurogenesis." "It's because you're actually creating new pathways in the brain. Not a new brain exactly, but new ways for the brain to fire," he tells me.

We're in my kitchen, just the two of us, while the rest of my guests sit in the living room, talking loudly, laughing. The menorah candles we've just lit burn merrily away. Two organic chickens roast in the oven, stuffed with apples and onion. I've laden a tray with *latkes*. I've made a honey-curry braided bread as my challah, studded with slivers of golden almonds, and I've got a white platter of raspberry-chocolate macaroons waiting on the sideboard. The kitchen smells of rosemary and cumin and paprika and oil and fried potatoes. We will eat around my coffee table and, afterward play a game of Taboo that will have us laughing so hard we'll be gasping for breath.

Neurogenesis. A new brain. A synaptic beginning. I let the dog outside and turn to my friend, my good friend for years now. He has had his own struggles with the brain. I turned fifty this year and have just started taking Celexa, an antidepressant that comes in the smallest pill imaginable. I'm talking to my friend, trying to describe how it feels: not so much that the medication has eradicated depression, but rather that my brain is being tilled, like soil, for some new crop to take root.

I had always resisted medication: I wanted my brain to be my brain, the brain I always knew, no matter how often and how regularly it turned against me. I once took Prozac for two days, fifteen years ago, and I ended up crouched in a corner with my head in my hands, calling the psychiatrist and asking for an antidote. "There is no antidote," she said impatiently. "Just wait for the side effects to pass."

So I had stubbornly refused to even consider medications for these many years. Besides, I thought, wasn't it normal to feel the way I felt? Wasn't it an ordinary condition: to be slightly blue most of the time, to feel terrible about yourself even when all evidence points to the contrary? Don't we all stare out the window, waiting for something to change?

"It's called neurogenesis," he says again, and smiles. I know what he's thinking; he has a biblical mind. Genesis: an origin. The brain washing itself clean. Expectant.

IV.

February 1963: I'm four years old and waiting for my mother to come home. I'm staring out the kitchen window; she's been gone two days, and I know something is up, something big. I've got a fat crayon clutched in my fist. I know my mother's in the hospital, giving birth to my baby brother, though I don't really understand what that means.

I would like to remember my mother's pregnant belly. I would like to remember touching that rounded, taut stomach, perhaps placing my lips against the belly button and kissing my nascent brother through this dome of flesh. I would like to imagine the smell of this belly, complex, layered with sweat and baby powder, and smooth against my own baby cheeks—my brother kicking me through the skin, and me babbling his name over and over so he would know me when he arrived.

But I remember none of this. Instead I see myself alone at a kitchen table, writing with a big blue crayon a welcome home card, or a happy birthday card for this new child that has been living inside my mother, generating cell by cell, alive and not yet alive. I want to touch him. I want to be touched by this ghost creature who's about to arrive.

A neighbor has been taking care of my older brother and me, and she slapped me when I cried for my mother too long. She apologized immediately, made me cinnamon toast, but her hand has left its mark. It has told me I'm not strong enough to be in this world alone.

I want my mother returned to me in her normal pressed slacks, her cotton sweaters, and her lipstick so perfectly applied with a brush. I hear a car turn onto the cul-de-sac, see the station wagon making its careful glide up Amestoy Avenue. I can see through the passenger window the vague shape of my mother, holding a bundle in her arms. Something flutters up in me: love, longing, excitement, anger, fear—all of them, all at once. I wait at the window to see what will happen next. I touch my own belly, the crayon still in my hand, and leave a mark there that will take forever to wash out.

V.

I wonder if Doris Taylor will rebuild a brain. Maybe wash away the one you have: all those cells with their unhelpful memories, all those flawed synapses, down the drain. You'd be left with a "ghost brain," pale and bland as Jell-O.

VI.

Perhaps *this* is what I'm after: an amniotic pause, a whispered hush.

I would like to put my ear up against the walls of my own cells. I'd like to listen to what they have to say. You need to stay in Geraldine Ondrizek's sculpture a long time to really get it: to hear the familial voices, the monastic chants, the whirring cells, and then—always behind it all—a vast silence. You hold your breath. You let time pass. Settle down. Hear a body regenerate itself within illuminated paper, the thinnest scaffold imaginable.

BRENDA MILLER is the author of three collections of creative nonfiction and has received six Pushcart Prizes for her work. She co-authored *Tell it Slant: Writing and Shaping Creative Nonfiction* and *The Pen and the Bell: Mindful Writing in a Busy World*. She is the editor-in-chief of the *Bellingham Review* and teaches creative nonfiction at Western Washington University in Bellingham.

Brenda Miller on "Regeneration"

I do my best writing when I'm not at my writing desk at all.

Put me in front of my computer, and I'll fritter away the time checking my email, watching cat videos, and making hotel reservations for trips I'll never take. Or I'll look up recipes using fennel pollen. Or I'll chew on my fingernails. In any case, not much actual writing gets done.

But put me in the kitchen. Give me a task that's challenging, but not too hard: maybe a layered winter stew. Turn on the radio, or switch my iPod to podcasts: *Splendid Table,* or *To the Best of Our Knowledge*, or *On Being.* Let me listen with one ear as I chop a carrot or caramelize an onion. The key is to be in motion, hands occupied, so only the intuitive mind can listen.

Or lead me to an art gallery, a small one that I can walk to with my students. Don't explain too much ahead of time, just allow me to enter, to see, to take out my notebook and sit on the floor. Don't tell me I'm writing. Tell me I'm simply observing with pen in hand. It's quiet here and students with notebooks array themselves around and within the art. None of us knows what we're doing. We've entered the mind of an artist who in turn has entered our bodies.

Or stand me up at a party, talking with a good friend. We can talk about anything. He is a poet. He knows the power of words. We roll words around together on our tongues, swallow them like food as the meal simmers on the stove. I'm listening, but with one ear as I wait for the timer to ring.

Or have the dog beg me for a walk. Gather up the harness, the leash; attach the iPod buds to my ears. Let it be a walk that demands a lot of sniffing, a lot of standing around, as a stranger's voice chats in my ear. I'm not really listening. I'm taking a walk with my dog. I'm not writing; I'm taking a walk with my dog.

Or sit me down in the artist's studio, surrounded by magazines, scissors, cardboard, and glue. Let me flip through the glossy pages, tearing out pictures of food, dogs, women, the brain. I'll get derailed reading recipes or tips on age-appropriate jeans. When it comes time to arrange the collage on my board, I have to just *do*. What catches my eye? I need to choose the background first: these colors, these images will determine everything that comes next. Give me patience to enjoy the snip of the scissors, the passing of time. Let the bits of paper arrange themselves on the board. Wait. Arrange them again. Discard some pieces, search for others. Do not be quick with the glue.

When I'm done, let me prop the collage up on the windowsill; allow me to consider it with fresh eyes. Let it divulge a story I couldn't know was mine to tell. One image escorts the next and the next, until together they whisper secrets that could never be told on their own.

BEDS

Toi Derricotte

*Trauma is not what happens to us, but what we hold
inside us in the absence of an empathetic witness.*

—Peter Levine, *The Unspoken Voice*

I.

The first was a bassinet. I don't remember what it was made
of; I think it was one of those big white baskets with wheels.
When I couldn't sleep at night, my father would drag it into the
kitchen. It was winter. He'd light the gas oven. I remember the
room's stuffiness, the acrid bite of cold and fumes.

My father didn't like crying. He said I was doing it to get
attention. He didn't like my mother teaching me that I could
cry and get attention. Nothing was wrong with me, and, even
if I was hungry, it wasn't time to eat. Sometimes, I screamed
for hours, and my father—I do remember this—would push
his chair up to the lip of the bassinet and smoke, as if he were
keeping me company.

After a few nights, he had broken me. I stopped crying. But
when he put the bottle to my lips, I was too exhausted to drink.

II.

My second was a crib in the corner of my parents' room. We
moved to the attic when I was eighteen months old, so it must
have been before that. I still didn't sleep at night. I'd see a huge
gray monster outside the window, swaying toward me and
side to side. I was afraid that, any moment, it would swoop in

and get me. But I couldn't wake my parents. What if it wasn't real but only the huge blue spruce outside the window? I was more afraid of my father than I was of the monster. As long as I watched, it couldn't get me.

III.

My aunt brought home a present for me every day when she came from work. I'd wait by the kitchen door as soon as I could walk. Sometimes, she'd fish down in her pocketbook, and the only thing she could find was a Tums, which she called candy. But mostly she'd bring colored paper and pencils from the printing press where she worked.

When I was two or three, I began to draw things and to write my own name. I wrote it backward for a long time: "I-O-T." I drew houses, cars, money, animals. I actually believed everything I drew was real; the house was a real house, as real as the one we lived in. I held it in my hand. It belonged to me, like a chair or an apple. From then on, I did not understand my mother's sadness or my father's rage. If we could have whatever we wanted just by drawing it, there was nothing to miss or to long for. I tried to show them what I meant, but they shrugged it off, not seeing or believing.

(This sideways escape—the battle between my father's worst thought of me and this proof, this stream of something, questioned and found lacking, which must remain nearly invisible— pressed into what leaks out as involuntarily as urine, a message, a self, which must be passed over the coals, raked, purified into a thin strand of unambiguous essence of the deep core.)

IV.

When I was seven, we moved to the Forest Lodge. We lived in D12 on the fourth floor. My mother and father slept in the living room on a bed that came down out of the wall. I slept on a rollaway cot kept in the same closet and pulled out at night. I helped my mother roll it into a corner of the kitchen, push the kitchen table back and open the cot, its sheets and blankets still tight. (Whatever I had, I kept nice. I had to. My bed was my bed, but it was in my mother's space. If she needed the space, my bed would go.)

Someone had given me a green blackboard with a sheet of see-through plastic to paint on. In the morning, my mother would set it up in a small area between the dining room and the kitchen. She didn't mind if the colors spilled, if a few drops fell on the newsprint she had put down. After she scrubbed every Saturday, she liked to put newspaper over the linoleum to keep it clean of our footprints. Halfway through the week, she'd take the torn, dirty papers up, and, underneath, the floor was like new.

V.

Most times I liked my food. I didn't mind eating until my daddy started making me clean my plate and either struck me off my chair if I didn't or lifted me up by my hair and held me midair if I was slow. He wanted me to eat faster; he didn't have all day.

He'd hold me off the floor until I pleaded. I'd sputter in fear and humiliation—I don't remember pain—but I had to button up before he put me down to do exactly what he had told me to do, fast.

Slowness was a sign of insubordination. If I missed a pea or a crumb, I was trying to outwit him. I must have thought he was stupid. And if I pleaded that I hadn't seen the pea, he'd know I was lying. "Your story is so touching till it sounds like a lie."

I swallowed it down; I wiped that look off my face. But still he would notice my bottom lip beginning to quiver or a single tear slide down my face. These were personal insults, as if I had taken a knife and put it to his face. If my brow wrinkled in a question—"Do you love me, daddy? How could you hurt me like this?"—this implied I was pursuing my own version of the truth, as if I was his victim.

It was a war of wills, as he so clearly saw, and these were my attempts to subvert him, to plant my flag, to make my will reign.

He was the ruler of my body. I had to learn that. It had to be as if he were deep in me, deeper than instinct, like the commander of a submarine during times of war.

VI.

Thinking was the thing about me that most offended or hurt him, the thing he most wanted to kill. Just in case my mind might be heading in that direction, here was a stop sign, a warning: "Who do you think you are?" But the words weren't enough. They'd bubble out of him like some terrible brew exploding from an escape hatch, a vortex that pulled in his whole body, his huge hands, which grabbed me up by my hair.

Where could I go? I was trapped in what my father thought I was thinking. I couldn't think. My thinking disappeared in case it was the wrong thought.

It was not the world that I needed to take in, but my father's voice. I had to see exactly what my father saw in me—and stay out of its way.

VII.

In the morning, I'd fold up my bed and put it away. On those days and nights when my father didn't come home, we didn't need the space in the kitchen for breakfast or dinner, so we didn't put my bed away. I'd make it without a wrinkle, the little pillow placed carefully on top.

Maybe the black phone had rung saying he'd be late. Or maybe she had put him out.

I didn't know how they slept in the same bed because they never touched. Once, I saw them kiss. Maybe it was her birthday or Mother's Day. They blushed when they saw I saw them.

VIII.

"Those caught in such a vicious abuse-reactive cycle will not only continue to expose the animals they love to suffering merely to prove that they themselves can no longer be hurt, but they are also given to testing the boundaries of their own desensitization through various acts of self-mutilation.

*In short, such children can only achieve a sense of safety and
empowerment by inflicting pain and suffering on themselves
and others."*

"The Animal-Cruelty Syndrome," *The New York Times
Magazine*, June 13, 2010

I am trying to get as close as possible to the place in me where
the change occurred: I had to take that voice in, become my
father, eternally vigilant, the judge referred to before any
dangerous self-assertion, any thought or feeling. I happened in
reverse: My body took in the pummeling actions, which went
down into my core, so that I ask myself, before any love or joy
or passion, anything that might grow from me: "Who do you
think you are?" I suppress the possibilities.

IX.

My mother used the small inheritance she received from her
mother to put my father through embalming school. She hoped
to raise us up—her mother had been a cook—and to become an
undertaker's wife, one of the highest positions of black society.
But when he came back from the school, my father wouldn't
take the mean five dollars a week his stepfather offered him to
apprentice. He wouldn't swallow his pride. He also wouldn't
take jobs offered by his stepfather's competitors. That, too, was
a matter of pride, not to sell out the family name.

My father knew the works of the heart. That's why so many
people—my grandmother; his stepfather; and even his best
friend Rad, whose heart he had crushed—loved him even after
he let them down completely and many times, even after he
abandoned them or did the meanest things. My father was
with each of them, holding their hands, when they died. My
handsome, charming father, the ultimate lover, the ultimate
knower of the heart.

X.

My father knew all about the body. He had learned in embalming
school. For a while after his mother died, he stopped smoking

and drinking, and came home at night. He'd get out the huge leather-bound dictionary (Webster's—the same as our last name!) that my grandmother had given him when he graduated. He would open to the middle of the book, where the pictures of bones faced each other, front and back, one on each side: on the first plastic overlay, the blue muscles; on the second, the red blood vessels; and, finally, on the third, the white nerves.

He loved the body, loved knowing how things worked. He taught me the longest name of a muscle, the sternocleidomastoid, a cradle or hammock that was strung between the sternum and mastoid. He taught me you could figure things out if you knew how to make connections. He'd amaze me with long, multisyllabic words; then he'd test me on the spelling.

My father always explained. He always showed me the little smear on the plate that I had set to drain before he'd make me do all the dishes over again. He'd explain how he had studied hard so he knew where to hit me and not leave a single mark. He'd brag about it. He wanted me to appreciate the quality of his work. Like any good teacher, he wanted to pass it down.

XI.

During the summer when my mother and aunt were cleaning and wanted me out of the house, I would go out to the side of the house with a fly swatter and command the flies not to land on my wall. There were hundreds of flies, and though I told them not to, they continued to land. I don't think I said it out loud. I think I said it—screamed it, really—in my mind. Sometimes, I believed that the things in the world heard your thoughts, the way God heard prayers. When I was very young, not even out of my crib, I'd ask the shades to blow a certain way to prove they heard me.

The flies were disobeying me. Whenever one landed, I would go after it with the flyswatter. I was furious that they would do what I had commanded them not to. I knew they understood, or would understand finally. I killed tens, hundreds—didn't they see?—but they wouldn't stop.

I knew I was murderous, and yet, was it murder to kill flies? My aunt and mother never stopped me.

XII.

My grandmother had three dogs before she died when I was ten. Each had a short life. Patsy was the "good" dog, who died of a chicken bone in her stomach, and Smokey was the "bad" dog, my grandmother said, who growled at people and would jump over the second-story banister on the porch and walk around on the outside of the rail. When my grandmother and grandfather were downstairs in the undertaking parlor, they would leave me alone with Smokey. I was about seven, and I had learned the voice the nuns used to say cruel things to the children who were slow. Sometimes, the nuns hit them over the knuckles with a ruler, but mostly they just humiliated them, made them sit in the back and never called on them to do errands. I played school with my stuffed animals and dolls at home, and when they'd slide out of their chairs, I beat them mercilessly. I tried to teach Smokey to stay behind the gate to the pantry. I would open the gate and tell him to stay, and when he went out in the kitchen, I'd hit him with his leash. I believe I hit him hard, maybe as hard as my father hit me. I wanted to feel that power.

I believe I did this several times, and though it seems impossible that my grandparents didn't know, no one ever stopped me. One time I came over, and my grandmother said Smokey had run away, jumped over the second-story banister and didn't die. He was never seen again. Was he that desperate? I felt sad and responsible. I felt glad.

XIII.

I was nine when we moved to a bigger apartment on the first floor. Now, my father had only one flight to carry me up by my hair. He didn't mind going public—the stairs were right in the lobby—but he refused to allow me to scream in terror when he grabbed me. Not because he was afraid people would see. My screaming made him furious because I knew he was only going to carry me up the stairs and scream at me, only beat me on the thighs and calves (where it wouldn't show), and only until I made every look of pain, confusion and fury disappear from my face. He knew I knew that. So what was up with all that broadcasting, as if something really bad was going to happen, as if he was going to kill me?

XIV.

Life is something you have to get used to: what is normal in a house, the bottom line, what is taken for granted. I always had good food. Our house was clean. My mother was tired and sad most of the time. My mother spent most of her day cleaning.

We had a kitchen with a little dining space, a living room, a bedroom, a bathroom and two halls, one that led to the bathroom and the bedroom, and one that led to the front door. There was a linen closet in the hall between the bedroom and the bathroom. I had a drawer in it for all my books and toys, which I had to straighten out every Saturday. There was a closet in the bedroom for my mother's clothes, a closet in the front hall for my father's, and a closet off the living room that held my mother's bed.

It was a huge metal apparatus that somehow swept out on a hinge. I can't imagine how my mother and I, as small as we were, brought it out and put it back every night and every morning, for my father was never there. We just grabbed on, exerted a little force and pulled it straight toward us. It seemed to glide by itself, swinging outward around the corner; then it would stand up, rocking, balancing, until we pulled it down.

XV.

My father and I shared the new bedroom, and my mother slept on the pullout in the living room so that she wouldn't wake us when she got dressed in the morning for work. We slept in twin beds, pushed up close together, as if we were a couple.

I could have slept with my mother in the bedroom, and my father could have slept in the living room on the pullout. I could have slept on the pullout, and my mother and father in the twin beds in the bedroom. It was a matter of what worked best. My mother knew what worked best. She would have liked to sleep in the bedroom, but she always put her comfort last.

I had special things given to me, special things she paid for: the expensive toys I got for Christmas that took a whole year to pay for and the clothes I wore from Himelhoch's while my mother wore an old plaid coat for eleven years. Now I was a big girl moving from a little cot in the kitchen to my own bed in a bedroom. My father and I always got the best.

XVI.

My mother shopped after work every Thursday, so my father would come home and fix dinner for me. He'd stop at Fadell's Market and get a big steak with a bone in it. He'd bring it home and unwrap the brown paper, slowly, savoring one corner at a time, like someone doing a striptease or opening a trove of stolen diamonds. He'd brag about how much money he had spent. He'd broil it right up next to the flame, spattering grease, fire, and smoke, only a couple of minutes on each side, cooked still bloody, nearly raw, the way we liked it, he said—different from my mother. He'd say he liked it just knocked over the head with a hammer and dragged over a hot skillet. His eyebrows would go wild, and he'd rub his hands together like a fly.

XVII.

Once, my father took me to the movies. We walked to the Fox Theater on one unusually warm Thursday evening during my Christmas vacation to see Bing Crosby in *The Bells of St. Mary's*. My father frequently promised things he didn't deliver, like the time he promised to come home and pray the family rosary every night for a week when I carried the huge statue of The Virgin home in a box something like a violin case. He never came home once. When I turned The Virgin back in at school, I had to lie to the nun. After that, I rarely asked for anything. But going to the movie was his idea.

I was never happier than when I was with my father and he was in a good mood. He liked to tease me and make me laugh.

He was so handsome that I felt proud when people noticed us. I thought they were thinking that my father really enjoyed me, that I was a very special girl. I acted as if I was a special girl, happy and pretty, until I almost believed it. I had dressed up as if I were his girlfriend, and we stopped for a Coney Island and caramel corn, which were his favorites.

XVIII.

By this time, my father didn't come home most nights. Sometimes, he and my mother wouldn't speak to each other for months. Sometimes, they wouldn't speak even to me when we were in the house together, as if we had to be quiet, like in church, and respect their hatred for each other.

My father thought I hated him like my mother did or else he didn't think I was worth talking to, for he'd often go months without speaking even when we were in the house alone.

I guess he was showing how long he could hold out, like a soldier who won't break. He was strong. I always needed him first. Finally, I'd break down. I'd have to ask for money for the bus or for lunch; I'd have to ask who was going to pick me up after school. He'd make me pay by not answering or make me stand at his closet door and wait or throw his answer as if it were a barb to catch my feet.

I tried to make him change. I'd make up special names like "D-dats." *Hi D-dats*, I'd meet him at the door when he came home at night. I knew he liked to feel young and hip. I'd make my voice happy, as if I weren't afraid he'd find a shoe or book out of place and beat me. I actually was happy when I was with him—I had to be! He could see inside; he could tell my moods; my unhappiness blamed him.

Maybe all that silence and beating was because he thought nobody loved him, not my mother and not his mother. He told me how his mother had knocked him down when he was a grown man. He told me how my mother always picked up his ashtrays to wash them as soon as he put his cigarette out. I tried to make him feel loved. Sometimes, we played "Step on a crack

you break your mother's back" when we were coming home
from his mother's house, as if the two of us were in cahoots.

XIX.

Once, when I was ten or eleven, he came home for lunch, and I
asked him if I could dance for him. I had seen Rita Hayworth
dance the Dance of the Seven Veils. I had stayed home sick and
practiced. I liked to dance on the bed so I could see myself in
my mother's dressing table mirror.

 I wore old see-through curtains and my mother's jewelry
on my head like a crown. I must have had something underneath for I knew some things mustn't show. I thought, maybe,
if he saw I was almost a woman and could do what beautiful
women do, he might find a reason to love me.

At the end, I spun around and around until most of the
drapes, towels and my mother's nightgown fell to the floor. I
don't remember what remained to cover me.

XX.

Sometimes, on the nights he came home, I'd sneak up on him
while he was reading the newspaper and pull off his slipper.

He'd put the paper down very deliberately, put on his
"mean" play-face and say, "Oh, you want to play, huh?" And
he'd grab me up like an ogre. He'd hold me down and jab his
fingers into my ribs.

"No," I'd scream, "I'm sorry," and I'd plead that I would pee
if he didn't let me up.

Finally, he'd relent. "You're not going to do it again?" And
he'd tickle me more.

"Never, never," I'd scream.

"Are you sure?"

As soon as he picked up the paper again and seemed to
turn his attention away, I'd go back. It hurt so badly, but it was
worth it. I was in charge this time.

My father could make me laugh. He knew just where
to hit the funny bone. Always, my father was the only
one who could make me swallow pills or sit still while he

administered burning iodine. When I fell or took the wrong step over a picket fence, I'd come to him, crying. "I'm going to have a big scar and nobody will love me." And he'd tease, "Oh, my poor little baby, all the boys are going to call her 'old scar leg,' and she's going to be alone for the rest of her life"; but he'd do what had to be done, hold the leg in place, put the iodine on the raw spot, right where it was needed, direct and quick, without flinching, never afraid to cause the necessary pain.

XXI.

On Saturday mornings, my mother and I would have toast and coffee in her bed. She let me lie there while she planned our day. She'd get up barefoot and put the coffee on and make me sugar toast. I loved those Saturday mornings near her: her big bed, her cold cream smell.

I had always thought my mother was frightened of my father. She never seemed to fight straight. She got him by going the back route, like the look on her face when she got in the orange and yellow truck that he bought when he started the egg business. She sat on the orange crate—he called it the passenger seat—and never laughed, never joined in on the fun as he took us around Belle Isle. He had been so happy when he jingled the keys, but you could tell she thought that old truck was nothing to be proud of, as if even a joke about such a poor thing was in bad taste.

Then one Saturday morning, I spotted a big roach, a waterbug, on the living room floor. I jumped up on the bed and started screaming; she came from the kitchen, grabbed her house shoe and got down on all fours. The thing charged her under the chair like a warrior. I was screaming like crazy. I realized she was my last protection. And she started punching at the thing, punching the floor, anywhere she could punch, as if killing it was going to be an accident. She didn't stop until it was flattened.

I had never seen my mother brave. It was a part of her she never showed—that she would fight to the death. I had thought she didn't stop my father from beating me because she was afraid. I was confused by her braveness.

XXII.

Life is something you have to get used to. My mother was sad. She didn't feel appreciated. I didn't do enough to take care. She hurt inside. Her body suffered. Her feet swelled black with poison. She had a dead baby. She had womb problems. They had to take the knotted thing out. The doctor rubbed her stomach for hours until she went to the bathroom. She got TB. She got a goiter. She shouldn't clean so hard; she should rest, at least late in the afternoon. But she wouldn't. She had to keep doing what hurt her.

My mother and father were at war; whoever loved the other first would lose.

XXIII.

Nobody thought the little marks were worth looking at. I cried and showed how they went up my arm all the way to my elbow, ran all over my ankles and the tops of my feet, even up my thighs. It was as if I could see them, but when anyone else looked, the marks disappeared.

Maybe they didn't itch. Maybe they weren't serious. Maybe I was causing trouble. (I had an active imagination, my mother and father said.) I couldn't sleep because something was happening in my bed—a misery—and everybody acted as if it wasn't.

It didn't hurt after a while. I could take my mind off it and put it somewhere else.

What was it that made me suffer? What made me see things they didn't, or see them in another way? I kept waiting for proof. I was invisible or invincible.

I think the only reason my mother finally believed me was because I kept showing her that Monday mornings, after I had spent the weekend with my aunt, I didn't have the marks, but Tuesdays, after I had slept in my own bed, I had the marks again.

In an instant of recognition, she raced into the bedroom, flipped my covers off the bed and saw the little bits of blood.

She turned over the mattress, and there, in the corners, were the nests of a thousand bedbugs, lethargic or crawling. She looked close. They had gotten so far inside that the room had to be sealed with tape, a bomb put in.

He had been sleeping with another woman. He had brought her dirt into his own home (though he said the bugs came in egg crates).

Bedbugs were what poor women had, women who couldn't do better, women who didn't matter. Some other woman's bedbugs were making my mother the same as that woman.

He had brought in everything she hated, everything she couldn't control: the helplessness of slavery, bad births, poverty, bargains with killers. Everything she had risked her life to clean out of our apartment.

My mother had reason for outrage.

I only had reason to itch.

XXIV.

The living room was off limits. There was too much that might get messed up or broken. I guess he chose rooms to beat me in honor of the sacrifices my mother had made to make our home beautiful.

In the bedroom, where could I go when I fell? I wouldn't fall on the wooden footboards. There was an aisle between my mother's closet and my father's bed. That was too narrow. On the left side of the doorway was my mother's dressing table, where I'd sit and put on necklaces, earrings, and nail polish and look in the mirror. There wasn't room for me to flail around, so my father had to be very specific about the direction in which his blows would aim me.

If my cousin was visiting, he would inform her, his voice sincere but matter-of-fact—as if he owed her an explanation— "I'm going to have to take Toi to the bathroom." He preferred the bathroom when she was visiting, except when my mother was in on it, and then we needed a bigger space. If, for example, my mother had told him I talked back, he'd say, "We're going to have to speak to Toi in the kitchen." He'd pull me by my arm and close the kitchen door, which had glass panes so that my cousin could see.

But she said she averted her eyes, knowing it would humiliate me. She remembers him sliding off his belt; she remembers me pleading each time the belt hit; she remembers him telling me, as he was beating me, in rhythm, why he was doing it and what I shouldn't do the next time. Then, I would come out of the bathroom, trying not to show how I had been afraid for my life, how I had pleaded without pride. I thought these things would have made her hate me.

I remember the hitting, but not the feeling of the hits; I remember falling and trying to cover my legs with my hands.

I remember the time I came home with a migraine and begged him not to beat me. "Please, please, daddy, it hurts so bad." I could hardly speak. I had to walk level, my head a huge cup of water that might spill on the floor.

Why couldn't he see my pain? My head seemed to be splitting open, my eyes bleeding. I didn't know what might happen if I tipped my head even slightly. He saw me walking like that, as if someone had placed delicate glass statues on my arms and shoulders. I begged him, not now. I knew I had it coming. I had gone out with the Childs, and he had left a note telling me not to go out.

The Childs lived on the fourth floor. Sometimes, they brought down the best rice with butter and just the right amount of salt and pepper. They had no children. They had a little bubble-shaped car. We all seemed glad to roll the windows down and go out to a place without many cars. Their niece turned her bike over to me. It was so much fun pumping it up and down the hill, letting my hair fly. I forgot my father, as I had forgotten the bug bites, as I forgot what it felt like to be beaten. I just thought, "I'm pumping harder so I will go faster and let the air hit my face and arms, and then I'll stop pumping at the top and fall down and down, my feet up off the pedals." And I didn't feel fat: My body lost weight—it just went with everything going in that direction, and the wind flew against me in the other direction. Though it blew in my face and began to sting, I couldn't stop pumping, couldn't stop trying, one more time, to bring myself to that moment of pleasure and accomplishment right before I'd let go.

I had never felt such power, earning it by my own work and skill. I could ride it. I was the girl in charge; I had the power to bring myself there.

XXV.

Shortly after I was married, we had a dog that kept shitting on the floor. Once, I took a coat hanger and was going to hit her with it, but she drew back her lips and snarled at me in self-defense and fury. I had no idea that she would defend herself. I was shocked. I thought she was going to attack me, and I put the hanger down. I respected her in a different way after that.

She lived for sixteen years and was a great mothering presence in our household. It seemed every dog and cat that came in the house had to lie beside her, with some part of its body—a paw, the hind—touching hers. Once, I heard a strange noise during the night and went to investigate. A kitten we had found on the railroad tracks was nursing from her, and she was sleeping, as if she just expected to be a mother. When I would come home, after I had been away for a while, she'd jump up on the bed and curl her butt into my belly, and I'd put my arms around her and hold her like a lover. When she died, I missed her so much I realized that she had been my mother, too. She taught me it was beautiful to defend yourself—and that you could be unafraid of touch.

I remember how, occasionally, my father's dogs would pull back and snarl at him when he was viciously beating them. His anger would increase immeasurably, as if they had truly given him a reason to kill them. "You think you can get away with that in my house?" he'd ask, the same as he'd ask me.

Once, to get away from him, one of his dogs leapt through the glass storm door in the kitchen and ran down 14th Street bleeding to death.

XXVI.

You would think that the one treated so cruelly would "kill" the abuser, throw him out of the brain forever. What a horrific irony that the abuser is the one most taken in, most remembered; the imprint of those who were loving and kind is secondary, like a passing cloud. Sometimes, I thought that's why my father beat me. Because he was afraid he would be forgotten. And he achieved what he wanted.

In the deepest place of judgment, not critical thinking, not on that high plain, but judgment of first waking, judgment awakened with perception, judgment of the sort that decides what inner face to turn toward the morning—in that first choosing moment of what to say to myself, the place from which first language blossoms—I choose, must choose, my father's words.

The twisted snarl of his unbelief turned everything good into something undeserved, unreal, so that nothing convinces enough—no man or woman or child, no play or work or art. There is no inner loyalty, no way of belonging. I cannot trust what I feel and connect to; I cannot love or hold anything in my hand, any fragile thing—a living blue egg, my own baby— in the same way that I never convinced my father I was his. And I must rest on it, as on bedrock.

XXVII.

The time I had the migraine, after my father had beaten me, he made me bathe. He drew the bath, felt the water with his fingers and made sure it wouldn't burn. He told me to go in there and take off my clothes.

The water, when I put my toe in, was like walking in fire. I stood there, holding myself.

And then—instead of letting my father kill me or bashing my own head against the tile to end all knowing—I crouched down, letting the lukewarm water touch me.

Oh, water, how can you hurt me this bad? What did I do to you? I was whimpering. I don't know if I still had hope he would hear me, or if I just couldn't stop the sound from leaking out of my body.

But my father came and lifted me out of the water in his arms, took me naked, laid me on my bed and covered me lightly with a sheet. Then he went away and left me in the dark as if to cool down, and he brought cut lemon slices for my eyes and a cool towel or pads of alcohol to put on my forehead. He bathed me in tenderness, as if he really knew I was suffering and he wanted me to feel better.

I wondered if he finally believed. If he realized from within himself that I had been telling the truth, that I wasn't evil. Maybe he had some idea of how much he had hurt me. I knew that, sometimes, men beat their women and then make up. I didn't know which daddy was real.

AFTERWORD:
I hear in myself a slight opposition, a wounded presence saying, "I am me, I know who I am." But I am left with only a narrow hole, a thin tube that the words must squeak through. Where words might have gushed out as from a struck well, now, instead, I watch it—watch every thought, every word. It wasn't my father's thought that I took in; it was the language. It is the language in me that must change.

TOI DERRICOTTE is Professor Emerita at the University of Pittsburgh and the co-founder of the Cave Canem Foundation, North American's premier "home for black poetry." She is the author of a memoir, *The Black Notebooks,* which received the Anisfield-Wolf Book Award and was a *New York Times* Notable Book of the Year. She has five books of poetry: *Tender, Captivity, Natural Birth, Empress of the Death House,* and *The Undertaker's Daughter.*

Toi Derricotte on "Beds"

I wrote the first draft twenty years ago. I had always wanted to write about the violence in my childhood in a more extended way than I had in my poetry. I had journaled about it for years, but I needed to find a form that would hold emotional complexity and, at the same time, give me a sense of freedom as I recalled memories and emotions as tangled as fine gold chains. I needed a container. I came upon a prose piece in which the writer had used the furniture in her childhood as a way of organizing memories. Reimagining the beds I had slept in helped me to locate the writing in specific places and times and opened up a range of memories and feelings.

I wrote many of the sections in one day. It was far from a work of art. As I worked through unburied trauma—as well as the trauma of writing about it—I had to reflect and re-see. After a hundred revisions, I saw that the writing was an object separate from my experience, something that existed between a reader and me. Often I'd find myself fearfully "out there" (I have been afraid of high bridges all my life!), in a place where I lacked emotional and/or artistic resources. But inspiration always arrived, like angels, and lifted me up so that my feet never did dash on a stone.

When I dotted the last "I," I truly felt the click of a box. My obsession had lifted. I had worked myself around to a different way of seeing my past, and to a different relationship with my father. Rather than being his victim, I had made something that had a kind of truth, clarity, and beauty.

"Beds," renamed "Burial Sites," is the central piece in my book *The Undertaker's Daughter*. Writing it changed my writing as well as my life.

THE HEART

Jerald Walker

For a decade, my brother struggled to save his marriage, but late one winter night, he accepted that it was over, right after his wife almost cut off his thumb. It dangled from a strip of flesh while his wife, still holding the butcher knife, flailed around in a spasm of remorse. My brother moved to console her, insisting that everything would be OK, displaying the kind of humanity perhaps common only in people who believe they can wed heroin addicts and have things turn out well.

She was, needless to say, high at the time. He, for his part, had had a great deal to drink, but he wasn't drunk, alcohol for him having become, over the better part of his thirty-eight years, more of a stabilizer than an intoxicant. His refrigerator was always full of malt liquor, forty-ounce bottles stacked neatly on the bottom shelf like an arsenal of small torpedoes. There was a lone bottle chilling in the freezer; he had been about to remove it when his wife tore into the kitchen, grabbed a knife from the drawer and accused him of being unfaithful. She frequently displayed this sort of wild paranoia, though it is true that, earlier in the day, he had flirted with one of the moms at a birthday party he had attended with his two daughters and son. His daughters were six and seven; his son, five. Now, having been awakened by their mother's shouting, they stood huddled together at the top of the stairs, quietly watching as she retrieved a plastic baggie from one of the drawers and proceeded to fill it with ice from the freezer, a remarkably astute response, all things considered. She even had the presence of mind to remove the bottle of beer lest it be forgotten and explode, as others had before. She offered it to my brother. He declined, on account of being busy holding his thumb together. She placed the bag of ice against the wound and began wrapping it in place with a dish towel. Seeing them standing so close together, with my brother's back pressed against the stove, a stranger entering the room might have mistaken this scene for something other than what it was—at least until after the thumb was wrapped, when my brother reached for the phone to call 9-1-1. "My wife," he said when the operator answered, "fucked me up."

The operator requested more specifics. He explained what had happened. Her voice heavy with boredom, as if my brother's predicament was a common one or simply low-ranking on the crisis scale, the operator told him to keep his hand elevated until the EMTs arrived. When she advised him to keep the thumb cold, my brother felt a surge of appreciation for his wife, for the way she had moved to preserve his finger, which was an example of how caring she could be. Deep down inside, she was a good person; he'd never doubted this. On the surface, unfortunately, was a troubled soul, which—despite his love for her—simply would not, and maybe could not, be soothed.

This realization was long in the making, having been delayed by periods of sobriety when she was soft-spoken and kind. He had met her during one of those periods. They were both studying for their GEDs, trying to reroute lives gone off track, because she didn't *have* to be on welfare forever, and he didn't *have* to be a hospital orderly always. So there they were, taking a class at the local community college, where she sat at the desk to his left, her body petite and fidgety, her skin the color of coffee beans, making it difficult to see, in her arms and legs, the tracks that he'd later tell her didn't matter. It was his unconditional acceptance of her that lengthened her abstinence longer than it had gone before, a full six months, so that when her relapse finally arrived, boring down on him like

a massive hurricane, he'd already taken shelter in the area of
the heart where reason does not venture. It was while there, no
doubt, that he'd decided to marry her.

Our family struggled to make sense of this decision. Sometimes, when we spoke of it in his absence, we offered the kind
of pop analyses one would find on a daytime talk show, using
phrases like "low self-esteem" and "nurturing complex," and
then, exhausted by the futility of this exercise, I'd simply hope
for her to overdose and die. It was an awful thing to do, and
I regret it now, but she seemed to have a death wish; I merely
wanted it to be fulfilled without also including my brother.
Every day, I feared receiving the phone call that would tell me
their bodies had been found in bed, both temples containing a single bullet in the manner of murders involving illegal
debts unpaid. Because while it had reached the point where
he was giving her money to get high, he could never give her
enough, so she was driven to find it by other means. Often,
this required dealing with the kind of people who would hold
you hostage, forcing you to perform sex acts with men clutching $20 bills until the account was settled—this happened to
her more than once. It happened, too, that thugs showed up at
their house looking for her; threatening messages were left on
their phone. So, yes, I wanted her to die. Instead, she gave life.
Three children in three years, each one born premature and
each one, like her, addicted and pleading for help.

One of them made a plea now. It was their son, whose
own thumb was crammed in his mouth, making it difficult
to understand him when he begged his mother not to hurt
his father.

His parents pulled apart.

"What are you doing up?" his father asked. "Go back to
bed. All of you, scat."

"But we heard yelling." That was the six-year-old.

The seven-year-old added, "And we saw Daddy's finger! It's
bleeding!"

"Go back to bed, damn it," shouted their mother, "before I
make *ya'll's* fingers bleed!"

Regardless of the effectiveness of the threat (the children did flee to their rooms without another word), my brother felt it was uncalled for. But there was no point in his saying so, because she was gone, replaced again by the addict who had thrust a knife toward his belly. It was the addict who yelled, *None of this would have happened if you had not been messing around with some hussy!* And: *You think I don't know what the hell you been doing all day?* And also: *You lucky only your* thumb *is on ice, motherfucker!* It was the addict who scampered from the kitchen into the living room, from the living room into the dining room, from the dining room back into the kitchen, over and over, like a panther in a cage. But it was the woman he loved who came back, crying now, professing her sorrow, cursing her life, wishing she'd never been born and then wrapping her arms around his waist and tilting up her head to snuggle her runny nose against his neck, and for an instant—but only for an instant, because this thought was interrupted by the blare of approaching sirens—he believed he could still make their marriage work.

Outside, the street swirled in festive lights, celebrating its end.

JERALD WALKER's work has appeared in magazines including *The Missouri Review, The Harvard Review, Mother Jones, The Iowa Review,* and *The Oxford American,* and has been widely anthologized, including multiple times in *The Best American Essays.* Walker is the author of *Street Shadows: A Memoir of Race, Rebellion, and Redemption,* recipient of the 2011 PEN New England/L.L. Winship Award for Nonfiction and named a Best Memoir of the Year by *Kirkus Reviews.*

Jerald Walker on "The Heart"

When my mother told me of my brother's stabbing, the details were still pretty murky—all she knew for certain was that it involved a butcher knife, his wife, and his thumb. Immediately, I pictured his thumb being severed. As a brother I didn't want this to be the case, of course, but later, as a writer, I saw its metaphoric value and included it in early drafts ("... his thumb lay on the floor," I wrote, "like a miniature hot dog, popped free of its bun ... "). This was a blatant case of my imagination running wild, never a good thing for a writer of creative nonfiction, but after letting it have its fun I reeled it in and focused on the facts.

The "facts," I should say, according to my brother, since he's the only person I interviewed who was at the scene of the crime. I'm certain if I'd spoken to his wife, or even to his three young children, I would have gotten a set of "facts" that conflicted with his. But because I knew early on that this essay wouldn't really be about his relationship with his family, but instead about our relationship with each other, I wanted his impression of the events to be primary.

True to his nature, the account he gave me was restrained and objective. True to my mine, I tossed restraint and objectivity to the wind; that was the only way I could write honestly about my affection for him, my resentment for his wife, and the anxiety both emotions caused me. But it's my very subjectivity—my attempt to confront and understand it, though not necessarily to overcome it—that provides much of the essay's tension.

Of course, stabbings have a tendency to bring a tension all their own. Because I didn't witness it, I had to recreate what happened based on my brother's account, my knowledge of his wife, my familiarity with the space where it occurred, etc., and so, in the end, my imagination did get to have some fun. This time, however, I allowed it to be the medium rather than the author.

WITHOUT A MAP

Meredith Hall

"Don't be mad," I telegram Steve, care of the American Express office in Amsterdam. "Heading off alone. See you in India." The telegram takes a startling $4.50 out of the $70 I have left after paying for my hotel. Steve has the other $600. I feel some concern about this, but I stuff the $65.50 into my jeans pocket and walk out of the telegraph office into the streets of Luxembourg. It is a cold, drizzly, metallic winter day. I am scared, but I like the feeling.

The city is just waking up: Delivery trucks park on the sidewalks, and men in wool jackets lower boxes and crates down steep stone steps to men waiting in basements below. Bare bulbs hang in the gloom; voices come in bursts of yelling and laughter. I can't understand a thing they are saying. I shoulder my new, red backpack—fifty-six pounds, including the lumpy cotton sleeping bag I bought at the Army/Navy store—and shift its weight on my small shoulders until it feels less painful. The men on the street stop their work and turn to watch me walk by. One of them smiles and tips his cap. There is a murmur among them and then laughter. I am twenty-two years old and afraid. I feel shaky and powerful, recognizing a reckless potency as it takes over decision-making. Nothing can hurt me. I smile back at the workers, lean forward against the weight of the pack and choose a direction. Luxembourg is silver in the morning mist. Men and women come out, one by one, onto the sidewalks to make their way to work. I walk among them, the human stream, but I have been outside that life for a long time and make my way alone now.

Steve and I had been playing for a few months at the edges
of love. It was winter, 1972. I lived on Dartmouth Street in
the Back Bay section of Boston, in a small, shabby apartment
with high ceilings and stained-glass windows in the bathroom door. At night, I sat in the big bay window at the back
of the house with the lights low, watching rats take over the
nighttime alley. A man, across the alley and up a story, stood
each night at his window, watching me through binoculars.
I stared back. Sometimes I filed my toenails for him or read
poetry out loud. I returned each night after work to the rats,
my books, the man who watched me. I resisted spending time
with Steve. He was a good and earnest boy who wanted me
to love him, but I had little to offer. Sometimes I left a note
for him on my door, saying I had taken off for a while and
would call when I got back. But when he came one snowy
December night and asked me if I wanted to go to India with
him, I immediately said yes. Maybe, on the road to a faraway
country, I would find release from the griefs of my past.

The plan was that Steve would fly ahead to Amsterdam.
I would follow two weeks later, flying to Luxembourg on a
cheap flight and taking a train to Amsterdam, where I would
meet him. He would simply wait at the station on Jan. 6th
until I climbed off one of the trains, and we would start our
four-month hitchhiking trip, joining the flow of American
and European hippies, young people seeking adventure and,
maybe, enlightenment in India. I was nervous as I flew to
Reykjavik and on to Luxembourg, anxious about getting
from the airport into the city alone and finding a place to
spend the night. I decided I would just sleep in a chair at
the train station, but when I got there, it was locked up.
It was a very cold and damp night. I didn't have the right
clothes; I had packed for India, forgetting the continents in
between. As I made my way into a nearby hotel, I felt inept
and alone. I went to sleep worried about the train ride to
Amsterdam the next day and what would happen if Steve, for
some reason, never showed up. He had almost all our money
and our maps. Our only line of communication was through

American Express, the hub for hitchhikers in Europe. Our plan seemed, in the damp, lonely room, flimsy and uncertain.

Before it was light, I was up, frightened. I washed in cold water at the stained sink behind the door, watching myself in the mirror. I was a girl in big trouble, and I knew this as I stared back at myself: at the guarded, haunted eyes; at the tight, closed face—a record of loss. I had a baby when I was sixteen. My mother kicked me out. Then my father kicked me out. I gave my baby away.

My baby, five years old now, was somewhere, maybe loved, maybe not. Mourning with no end and a sense that I had lost everything—my child, my mother's love and protection, my father's love and protection, the life I had once imagined for myself—hollowed me out. Every day, I floated alone and disconnected, and could not find comfort or release. I understood clearly that my history had harmed me, had cut me off from the normal connections between people. Every day for five years, I had been afraid of this disconnection, feeling the possibility of perfect detachment within my reach, like a river running alongside me, inviting me to step into its current.

Something shifted in the early morning's coming light as I looked back at the broken life reflected in the mirror. In that moment, the river swept in close beside me, the current smooth and swift. I stepped in finally, reckless and grateful, a calm giving up. I had nothing more to lose. I walked toward the telegraph office. I did not care what happened to me anymore.

The winter air is heavy with sweet coal smoke as I walk and hitchhike, following the Rhône River through eastern France. I am walking blind, with no maps, and learn the names of the cities I am passing through from small, brown signs: Nancy, Dijon, Lyons, Montelimar, Arles. Everything—buildings, fields, chugging factories, workers' faces and clothes—is gray. Snow falls and turns to slush. I am cold and wet, but I am strangely excited. My money is going fast on bread and cheese and hot soup. Each late afternoon, I have one purpose—to find a dry place to sleep where no one will find me.

I am furtive as each day closes, slipping into farm sheds and factory storerooms and derelict warehouses. Sometimes I am caught, and an angry or indignant man or woman sends me back into the night. I sleep lightly, listening for footsteps. If I am near a town in the morning, I like to find a public place—a cafe or market—and spend a few minutes warming up, my backpack resting against my legs near the sweaty windows. Often, the owner realizes I have no money to spend and shoos me out. Sometimes a man or a young woman—a mother with a small, wide-eyed child, perhaps—smiles and motions me to sit down. My French is poor: "Yes, I am walking to India," I say. "Thank you," I say, again and again. I eat a pastry and drink a bowl of steaming coffee. Sometimes the men who pick me up in their green Deux Cheveaux or blue Fiats or black Mercedes pull over at a market and buy me bread and tins of sardines and cheese. The world feels perfectly benign, generous even, and I go on my way, following the river.

I think of Steve, hoping he did not sit long in the train station waiting for me before he realized there was trouble, before he made his way to the American Express office and ripped open my telegram. I half-expect to see him waving at me across an intersection where roads meet and part again. I have no idea where I am.

One cold, windy day, as I walk through another little town with no name, I meet a man named Alex, who is absent without leave from the British Army. He is tall and very, very thin, with hollowed-out cheeks and sunken eyes. His boots are rotting away; he has tied newspapers around the soles. In his dirty, wet canvas satchel, he carries a brown wool blanket, which is thin and filthy, and a miniature chess set. He has no passport. He has not contacted his family for over a year. He looks haunted, as if he no longer belongs to the world. He teaches me to play chess in the back stairwell of an apartment building. He is curt with me and never smiles. He smells unwashed, but, more than that, he seems to be fading from the world. I feel as if I am looking at myself a year from now.

The next morning, Alex points down the empty road and tells me, "Go that way until you reach the Mediterranean Sea. Turn left there. It will take you to a warmer place." I leave him sitting on a heap of stones at the edge of a field and head in the direction he pointed.

My backpack is lighter. In dirty Genoa, I sell two pairs of Levi's; my tall, red suede boots; a black lace shirt; and a bra to a girl from Chicago who is hitchhiking with her boyfriend. She gives me $20, and the rising worry about money, which I have been trying to ignore, eases. I have lost weight in just three weeks and think about food as I walk.

Now that I have reached the warmer Mediterranean coast, I see lots of kids traveling together. Like me, they carry heavy backpacks and stick out their thumbs for a ride. They look happy and well-fed, and each night, they sleep in youth hostels they have chosen from their "Europe on Five Dollars a Day" guide. They congregate—little international communities—in cafes and clubs and parks in the centers of the quaint southern towns, finding a common language and sharing tales of their adventures. I avoid them, feeling detached from their youth and the ease with which they travel through the world.

The hole in me grows. I am becoming more and more isolated and recognize that I am walking my way into perfect disconnection. I think of my baby, a boy, every single day now. I make up stories: My baby is a boy named Anthony, with black, black hair. My baby is a boy lying on his back under a maple tree, watching clouds—just like these above me—spin by on an easterly wind. Like me, he has blond curls and crooked fingers. He is shaped like this hole in me. I think of my mother. I think of my father. Under the weight of my backpack, I walk away from home.

The cobbled sidewalks in Florence have been worn down in the middle by centuries of people walking to the market or to work and back home, people who have carried burdens on their backs and in their string bags and in their hearts. The ancient stone steps of the Palazzo Medici and Pitti Palace are worn so deeply they seem to sag in the middle, as if the weight of all those lives has made its mark forever. I am at peace here, trudging down the center of the sidewalks.

I learn to steal oranges and bread and dates from indoor markets, leaving my backpack outside by the door so I can make a fast run with my day's food. At night, I comb my hair and present myself as an American college girl at the doors of *albergos*. Skeptical women in black dresses and stout shoes size me up, but each night, someone agrees to take me in. In rapid-fire English, I refuse to leave my passport with them, arguing that I am going to meet friends later and will need my identification on the city streets. I cannot understand their answers, but if I get away with it, I find myself in a clean room with stiff, white sheets on a high bed and windows looking over a quiet side street.

I request that the hot-water burner in my room be turned on, an extra cost. While the widow turns the gas valve and lights the match below the heater, I smile my gratitude. The woman doesn't smile back at me. Left alone, I put the lamp on and ease into the long tub. I soak clean in the deep, steaming water, easing some of my aloneness in its embrace. I climb out then wash my clothes in the tub and lay them across the chugging radiator for the night. In the morning, the woman brusquely brings me a tray of hard-crusted toast and sweet butter and strawberry jam in a little white pot. Later, of course, I lift my backpack onto my shoulders and quietly take the stairs past her rooms. Clean, my hunger appeased and troubled with guilt, I enter the day in Florence. The beautiful old city wakes slowly while I watch, the red tiled roofs catching the coming sun as it rises over the Arno River.

I make my way toward the rising sun. I no longer care about India. I have no destination. Most days, I speak briefly to one or two people, but I am worlds away. The road is leading in. The walking is a drug.

I cross mountains and find myself again on a sea. Rimini. Ravenna. Ferrara. Venice in the springtime—a liquid, pink city. I am a reluctant but accomplished thief in these cities, stealing food and a bath and sleep. I sell a red dress I like very much and black tights and four T-shirts. I put the $15 in my pocket. I study a French girl's map and see that I am headed away from tourist cities, from food and beds, a roof. Worry nags at me. I linger in Venice, sitting in San Marco Square or on the boulevard looking across to the Lido. Men on the freight boats in the canals call to me with white smiles. Sometimes I smile back, and a man throws fruit and small parcels of nuts or olives to me. I wave my thanks. I am thin and wonder if they see, yet, the hollowed-out look I met in Alex.

My child turns six on Memorial Day as I walk out of Venice. I will not try to hitch a ride today. I feel my son with me, a light, and I want to be alone with him.

It has been several months since I have had a real conversation with anyone. I am not at all lonely. I choose this way of being in the world. I know I would scare people at home. But I have nothing to say to anyone. I have not been in touch with my family since I left to meet Steve in Amsterdam, and their voices are finally silent in my head. My backpack is lighter. I hum Bach's Partita No. 2 and head through Trieste to the next place that waits for me.

Beograd: I am up to my old tricks—thieving food, a bed. I hoard the $36 in my pocket. Summer has come to Yugoslavia. I like this enormous country very much. Tito watches me from posters and framed photos in every building and home. The Danube makes its lazy way past the city, to mysterious places far away. I get rested and ease my constant hunger. My jeans hang from my hips. My legs are strong. I ask a soldier, "Which way is Greece?" and follow his finger.

There are fewer and fewer hitchhiking kids as I move from farm town to farm town. Boys drive oxen with goad sticks, stopping to stare open-mouthed as I walk past. I sneak into barns and sheds at night, pulling my old sleeping bag snug against my neck because of the rats and mice I hear in the hay and chaff. The nights are still cold, and my Army surplus bag offers no warmth at all. I curl my legs tight to my chest, trying to get warm enough to slip into a tired sleep. I have learned the arc of the sun: Each morning, before the roosters call the day to a start, I slip out into the dewy, gray light, orienting myself, continuing on my way.

Athens is beautiful—crisp green and white in the brilliant summer sun. It is crawling with travelers, and after weeks in the quiet countryside of Yugoslavia, I feel thrown back into a forgotten world. People speak to me in English and French, and I understand what they want of me—momentary connection, shared experiences. I pretend I don't understand and back away without smiling.

I sell my boots to a shoe vendor on a dead-end street and buy a used pair of sandals from him, giving me an extra $7. I sell my red sweater and all my socks and a yellow jersey. I have $21 left. I sit for long afternoons in the little parks lined with orange trees, considering what will happen when I can't raise more money. Going home is not an option I consider.

I have lived inside my brain for months now. The walking is an underlying rhythm for my thoughts, like an obbligato, persistent and reassuring. I have accomplished the disconnection, and my wanderings are entirely solitary, free of any voices from the past. Grief is my companion. As the child grows bigger, the hole carved in me grows, too. Silent, solitary, moving—step by step, I measure the distance between me and the woman I thought I was going to grow up to be.

Three times I try to cross the Bosporus and enter Istanbul. Gathering speed in Athens, I sweep up the coast of Greece, through Larisa and Lamia, up through Thessaloniki, through Alexandroupolis, walking, catching rides, and each time, I balk at the border, unable to broach Turkey. I am hungry. I have less than $10 left. Each time, at the door to Asia, facing the dark mystery of Turkey, I stumble at the threshold, afraid.

Asia lies behind a curtain, masculine and remote and secretive, having absolutely nothing to do with me. In northern Greece, as Europe gives way to Asia, dark men sit outside their shops, smoking *hookahs* and drinking tea from small glasses. They stare as I walk past. I feel naked, lost. There are no women anywhere. Small, dusty-legged boys run in packs beside me, screaming their excitement as they jump to touch my sun-bleached hair. I am all white, a floating apparition; their dark hands and shrill voices chase me in the village streets. Nasal prayers blare from minarets, and the sun sears the land.

I slide back down the coast to Athens, confused and worried because, even here, there is not enough room to move. I feel trapped. Remembering the freehand maps we drew in seventh grade, I know the world opens and extends beyond the Bosporus, and I want to be lost in its expanse. Again, I roar up the coast. I walk fast. Sometimes rich men in Mercedes pick me up. They feed me at restaurants hidden in the hills and smile at me, baffled and aroused. Again and again, I approach the shadowy world that sprawls beyond Europe.

Finally, too tired to turn around, I slip into Istanbul at night and let a kind, young student lead me to the cellar where he rents a room with four others. I do not go out for three days, paralyzed with fear. And then one morning, sliding to recklessness again, I leave the dark hideaway. Muezzins chant their minor-key call to prayer from the minarets of the mosques. I gather my things and enter the old bazaar. It is dark and dreamy and heavy; wool rugs and pungent spices and dates and plastic dolls tumble from doorways into the alleys. I spend $1 on a length of dark cloth and a needle, and, sitting in a wavering pool of light within the gloom, I sew a shapeless shift, long and loose. I sell my last blue jeans and my bra and my sandals and, finally, my pack. I save my belt, which I pull tight around my rolled sleeping bag.

I have heard I can get $300 for my passport. I make my way slowly through the labyrinth of shops and paths, watching for men who might return my gaze and invite a deal. I wander slowly in the maze, making eye contact with the dark men who embody danger. Everywhere, men slide next to me, touch my arm insistently and whisper, "Hashish? Hashish?" "No money," I say, emboldened, and then, "Passport? Passport?" The men move away quickly. I know I have scared them.

I am lost. The bazaar is an ancient city of stone tunnels, roofed with great vaulting domes. It is dark and very noisy. Children run past, barefoot and dark-eyed. They pull back against the scarred walls when they see me, so different from the brazen village boys. I walk slowly, watching the men. "Hashish?" "No. Passport?" Finally, a man stares back at me and signals for me to follow. A small man with a sharp nose and scuffed shoes, he leads me through the maze for five minutes, without once glancing back at me. He stops at a stall selling spices from big wooden barrels; the bright orange and green and yellow and red and brown spices fill the alley with a rich, heavy smell, mysterious and seductive. The man speaks to a younger man sitting high behind the barrels. That man stares at me coolly. I make myself stare back. He nods then says something to the older man, who turns to me and says in English, "Twenty-five dollars."

"No," I say. I am shocked. I know that what I am doing is a serious crime. It has to be worth it. "No, $300."

Both men return my look of shock. They shake hands with each other, and the younger man motions me away. I hesitate, but he yells something at me, and I turn away. I am shaken. My plan seems naive and unworkable. Later, I spend $4 on a large, peaty chunk of hashish; I sew it into the hem of my shift to sell when I need money.

I need food. A fat man watching me from his stall with serious eyes calls me to him. He doesn't smile as he puts me in a chair and lays a tin plate in front of me. He hacks the head off the lamb roasting on his brazier and places it on the plate. I spend an hour picking and sucking every sweet bit from the skull. The man shakes his head when I offer him money. I wander through the bazaar, watching the end of each tunnel for the light outside, the path out. Then I head south with $17.

Beyond the city, across the Dardanelles, I am free in that vast far-off space I remember from my childhood maps. This is where I want to be. Nothing here is like home. The disconnection is complete. I sleep alone under the trees at night. It rains some nights, and I am cold and wet. I share dark sheds with small animals—rats, I think—and I sneak out before dawn when men come to do their chores. The land is spare and mimics my stripped life. Voices—shepherds as alone as I am—call across the hills. Goat bells answer. The call to prayer. Wind. Everything has slipped. I am not me anymore.

It is mid-summer. I have been walking since January. In southern Turkey, it is warm and very dry. I am always thirsty. My bare feet are strong and calloused. The land is beautiful, rolling and arid and silent. This is an enormous place. I am lost in it.

For several days, I have been following a dusty track that winds south. I don't know how far away the coast is and can't remember how it fits on the planet. I think the Middle East comes after Turkey, and I head that way. I have forgotten about India, the hitchhiker's mecca. I am wandering. The track has been getting smaller and smaller, and now I know I am on an animal trail or maybe a shepherd's path. It winds up and over the dry, brown hills. I have not seen a house or shepherd's hut for two days. Sometimes I hear the heavy tonk of goat bells on the distant hills. I am not lonely. I hear my steps muffled in the stone-dust and the pulse of blood in my ears. I hum a fragment from Bach, the same bit over and over. I am hungry.

Night comes quickly here. In the near dark, I feel the clinking of pottery under my feet: I am walking on tiny mosaic tiles. Fragments, brilliant blue and yellow even in this erasing light, stretch for hundreds of feet in the sparse grass. I know nothing. I know no history. When did Homer live? The Trojan War—could that have been here? Cretans,

Minoans, Phoenicians—did they lay these bits of clay? I have no sense of what belongs where, or when. I am old, an old woman walking across time in the dust. Other women have walked here. Other women, I know, have been alone. I feel a momentary jolt of connection, of steadying order.

A small, stone building, round and low, rises in the dark. I feel my way to a door. I have to step down three feet to the floor, where more tiles crackle each time I step. It is damp and smells green inside. I feel for the roof—it is a low dome, and tiles clap to the floor when I touch them. There is a raised platform in the middle, an oblong, covered in tiles. I listen but hear no rats. Pleased with my find for the night, I spread my sleeping bag on the platform and wrap myself up as well as I can against the coming cold.

I wake abruptly, knowing suddenly that this is an ancient tomb. I am a trespasser. I am in over my head. The old, deep shame creeps back to me. Glued to the altar all night, I stare straight into the pitch-black dome. At dawn, I crawl up into the faint light, the air, the patterns of lives etched for millennia in the soil. On my hands and knees, I study the mosaic design, searching for clues, a map for how a life gets lived, how it all can be contained, how the boundaries can hold against the inexpressible and unnamed. How I can hold against the past. People called to God in this place, a god who was, I think, furious and harsh. I am not ready. I may never be ready. I gather my sleeping bag and walk toward the rising sun.

Night is coming. I am somewhere in southern Lebanon, on the coast, in a place I can't name. I need to find somewhere to sleep before it is dark. On a narrow beach, I discover a cement-block house still standing, its roof and one wall blasted away. Its whitewash gleams in the dusk, and it is oddly tidy. The shattered glass, the splinters of wood, the furniture and clothes and dishes that must have been left behind when the Israeli mortar shells flew through the night—everything has been scrubbed clean by the winds and shifting sand. Eddies in its corners have left tiny dunes. I push them flat with a sweep of my arm and drop my sleeping bag. It is all I carry now, this bag rolled and bound with my belt; my passport, my pocketknife and matches are tucked into the foot. I shake out the bag, dirty and musty, and lay it neatly in the corner of the ruins. I slide my passport back inside and lay the matches on top. I keep the knife in my hand. In the deep dusk, I wander the beach, gathering driftwood. The little fire whooshes up, and I am home.

I have not eaten today and have no food for tonight. The bats are out as always, their syncopated bursts felt but not seen. The Mediterranean Sea is not dramatic. It pulses in and out softly in the dark. Sparks snap and rise. Although it is August, the nights are chilly, and I am cold. I am always cold at night, my body too thin now to generate enough heat. My bag is lumpy with wadded cotton batting and only serves to keep the bats from touching my skin. I am almost content. I am free from most things. Recklessness has become a drug, and I am walking stoned. I have not had a conversation with anyone for several months; I live in my head, all eyes and ears, a receptor with nothing to return. I have no heart anymore and cannot be afraid.

I hear men shouting suddenly. They come nearer. I can hear their pant legs swishing up the beach and the clatter of what I instantly know are weapons. I wait in the dark, hoping they will march past me, past my small fire, past this already ruined house. They stop in the gaping hole that was a wall. There are six of them: soldiers in camouflage with automatic weapons drawn. I stay seated, wrapped in my flimsy bag. They are very young, some with no hair at all on their cheeks. One of them, short and thick, is older, my age, maybe twenty-one or twenty-two. He shouts at me. I cannot tell if they are Israeli or Lebanese. Maybe I have walked out of Lebanon and into Israel along the shore. I don't know where I am or what the soldiers are protecting, but I know I am in trouble.

"Passport?" the stocky one demands. I know enough not to hand it to them. It will bring them quick cash, and I will never see it again. My answer is long, as if there is a logic to my presence on their beach, as if there has been no War of '67, as if I know what I'm doing here. He shouts at me. I don't know if it is Hebrew or Arabic. "Passport!" I hear in English.

Suddenly, one of the boys jostles another, points at me with his elbow and says something. I know what it must be. They all laugh, excited and a little embarrassed. I flare to life after all these months, and I am afraid. I do not dare to stand up. My dress is thin, and I have no underwear.

My fire has died to a glow. They shove each other and giggle and jostle as if they are drunk, but they are not. They are soldiers, a team, and no one knows I am here. They sit in a semicircle around me, their rifles across their laps, their smooth, olive hands and cheeks luminescent in the night. They are quiet for minutes at a time, watching me. Then they burst into joking laughter. I sit silent, tense, surprised that I suddenly care so much what happens to me. The bats flick down onto our legs and heads and shoulders. The stars are out, the Milky Way stretching across two seas to my other life. I am sitting on my passport, my little knife gripped in my hand. I stare back at these boys, these boys with guns, and I am puffed like a frightened bird to make myself seem brave.

I sit, stiff and cold. Suddenly, all the walking away from my past—from my home; from the baby, just born and alone, that I abandoned in a hospital; from my mother, cold, her love evaporated; from my father, his love withdrawn; from the child I was myself—all the walking has taken me no-where. Here I am, alone and scared. I remember the days after my baby was born. My young breasts, still a girl's, were large and tight and hard, swollen with milk. My shirt was soaked. I stood over the bathroom sink, crying, pressing the milk from my breasts. I could hear my lost baby cry for me from someplace far away, as if my own cry echoed back to me. My milk flowed and flowed, sticky and hot, down the drain of the sink.

I clutch my arms tight to my breasts and face the soldiers who surround me. The night goes on slowly, hour by wary hour. The tides are small here, and the creep of the sea is no measure of time. Occasionally, the stocky leader shouts at me, asking for my passport. "American?" he asks. "Yes. American," I say, emphatically. "Passport!" he demands, again and again. I shrug my shoulders, gesturing no, as if these are my lines in the play we are all rehearsing. Not one of us moves. The constellations reel around the polestar, and we sit through the deep night. In the quiet minutes, one or another lifts his rifle, clacking and clipping metal against metal as he opens and closes the breach. The sound bangs against the bombed-out walls and echoes back to us. They laugh.

At the first seep of light, the leader suddenly rises. The other boys jump to their feet, brushing sand from their laps. They all look frayed with sleeplessness. The leader stands upright and nods to me. They all turn without speaking and move back down the beach in a slow, drifting line. I shake my bag out, place my passport and matches and knife in the foot, and strap my belt around it. Images rise: my mother's face turned from me; the white and metal hospital where I left my baby; my swollen breasts; my milk slipping slowly, in thick lines, down the sink. The sand in the bombed-out house is scuffed in a half-circle around me. Suddenly, I don't know if these boys spent this long night threatening me or protecting me.

I don't know where I am. My fear settles again as I walk. I head north, pretty sure I'm in Lebanon.

It is my birthday. I want ritual. This place in Lebanon is called Jbeil, "the beautiful place." I wash slowly in the Mediterranean Sea at dawn, dipping my head back into the cool, still water, an anointment. I wash my dress and sit for the rest of the day on a long, smooth ledge that falls away into the water. I have been feeling the silence acutely, the absolute lack of attachment. It frightens me because I know I have slipped into the deepest current and may not come back. But I like the narcotic of walking and will not stop. I know the roads to Damascus and Latakia and Tyre. The walking claims ground as mine, and I am as much at home here as I have been anywhere since I was sixteen.

Between me and my mother, me and my father, me and my castaway child, beyond this quiet sea, is the dark and raging Atlantic. The sun on the Mediterranean stuns the mind. I am blank. I am here in this beautiful place. I am twenty-three. I am alone. I have nothing.

It is late summer—dry, brown, peaceful in the hills. I wander from Syria to Jordan to Lebanon to Syria. I am among Palestinian refugees. Soldiers with machine guns lie behind sandbag bunkers on every corner in every country. The low, flat roofs are sandbagged, and soldiers train their rifles on the dusty streets below. I know that Israel invaded Palestine in 1949. I know that Israel occupied Jordan's West Bank and Syria's Golan Heights in the War of '67; armies of American kids joined the kibbutz movement to help Jews come home. I don't know anything else, except that the Palestinian refugees suffer. They live in vast tent cities along every highway and in crowded warrens of shacks in every town. Everyone, Arab and Jew, has lost someone; some have lost everyone. They try to tell me their stories and weep. My own grief feels smaller here.

I walk, with no plan, through Baalbek and Masyaf and Saida and Sabkha and back through Masyaf. In every place, men and women greet me with hands extended. They smile, drawing me in as if I belong to them. I have no idea who they think I am. They share food with me: flat bread and warm, tangy yogurt from the bowls on their door stones. It always means they leave their own meals hungry. A woman beating a rug in her yard calls to me as I walk by her house. She looks sad and tired, like all the people here. She holds up her hand: Wait. I sit against the low cement wall surrounding her dusty yard. In ten minutes, she comes to me with two eggs—fried warm and runny and lifesaving—and flatbread to sop them up. She stands, smiling, while I eat, her black skirt and thin, black shoes powdered with dust, her hens wandering near us, pecking in the dirt.

Several teeth ache. Sometimes in the city I steal packets of aspirin from vendors. When I can't sleep, I lay one against the gum. It burns the tissue, but I sleep.

I sell my blood to the Red Cross whenever I am in a city. I get $3, enough for a visa to cross back into Syria or Lebanon or Jordan. I try to hide the bruise from the last time. Sometimes they scold me and send me away; sometimes they need the blood badly and reach for the less-bruised arm. I feel vestiges of a familiar shame, broad and deep, with these American and European workers. They ask me if my family knows where I am. I always say yes. They ask, "What are you doing here?" But I have no answer for them and leave quickly with my $3.

Abrahim offers me hot bread from the doorway of his shop. He speaks some English and tells me he is getting married. He brings me home to his mother in As Sarafand, the refugee camp south of Beirut. She chatters at me in Arabic while she and four other women crowd around the pit-fire to cook for the feast. There is joy here. I have forgotten this kind of happiness, happiness that looks forward. I stay in this tiny, plywood and tin house for three days, basking in the large, soft peace of family. I sleep with Abrahim's sisters on mats on the floor; his father snores, and his mother murmurs to him in the night until he stops. I leave on the morning of the wedding. Abrahim's mother wraps a black and white *kafiyeh* around my shoulders as I leave. I feel a new stab of dread as I walk away, unsure in which direction to head.

I am stopped at the border. I never know which country I am leaving and which I am entering. I cross these boundaries as they appear before me. I have no plan.

It is still light. A French businessman has picked me up on the road and has driven with me, in silence, for the past several hours. He knows where he is going. At the tiny border station, he is motioned through, but I am held by the two soldiers in the guardhouse. The driver looks very concerned; his fear is contagious, and I try to get back into his car. Rifles come up, and the guards shout at him to drive on. He leans across the front seat, closes the door and drives away, looking back at me in his mirror as if he is memorizing my face.

The guards speak to me in Arabic and motion me to sit on a small bench inside the hut. It is late summer and very hot in their shack. I think I am entering Syria near Al Qusayr. A few cars pull through; then, after dusk falls, there are no more. The soldiers come inside and close the door. A bare bulb hangs in the gloom. The men sit in chairs facing me, our knees almost touching. They still have my passport. I want to sleep. I am hungry and suddenly feel too tired to face them. It is absolutely quiet outside, and I can't see lights anywhere in the no man's land of the border.

They talk, pointing the ends of their rifles at me and clicking their tongues. They burst into laughter. I sit, hugging my sleeping bag to my chest. Finally, one of the men gets up and goes outside. The one left with me taunts me and stares silently and taunts again. When the first man returns an hour later, he has a young civilian with him, a buddy. They are agitated and make jokes for each other. Sometimes the civilian touches my face or arm, or pulls my hair tight in his fist, and they all laugh, their teeth white and shiny in the hard light. One makes me stand sometimes, and the two others speak in low, rough voices behind me. The clock over the door ticks the seconds and the minutes. It is 2:30 in the dark of the night.

A car pulls up to the gate, and the soldiers jump up as if they have been caught at some-thing. I stand quickly and demand my passport. The guard hesitates then hands it to me, smiling ingratiatingly, and lets me push past him out the door. Without asking, I climb into the front seat of the car. People here know trouble, and the driver, a middle-aged Arab in a white *jalaba* and red *kafiyeh*, never says a word. They pass him through, and we drive on into Syria.

The air has changed. It is October, and the nights are very cold. I have no jacket, no sweater, no shoes. I squat by my little fire, the *kafiyeh* wrapped around my head and neck. I am always hungry. I have slept on this rocky beach in Syria for two weeks. The first few days, just before dusk, a very old man walked the length of the beach with his sheep; he murmured to them as they rustled, grazing among the debris of seaweed and trash. He didn't look at me.

Then one night, he came across the beach toward me, his sheep following. He was very thin, and everything about him was dark—his frayed wool jacket and old shoes and dirty cap and lined face. He smiled at me; he had two teeth, both on top. He spoke softly to me in the same vowelly voice he used to herd his animals. Kneeling by my small fire, he took a leather sack from his belt. He used the dented, little pot inside to milk one of the ewes, the milk hissing again and again against the tin. She stood for him without moving. His voice hushed in the falling light; he put the pot on the fire. The milk quickly boiled. He jerked it off the fire and dumped a brown clump of sugar into the creamy foam, stirring it with a stick. Sitting back on his heels, he waited while the milk cooled then gave it to me, smiling and nodding and talking. He watched me drink it down, delicious and sustaining. I came to life. He nodded and smiled and smiled.

Every night now, he stops and warms ewe's milk and sugar for me, talking to me softly like my father did when I was a child. His old hands are creased and knobby. I don't want him to leave, and I drink the milk slowly, holding him to me. I am nourished and feel a father's care. All day, I wait for him, feeling how mute I am, how distant I have become from anything I once knew.

One night, I try to tell him I have a child. I hold up six fingers and mime a belly, large and round. I point to the West, across the sea. I very much want him to understand. He finally makes a loud, kind noise of understanding, laughing knowingly, smiling and nodding. But I know he cannot imagine what I am talking about. That night, I feel very alone under the black sky.

I leave the beach the next night. I say goodbye to him after I have drunk the milk he offers. He smiles and nods at me and turns several times to wave goodbye as he makes his way with his sheep, their bells tonking their hollow, peaceful course along the shore.

It is always almost night, the time when I must find a place to lay down my sleeping bag, a place to attach myself for a few hours. The decision feels enormously important every night. When I am tired, the unspoken thoughts that ride under the rhythms of my walking begin to seep out and over an edge I cannot protect. At this haunting hour, I feel like a stray animal, desperate for warmth of any kind. Each night, I watch the countryside go gray then black. I keep walking. Voices I know—my mother's, my father's, mine, the cry of a child— press at my back.

I move in the dark, alone. I search for lights on the arid hillsides, in the steep valleys. I float toward them with an intensity of longing; my outsideness feels contemptible, a failure of great magnitude, which hits each day at this time. There are voices coming from the lights, from behind secure walls—fires and food and entangled lives. The oncoming night leads me to them; I want, for a little while, to weave myself into their web. I do not want to sleep out in the open again, cold and apart, the dry wind swirling the stars out of place. I do not want to be alone. I creep toward the lights. Some nights, I sleep in the dirty sheds with chickens and goats. Some nights, I lie against the low cement walls, close enough to hear the voices, hushed or shrill. Most nights, there are no lights anywhere, no secure walls, and I lay my bag down where I am and curl against the cold.

I walk. It is November. I have been moving for eleven months. In a dusty field, twenty women stoop, preparing the rocky soil for the fall planting. Many of them have babies tied with bright cloths to their backs. Small children stand listlessly by their mothers in the sun. I am walking on a track from nowhere that skirts the field. Heads come up and watch me, but they continue their work. The children stare, slowly turning to follow me with their eyes as I pass. The dust rises. The barren hills lift behind us onto the high plain. Suddenly, at a signal I cannot see, the women stand and call their children out of the field for their midday meal, moving together toward me on the path.

I am struck with shyness. I cannot remember how I got here, what it is I am looking for. I don't know if I have found it, if it can be found. I am outside the world, drifting. I don't think I am lost, but I cannot explain where I am. I want so much all of a sudden, but I cannot name what it is. I am empty and very tired. I don't know where to walk next. I don't want these women—with their babies and their gray, dusty feet and hands and careful eyes—to wonder what brought me here. Things gone rise up in a flood. Suddenly, I am scared of myself and of how far I have drifted.

The women do not speak to me. They lift the baskets they have left by the road and sit to eat their meals on the little ridge of hard dirt beside the field. I walk along in front of the women and children, feeling exposed. We eye each other; the children lean against their mothers. Goats bleat far off in the hills.

Suddenly, a woman smiles up at me and wags her hand: Stop. She is wearing a 1950s short-sleeved sweater, bright red. She swings her dark-eyed baby onto her lap from her back and opens her bag. She lifts her sweater over her swollen breast, her skin the same soft dusk as the soil around her. Holding a dented tin cup under her breast, she presses milk—creamy white, hissing again and again—into the tin. She smiles against the brilliant sun as she hands it to me. I hesitate then take the cup, sitting down beside her in the dirt. She lifts her child to the same breast. The other women nod and smile while I sip the milk. It is hot and thick and sweet. For a few minutes, I am bound to this mother and her baby, to these women and their children. I remember what it is to belong, to be loved. I imagine my child loved somewhere.

For a few moments, I am suspended within this circle. But I do not belong here, and when the cup is empty, I slowly get up. Nodding again and again, I wave to the woman in the red sweater. A different hunger steals into me. Memories of my old life—when I was a girl in a family, a girl with dreams of the life coming to me—flash white and clear as I start to walk away. I want to go home, home to my adult life, with its losses carved forever in my path, with its possibilities, like unformed clouds, calling me forward. I head back the way I came, against the current, orienting myself north and west, toward the Atlantic. The sun is warm. Behind me, I can hear the women and children talking and laughing as they eat and rest. Their voices rise in soft, floating prayers as I walk.

MEREDITH HALL's memoir, *Without a Map*, was a *New York Times* Bestseller and was included on Oprah's Top Ten Memoirs list. Hall won the Pushcart Prize and was noted in *Best American Essays*. She was awarded the Gift of Freedom Award, a two-year fellowship from A Room of Her Own Foundation. Her work has appeared in *Creative Nonfiction*, *The New York Times*, *The Southern Review*, *The Kenyon Review* and many other journals and anthologies. She teaches in the MFA program at the University of New Hampshire.

Meredith Hall on "Without a Map"

Goat bells tonk, tonk from the brown, arid hills. Their hoofs scatter stones in a steady, soft clatter. Goatherds scold and coax. Their voices wake me to a great hunger. I search the hills for a figure, and raise my hand in greeting. I do not escape notice anywhere, and always there is a greeting in return, a startled *hello* called across the valleys, and then the echo, *hello, hello*. The sun is clean and sharp on my head and shoulders and arms. I am barefoot on the same stony paths the goats wander. The dusty ground is warm beneath my feet. My sleeping bag, dirty and very worn, bumps against my back, the belt cinching it slippery in my sweaty hand. I am thirsty. The hills are laced with paths, sometimes running off in the distance to a cluster of small, worn buildings which might offer food—eggs fried in beaten up flat pans, warm, runny yogurt, bread. I am hungry, always. Mostly, the hunger is for people, women brought from their chores to stare at me, their shy smiles and bobbing heads, their hands stroking my arms and hands, their children hiding in the small dark doorways.

I carry these memories of my walk through Lebanon and Syria and Jordan in my body. Simply calling back to any moment during that time causes powerful physical memory to arise, pure and unmediated. What startles me is the depth of the emotional memory carried in those sense-memories. As I started to write this essay, I worried that I would not be able to render the extraordinary events convincingly, would not be able to evoke the power of such aloneness and disconnection. A friend calls this my "suicide walk." If that is true, how could I speak that story without melodrama, without explanation and analysis?

I know this: writers must trust the story, and the story is enacted in our senses. The body perceives the world and records it as memory. In order to remember what happened, I started to walk again on the land with its great, sere beauty and gentle, generous people. The stories were waiting, here in my physical being: heat and stone and brilliant light, frigid nights and goat bells and boys calling to them and to me, yogurt and fire and the clack of gun parts, needle pricks and bruises at my elbows, cool dirt floors, dry seaweed and ancient broken tiles crackling underfoot.

My physical self recalls my story of alienation and loss and hopeless-ness, and here it is in "Without a Map." But my body also recalls hands offering sustenance, physical and emotional. Offering a small, obscured suggestion of a passageway back, a reminder of myself, of a previous world still there. Before I sat to write, I did not remember the power of those offerings, but my senses did, the stroking of hands, the murmurs of worried women.

I do not generally share my writing with anyone. I find that any response, applauding or critiquing, confuses me and distances me from my work. But I did show the draft of this essay to other readers. One woman responded, "I love the way milk is working here as a powerful theme." Milk? I asked. I had no idea that I had written about milk. What milk?

But my body knew what milk: my own, swirling down the bathroom sink after I left my baby at the hospital; sheep milk, warmed over a fire, sweetened and handed to me by a very old man distressed by my presence on a forgotten stretch of rocky beach; a woman's, pressed from her breast as a hollow-eyed girl wandered by. My physical self remembers milk, and I know—my body taught me—that milk binds mother and child, and once, a long time ago, bound a lost young girl back to the world.

As I wrote this essay, I did not have language for such desperate hungers and fears, or, at least, I understood that whatever abstractions I tried to name could have little effect on readers. I often receive notes from people thanking me for this singular and irregular story. They tell me that they have never lost a child, or a mother and a father. They have never wandered recklessly as I did. They have not been hungry. But they tell me that I have told their stories. Concrete details carried as memory are able to tell the largest truths. Those truths, written from my body, are recognized and shared: we all know loss, and we all know the desire to belong, and we all know the great hunger to be loved.

TWO ON TWO

Brian Doyle

Once upon a time, a long time ago, I rambled through
thickets of brawny power forwards and quicksilver
cocksure guards and rooted ancient centers, trying to
slide smoothly to the hoop, trying to find space in the crowd to
get off my shot, trying to maneuver at high speed with the ball
around corners and hips and sudden angry elbows, the elbows
of twenty years of men in grade school high school college the
park the playground the men's league the noon league the summer league, men as high as the seven-foot center I met violently
during a summer league game, men as able as the college and
professional players I was hammered by in playgrounds, men
as fierce as the fellow who once took off his sweats and laid his
shotgun down by his cap before he trotted onto the court.

I got hurt, everyone does eventually; I got hurt enough to
quit; back pains then back surgery then more surgeries; it was
quit or walk, now I walk.

The game receded, fell away, a part of me sliding into the
dark like a rocket stage no longer part of the mission.

Now I am married and here come my children: my lovely
dark thoughtful daughter and then three years later suddenly
my squirming twin electric sons and now my daughter is four
and my sons are one each and yesterday my daughter and I
played two on two against my sons on the lovely burnished oak
floor of our dining room, the boys who just learned to walk
staggering across the floor like drunken sailors and falling at
the slightest touch, my daughter loud lanky in her orange socks
sliding from place to place without benefit of a dribble but there
is no referee only me on my knees, dribbling behind my back
and trick-dribbling through the plump legs of the boys, their

diapers sagging, my daughter shrieking with glee, the boys confused and excited, and I am weeping weeping weeping, in love with my perfect magic children, with the feel of the bright-red plastic tiny ball spinning in my hands, my arms at home in the old motions, my head and shoulders snapping fakes on the boys, who laugh; I pick up a loose ball near the dining room table and shuffle so slowly so slowly on my knees toward the toy basket eight feet away, a mile, a hundred miles, my children brushing against my thighs and shoulders like dreams like birds; Joe staggers toward me, reaches for the ball, I wrap it around my back to my left hand, which picks up rapid dribble, Joe loses balance and grabs my hair, Lily slides by suddenly and cuts Joe cleanly away, he takes a couple of hairs with him as he and Lily disappear in a tangle of limbs and laughs, a terrific moving pick, I would stop to admire it but here comes big Liam, lumbering along toward the ball as alluring and bright as the sun; crossover dribble back to my right hand, Liam drops like a stone, he spins on his bottom to stay with the play, I palm ball, show-fake and lean into short fallaway from four feet away, ball hits rim of basket and bounces straight up in the air, Lily slides back into picture and grabs my right hand but I lean east and with the left hand catch and slam the ball into the basket all in one motion; and it bounces off a purple plastic duck and rolls away again under the table, and I lie there on the floor as Joe pulls on my sock and Lily sits on my chest and Liam ever so gently so meticulously so daintily takes off my glasses, and I am happier than I have ever been, ever and ever, amen.

BRIAN DOYLE edits *Portland Magazine* at the University of Portland. He is the author of fifteen books of essays, fiction, poems, and nonfiction, most recently the essay collection *The Thorny Grace of It* and the sprawling novel *Mink River*. His essays have been reprinted in the annual *Best American Essays, Best American Science & Nature Writing,* and *Best American Spiritual Writing* anthologies. Among various honors for his work is the John Burroughs Award for Nature Essays and an Award in Literature from the American Academy of Arts and Letters.

Brian Doyle on "Two on Two"

Often, when I turn back to a piece I wrote years ago I recoil in horror at what a fervent idiot I was, preening and bloviating, missing the point altogether, overwriting at high speed, not yet aware that the great achievement in writing is knowing what to leave out—but not with this essay. This one sings ever louder to me over the years. Partly that's because the principals in it are now long and lanky and dewy adults, and I miss the years when they were small and wild and hilarious and not yet surly and supercilious and veterans of strife and struggle; but also here's a case of a piece that is exactly what it should be, seems to me. As a schoolchild in Brooklyn wrote to me after she "had" to read it in class (ouch), it begins as a fable and ends as a prayer, and she was right about that, although I had to admit I had not done that consciously. But now I think perhaps that's the nut of some useful thoughts for writers: relax, stop thinking, write with your lightning fingers, write like you think and speak and dream, not like you think Writers write; write with the cadence and music of all the hymns and fables and songs and poems and curses and slurs you ever heard swirling in your memory; write fast and let the sentences sprint and whirl as they will. You can always tinker later; you can always give up snarling and feed the draft to the fire; but you cannot always catch the way something spills out of your belly and your bones through your fingertips onto the page, unless you learn to let go, turn off your brain, take ideas and feelings out for canters on the open beach of the empty page and see what happens. Sometimes what happens is that you write something you never imagined before, something that surprises and moves you, something you felt so deeply you had never been able to articulate it before your fingertips, shockingly, did so; and sometimes then you sit back amazed and delighted that this pile and jumble of sentences, which was never in the world before in this motley parade order, actually did catch something of love and pain and prayer and miracle and diapers and time and holiness. That's a great feeling. It's happened to me a few times, and it's glorious, although even better is the feeling you get when someone reads a piece you wrote and is moved by it, startled and shivered somehow; that's the best, as connection is what writing is all about. It'll happen to you, if you keep typing. And when it happens, dig it for a while, and then start another piece, and see where it wants to go.

PESÄPALLO: PLAYING AT THE EDGE OF THE WORLD

Caitlin Horrocks

We're leading by one, but with two outs, when I come up to bat. The staff-student baseball game is a yearly tradition at Päämajakoulu, and part of the tradition is that the game isn't played for any set number of innings. Whoever is winning when the bell rings for the next lesson is that year's champion, so the game's normal rhythms are speeded up and slowed down, tense, the leading team moseying through the batting order and the trailing team fielding with a frenzy. Our opponents are a hand-picked lineup of sixth graders, mostly the boys who are hitting puberty faster than their peers. Finnish sixth graders are the age of American seventh graders, and a few of the boys are already much taller than I am, which admittedly is not saying much.

I am buried somewhere in the middle of the batting order, but there's only one runner on base, the school handicrafts teacher, when I come up to bat. I don't remember now which student is pitching, but I believe it was Jukkis, the monosyllabic nemesis of my Conversational English classes. Tall and broad and sullen, with spiked, naturally platinum hair, he's barely talked to me all year. This wouldn't be such a problem except that being talked to is nearly my only function here at Päämajakoulu. Jukkis, I imagine, after nine months of being asked about his favorite animal, his favorite sport, his favorite flavor of ice cream, finds me as infuriating as I find him. We eye each other balefully, the bright yellow ball seeming to glow in his hand.

Because this is a game of pesäpallo, Finnish baseball, Jukkis is standing beside me, across home plate and just out of range of my swing. To pitch he will throw the ball in the air, at least three feet above my head, and I will try to hit it on its way down. If it falls and hits the asphalt of the schoolyard, that's a ball. Two balls and the batter walks. If it falls and hits the base, that's a strike. Three strikes are an out. I have no intention of missing the pitch, but bats and gloves and balls of all kinds have traditionally not paid me much heed. As a clumsy, pudgy kid, a girl who really did throw like a girl, I long ago convinced myself not to care. On this May morning in Mikkeli, Finland, sixty miles west of the Russian border, one hundred and forty miles northeast of Helsinki, three hundred and twenty-five miles south of the Arctic Circle, eyeing a thirteen-year-old student across the plate, I care desperately. I bend my knees, raise the bat, my stance the same as in the American game, and wait for Jukkis to fling the ball upwards. I concentrate on its speed, its height, and at the same time keep repeating to myself: *Remember to run towards third! Run towards third!*

The pitching style is not the only thing that separates American baseball from the upstart Finnish version: the base running pattern is also radically different, with first base roughly where third should be. Second is over by first, and third is across the outfield, somewhere in left field close to the foul line. The distances between each are different: approximately sixty feet from home to first base, then ninety-six, one hundred and eight, and a long one hundred and fourteen feet from third to home.

The rules for running the bases are different, too. Technically, I don't even have to run after hitting the ball; according to the rules I can hit both my first and second pitches and just stand there, making it possible to advance two runners while remaining at-bat. If I hit a fly ball and a fielder catches it, I will be "wounded," not out. (Three outs or eleven woundings end an inning.)

There are other quirks, too: a triple counts as a home run for scoring purposes, but the batter gets to stay on third and try to score again. Stealing is generally not a good idea; anytime a hit is caught, any runner not touching a base is automatically out. If a runner leads off at second and the pitcher throws to third, the runner is out unless he can physically get back to touch second before the pitcher's throw is caught by the third baseman.

Here in the Päämajakoulu schoolyard we are hardly playing a professional game, and most of these rules are irrelevant, which is just as well—it's all I can do to remember which way to run. It's also a burden to know that I am playing to uphold faculty honor, my honor, the honor of "grownups," the honor of the English language, the honor of Americans. This year, the year of the Iraq invasion, being an American has been complicated. In Conversational English classes my students have mustered their best English, their best understanding of global politics, to ask me *why*: Why is America doing this? Why are *you* doing this? Without consistent access to English language news, only dimly aware that the war is even happening, I am the wrong person to ask. But I am the only American my students know, and so they assume, surely, I can explain American foreign policy, and surely, I am brilliant at baseball. In their minds, America is a nation of warmongers and ballplayers.

The crowd of students has been booing the teachers proudly and powerfully, rooting for their classmates, but I seem to divide their loyalties. They are used to encouraging me, soothing my embarrassment, watching me climb back on my skis or stumble through a discussion about the school cafeteria porridge with their "real" English teacher, who thinks it's hilarious to test my Finnish in class. They tried to console me when I got so lost during the Official School Skiing Day that the headmaster was dispatched to look for me in the woods. (In my defense, I had been on skis only four times in my life, all of them in the two weeks before the Official School Skiing Day.) They want their team to win the pesäpallo game, but they also want me to do well. Their enthusiasm, their confidence, is palpable: this is baseball, she's American. Finally, *something* she can do.

"Go, Caitlin!" they yell as I wait for the pitch, and I wonder where they've learned the cheer. Video games, perhaps—a lot of their English is from video games. "Game over!" they occasionally shout at each other on the playground. "Finish him!"

This is the home of Nokia, the neighbor of IKEA and Volvo, a social welfare democracy full of tall, trim, well-educated blondes. Finland's educational system has been ranked the best in the world, its standard of living among the highest. Most of my students look like extras from *Children of the Corn*, pale and golden-haired and hauntingly wholesome. They love the place they were born with an innocence, a straightforward pride I envy. I check over their sentence-completion exercises: Finland is_____. *The most beautiful country in the world. The country with the most beautiful nature. The best country on Earth. A place with excellent four seasons.* They are very big on this, the fact that Finland has four seasons; I try to tell them most of the United States does, too, except our winter does not last six months, our summer two.

My students speak of "going to Europe" on vacations. When I tell them that to Americans, at least those Americans who could find Finland on a map, they're already *in* Europe, they shrug. "Sort of," they say. "But not really." This is a country that for hundreds of years was a backwater of the Swedish empire, then a backwater imperial Russian duchy, then a fledging independent state in the shadow of the Soviet Union. This is a country that has been left to its own devices when it comes to language, cuisine, literature, sports.

Pesäpallo was imported and reinvented by Lauri "Tahko" Pihkala, a Finn studying in the United States who happened to watch a 1907 Red Sox game. He found American-style baseball frankly boring, but upon his return to Finland, he noticed how many traditional sports were losing ground to modern imports. He decided to create a new game, loosely based on a nineteenth century Finnish game called Kuningaspallo (Kingball) but named after American baseball—and more exciting, faster-moving, and more competitive than either. Pesäpallo was officially introduced in 1922, and the Finnish National Baseball Association (Pesäpalloliito) was formed in 1930. After a name change or two, the sport settled on pesäpallo, a direct translation (base-ball) and transcription of how it sounded to Finnish ears: to the Finnish, the English 'b' and 'p' sound exactly the same. (Hence my third grade students' hysterical laughter at the phrase "big pig," and their teacher's enthusiastic shouting at an exhibition match at Päämjakoulu's sister school in Britain: "Good bitch! Good bitch!" she praised the English schoolgirls.)

Pesäpallo eventually became known as the *kansallispeli*, the Finnish national sport, and at least during the spring and summer the title is earned. During the winter, ice hockey takes over; losses, particularly to Sweden, could plunge the entire country into a day of mourning. I never saw pesäpallo inspire such heights of despair or triumph, but it is universally taught to schoolchildren, and in the warmer months it is played in many small town and community leagues, as well as in the professional Superpesis league, which prides itself on its separate-but-equal tournaments for male and female players.

Outside the country, it's another matter. Baseball has the United States, Canada, Japan, the Caribbean, and most of the Western hemisphere. Pesapällo has Finland, Sweden, Germany, and Australia. There's a team in New Zealand, too, but it doesn't have the money to compete abroad. The Pesäpallo World Cup in 2006, held in Munich, had only four participants. Fortunately for national pride, Finland won the gold. Indeed, there has been a proposal that in the next World Cup, Finland be allowed to field twelve separate teams, one from each of its provinces, to increase participation and create more competition.

As a small country with a pool of potential athletes only five-million deep, Finland has had to make its peace with almost never being good at anything on the world stage. I once asked a Finn if the national soccer team had qualified to play in that year's World Cup. He burst out laughing. And yet Finns are ferociously proud of their Formula One race car drivers, their curling team, their ski jumpers, the long distance runner Paavo Nurmi, who has been dead for decades, and a sixth place finisher at the 2006 European Championships in women's singles figure skating. In 2002 a sprinter named Markus Pöyhönen won his heat and made it into the finals of the men's

100m at the European track and field championships, the first Finn ever to do so. He finished fifth in a field of seven, and the country went wild. This was more than respectable. This was enough to get him on the Finnish version of *Dancing with the Stars*, and to keep the sixth grade female students at Päämajak-oulu swooning over celebrity magazine pictures of him for the next nine months.

Pesäpallo is one of few venues for athletic prowess Finns have to themselves, or nearly so. By having their own brand of baseball, they have ensured both that other countries will have to compete on their terms, and that they will never have to compete on those of the United States. But they don't see pesäpallo as a consolation sport; Finns fiercely defend the superiority of pesäpallo to American baseball. They won't even be diplomatic about it. To them, there is no contest. They claim pesäpallo is more entertaining, more physically and intellectu-ally demanding—basically, smarter, fitter, faster, better—than baseball. "Are you tired of watching boring baseball?" demands an international rule booklet. "Do you prefer faster and more tactical batting sports?"

To some extent these claims are demonstrably true—pesä-pallo games are shorter, with two periods of four innings each, and the ball stays in motion much more. Finns are proud that pesäpallo doesn't reward power hitters: a ball that goes over the fence is counted as a foul. The goal of a skilled batter is to hit the ball to certain parts of the outfield—where the fielders aren't, yes, but more than that, there are very specific plays that require highly accurate hitting to move all the runners into po-sition. At the game's highest levels, teams have playbooks and plans closer in complexity to American football than baseball.

To present the American side of this argument, I defer to sportswriter Red Smith, who had the (mis)fortune of watching a pesäpallo match when it was an exhibition sport at the 1952 Hel-sinki Olympics. Pesäpallo's inventor, Pihkala himself, threw out the opening pitch. Smith titled his article "Monstrous Infant": "They played a ball game here last night, and if there's a stone left upon a tomb in Cooperstown today it's an upset. . . . [The game] was invented by Lauri Pihkala, a professor who wears a hearing aid. . . . Somebody must have described baseball to him when his battery was dead." Smith thought the game lacked elegance, sense, a coherent strategy, or anything to differentiate it from a bunch of far northern yokels running in zigzag patterns across a field. It is hard to tell, though, whether the game offended Smith's sensibilities simply by being so different from its namesake, or he found it unpleasant to watch, or, perhaps most likely, he simply couldn't get over the most outwardly bizarre aspects of the game. I suppose any true devotee of a sport has a point at which his sensibilities are irrevocably offended. Even Finns look askance at the Swedish brannboll, a version of baseball in which, among other oddities, an unlimited number of players can stay on any one base—the entire batting order, for example, can huddle on first.

Smith also had the luxury of having grown up with the American version of baseball, *the* baseball. But what makes the Finnish sport less legitimate than its precursor? Why is pesäpallo seen as a freakish offshoot of its parent sport, while baseball is given the respect of long tradition and sanctified rules? After all, someone had to come up with baseball, or we'd still be playing "stoolball" on village greens. We just don't know who, despite long-cherished myths like the one about Abner Doubleday's field in Cooperstown. Baseball has a long history and idiosyncratic evolution, as opposed to being the invention of a single man in the 1920s, but baseball is not sacrosanct. Much as Americans complain about the snooze-factor in a five-day cricket test match, I never met a Finn who thought American baseball was anything other than the slow-moving dinosaur of the sports world, a woefully unevolved predecessor of his own sport. Even Finns who don't particularly like pesäpallo think it is a sport far superior, in design and execution, to the American version. Surely, if the rest of the world would just sit up and take notice, if pesäpallo boosters had one one-hundredth of one percent of the money and resources of American Major League Baseball, pesäpallo would conquer the world.

Finland doesn't hold out much hope of this happening, but that doesn't stop the Finns from trying to spread the gospel of pesäpallo, or, as it's now known in younger, hipper circles, pesis. There are a few teams playing now in Estonia, Japan, and Switzerland. The next World Cup is in 2009, so the Finnish Society of Auckland might have time to raise the money to send the New Zealand team.

In fact, there is an entire world of baseball offshoots and progenitors, a family of fringe sports played with bats and balls. Pesäpallo is hardly on the farthest fringe; it already has thousands more adherents than British baseball, for example, a sport played in three cities that touts its yearly "international" championship: a match between Cardiff, Wales, and either Liverpool or Newport, England. Pesäpallo has also outlived some of its sister sports: while nineteenth century Finns were playing kuningaspallo, Russians were playing the closely related lapta, Swedes were playing langboll, and Germans were playing schlag-ball. Lapta, Russian baseball, dates all the way back to the fourteenth century, as evidenced by the discovery of seven-hundred-year-old leather balls and wooden bats; the pitcher placement is the same as in pesäpallo (perhaps this is where Pihkala got the idea), but the batter must begin his swing with the bat held between his legs. The game survives as an activity for schoolchildren and an official "Traditional Russian Sport." Schlag-ball is similarly hanging on, and even stoolball is still played, if only in Sussex, England. Langboll, alas, has gone gently into the great sports beyond.

It's hard for Americans to realize this anywhere except a dirt playing field in Russia, or an English city green, or a concrete Finnish schoolyard, but American is the not the only flavor of baseball; it's just the one with the largest reach and the most money, and the only one most Americans are aware of.

And yet Finns, as proud as they are of their homegrown sport, understand that it has a clear kinship with the American version, that eight-hundred-pound gorilla. Finns see pesäpallo as a starter experience for foreigners, especially Americans. It is what a Finnish person will try to teach you to bridge the cultural gap; if the two of you can't talk about curling, there's baseball. They bring it up when they aren't sure if you're ready for something like *avantouinti*, a single verb that means going-swimming-by-jumping-in-a-frozen-lake-through-a-hole-cut-in-the-ice. Have you gone avantouinti? Would you like to avantouinti? Did you avantouinti and get hypothermia and nearly die? The Finns understand that avantounti is approximately an 8.4 on a ten-point scale of cultural adventurousness and assimilation. Pesäpallo is a 1.2. Pesäpallo is to avantouinti what karjalanpiiraka is to kalakukko, both of which are specialty Finnish foods. The former is a rice pastry with butter and the latter is a baked bread bowl full of lard and fish heads.

Since I arrived in Finland at the beginning of the school year, I didn't encounter pesäpallo until the start of the new season the following spring. By that time, I had tried kalakukko and karjalanpiiraka and mämmi, a delicacy that looks like a lump of tar and is a traditional food for Lent partly because its laxative effects help purify the body for Easter. I had also slurped koivunmahla, a traditional spring drink harvested by sticking spigots in birch trees and drinking what comes out. I'd tried to learn to ski, and learned both the Finnish word for javelin-throwing (keihäänheitto) and the location of the world's tallest ski jump (Lahti, Central Finland). I'd attended events including a Moose Raffle and a First Aid Championship, been beaten with leafy birch branches in a sauna, and had a Russian border guard joke about shooting me in the head. By pesäpallo season, I was ready for anything.

The previous spring, with an English literature B.A. in hand and no clue what to do with myself, I had applied for exactly two jobs: teaching English in Finland, and being an apprentice pastry chef at a bakery in Michigan. I didn't speak Finnish, didn't have any Finnish family background—I had stumbled onto the job advertisement online. *Why?* everyone asked me, both Americans and Finns. *Why not?* I answered. Eventually I came up with an answer involving my passionate commitment to teaching and cultural exchange, but "Why not?" was more honest. I was unprepared and underqualified for the job. I'd made it to my second round of interviews at the bakery when, one morning, the assistant headmaster of a Finnish elementary school was on the phone, telling me Mikkeli was a nice town with only one bear. "I think you will not meet him in the forest. It is not sure that he exists. Maybe you will. But probably not. And if you do you will run away!" This was my job interview: apply for a visa, arrive in August, run from the bear.

My job title is "Assistant Teacher of English," which means various things as the year unfolds. I start out visiting other teachers' lessons: math, science, Finnish, handicrafts, physical education. I'm supposed to engage the students in conversation about anything—numbers, animals, yarn, javelins. I am the school's pet English speaker, the pet American. My job is primarily to be unintimidating, and I trip over my own feet and tongue so often I can't imagine this could really be a problem. By winter I've graduated to holding my own Conversational English lessons with the older students and teaching the younger ones English songs and games. When a fifth grader tugs on my sleeve one day in the middle of a conversation group and tells me the assistant headmaster/fifth grade teacher wants me to join his phys ed class out in the schoolyard, I worry I've been demoted.

I help haul boxes of equipment out of a shed into the yard that is finally, in late April, free of snow. The kids open the boxes and distribute bats, balls, brown leather mitts. I have heard rumors of Finnish baseball but have never seen a game or the equipment. I allow myself a hint of anticipation. This is not tearing through the forest standing on a pair of someone else's waxed sticks. This is baseball. This I can do.

The teacher tells me he wants me to play, play to win, like I'm one of the eleven-year-olds. He puts me on a team and hands me a glove. For once, he seems to be doing this not as some new way to humiliate me, but because he assumes I will be good enough at the game to provide a productive example for his students. The Finnish winter being as long as it is, there are very few baseball-friendly weeks in the school year, and his students have played only a handful of times in the past few years. No one even asks me if I can play baseball. "Since Finnish baseball is so much easier, you will be very good at this game," he says. "Don't all Americans play baseball?"

For once, I'm glad my father made me play baseball. It was his sport, the one he followed, the one he would have loved to be really good at, the one he would have loved for one of his kids to be good at. My father has two daughters, no sons, and to his credit, the only time I have detected any regret in him over this is when it came to baseball. He had been a rising Little League pitcher, poised to be a large fish in his small hometown pond when his arm was badly broken in a school-yard fight. He still can't pull his right arm all the way back, but he could spend weekends pitching softballs to his kids, and he still speaks with embarrassing pride about my single moment of sports glory, which happened when I was nine. I don't remember it, but according to him, I pulled off a double play during a game with my summer softball team. I think it was apparent very early on I had no innate athletic skill, but my father didn't lose heart. Our baseball playing, our occasional tickets to Detroit Tigers games, were reflexive but sincere: this was what fathers did with sons, or daughters; this was what Americans did with each other. Faced with a child who read a lot more books about unicorns than she caught fly balls, my father still thought I should at least be able to play catch, to hit an easy pitch.

In American baseball, that's about all I can do. But as it turns out, I can beat the pants off a bunch of Finnish kids. Finnish baseball gloves are larger and rounder than the American version; so is home plate. The pitching style makes it much easier to hit the ball. A reporter from the *Chicago Tribune* once asked avid pesäpallo player and Olympic curler Teemu Salo if he thought he could hit a U.S. major league pitch. "I think never," he said. In fact, everything about the Finnish version of the game seems easier. It's like we're playing on the moon, or in some parallel universe. Not only are we all running backwards, swinging at pop-ups, constantly moving, but I'm good. It also doesn't hurt that the opposing team is made up of eleven-year-olds.

After my first at bat the kids back way into the outfield every time I'm up. I'm still not a power hitter, so the balls don't foul out by overshooting the edge of the field. I can bring runners home without ever going to first base. The only thing I have to concentrate on is remembering to run towards third, instead of the ingrained instinct to run right. My only slip-up is missing an easy grounder in the outfield. "Fuck!" I instinctively shout as the ball rolls past me. I look up at my fifth grade teammates, who grin at me. "Don't tell your teacher," I say. Then the bell rings and I go back inside to talk about fourth grade girls' favorite animals: dolphins, always dolphins.

I never did see a live professional pesäpallo game—only televised ones, flipping though the state-owned channels on weekends. The players compete in small dirt stadiums, more like a high school facility than even a minor league ballpark in the U.S. They wear light helmets something like bicycle helmets, and full-body uniforms covered in advertisements, like the ones worn by race car drivers. It's been harder to find sponsors, though, since a gambling scandal a few years back. Some Superpesis players, frustrated by and struggling on professional players' meager salaries, started betting on and then purposely throwing their games. Like the U.S. MLB strike, the scandal disillusioned fans and drove down attendance.

Although professional pesäpallo is suffering, the amateur version is alive and well. Attendance at the Päämajakoulu staff-student game is universal. A crackling announcement goes out over the PA that I don't fully understand, but I know enough to follow the exodus down the hallway and out into the yard where the children overflow, climbing the wrought-iron fence to stand on the sidewalk outside; they aren't making a break for it, just trying to claim a better view. Another teacher spots me and summons me over to the bike racks, where the rest of the staff has congregated. They have heard I am very good at pesäpallo.

"Yeah, against eleven-year-olds," I say.

My co-workers look disapprovingly at my sandals. Today, everyone except me has brought sneakers. Apparently, my grasp of the Finnish language has not improved as drastically as I might like to think. I shrug and tell them it's all right; I'll run and field as best I can. The game has been delayed by a choir performance for the retiring woodshop teacher, so it's already unlikely I'll see much playing time. Like baseball, pesäpallo uses nine men in the field; there are lots more than nine teachers, so we send out our best. I insist I am not among them, and to my relief, they believe me. A sixth grade teacher who also happens to be a star player on a regional soccer team makes the first out in the first inning, but the sixth graders manage several runners on base, and one run. The students are making a good showing, and the crowd is ecstatic.

My non-renewable contract at Päämajakoulu is up at the end of the school year, and I'm not legally eligible to look for work elsewhere. I'd begun applying for teaching jobs in other countries when there was still snow on the ground, when the sun set at two p.m., when I thought I'd vomit if the cafeteria served one more tater tot made of shredded beets. But now, with the beautiful spring weather and hundreds of students laughing and cheering in the sunshine, my heart starts to break a little. Not for the Finnish man I am dating—by spring we both know the relationship won't outlive my job contract—but for this country, for the fifth-place sprinter everyone adores, for lard and fish bowls, for drinking the clear blood of a birch tree, for my generous, self-confident students. *Finland is the most beautiful country in the world. Finland is the best place on earth.* I love them and their moon-baseball, their sport played proudly in four lonely countries. I love them for hitting easy pitches and running backwards and not apologizing for it, for saying *this*, this is the best kind, the truest kind of baseball.

The teachers get two more outs, and the sixth graders grab gloves and take the field. We lead with our best: the soccer star, the lanky assistant headmaster, the school caretaker. Both sides have been playing fast and loose with the batting order; the heavyset headmaster is allowed to bow out cheerfully while I get shoved up to the plate, even though I haven't fielded. We've scored two runs but have two outs and a single runner on base. The children are disheartened, but think they'll have enough time in the next inning to turn the tide. They can afford to cheer for me.

I don't want an American to lose the pesäpallo game for the teachers; I don't want an American to screw up at baseball in front of a bunch of Finnish children. I shoulder the bat and connect with the yellow ball. It bounces in the outfield, and I make it to first/third easily, even with my feet slipping in sandals. Two more batters, two more hits: the woodshop teacher, the long-term substitute for a third grade teacher on maternity leave. The next teacher is thrown out at first as I'm running down the left foul line towards home. The inning ends with the teachers still leading 2-1, and with American honor intact. Our fielders go back out and the next inning begins. Two students make it on base, but two more strike out, and before their side can tie the game, the bell rings. The students howl—not only have they lost until next spring, but they have to go inside to class. The teachers have to go back into class, too, but we march into the school victorious.

In the staff lounge I check my phone minutes and try to decide whether I can afford to make an international call to my father, to tell him I upheld our national reputation in an international exhibition match. I try to figure out how to tell him, if I should tell him, if he will be pleased or offended to learn this: after all his efforts, after being born and bred—every one of us, the athletes and the fans and the clumsy and the dispassionate—to believe that baseball is America's national sport, it is only here on this May morning in Mikkeli, Finland, an hour from the Russian border, three hours from Helsinki, five hours south of the Arctic Circle, running left towards third base, that I am finally the grateful citizen of a baseball nation.

CAITLIN HORROCKS is the author of the story collection *This Is Not Your City*. Her work appears in *The New Yorker*, *The Best American Short Stories*, *The PEN/O. Henry Prize Stories*, *The Pushcart Prize*, *The Paris Review*, *Tin House*, and elsewhere. She is the fiction editor of *The Kenyon Review* and teaches at Grand Valley State University in Grand Rapids, Michigan.

Caitlin Horrocks on "Pesäpallo: Playing at the Edge of the World"

This story started as a class assignment for a creative nonfiction workshop at Arizona State University. I was in the last semester of an MFA in fiction and seizing my final opportunity to take classes in other genres. I turned out to be a terrible poet, but I really enjoyed creative nonfiction, even though I was intimidated by an assignment that asked us to attend a spring training baseball game, then research and write about some aspect of the sport. American baseball already has hordes of talented writers to do it justice—people who play the game better, know the game better, love the game better than I ever could. On the field, I'm liable to drop the ball. In the stands, I'm easily distracted by soft pretzels. I don't have a head for statistics, either; I've lost many games of Trivial Pursuit trying to earn that Sports & Leisure wedge.

As I struggled to find an aspect of baseball I was possibly qualified to address, I found myself thinking about pesäpallo. That sport was the first species of baseball I encountered that I was actually good at, and I felt I could say something about it that people hadn't already read. This essay also marks the first time that I tried to look at any part of my own life through the lens of sports, and nearly the first time I tried to write about my own life at all, at least without the veil of fiction. Why did my father spend so many hours playing catch with his clumsy daughter? What did it mean to be one of the only Americans in a small Finnish town? Was I ashamed of taking joy in being the twenty-something pesäpallo MVP of the fourth grade? (No, I was not.)

After workshopping a draft of the essay, I cut the spring training scenes that had originally triggered the piece. I also learned many of my first lessons about balancing researched information and personal narrative. "Pesäpallo" then benefited from the excellent editors at *Creative Nonfiction*. To be such a newcomer to the genre and have my essay not just selected for publication, but treated so well and thoughtfully, was a mindboggling stroke of good fortune.

"Pesäpallo" remains my only essay about sports, but I've continued to write creative nonfiction, and to explore the places where the genre bumps up against my first love, short stories. I love the opportunities that nonfiction offers to include information and ideas openly and unapologetically. Structuring essays, without the convenience of constructed plots to order the paragraphs and hold them together, remains a rewarding challenge. I'm a more articulate, self-reflective person for the act of trying to interrogate and record my own experiences in ways that will be meaningful to an audience. Coming to creative nonfiction from fiction has also probably made me something of a traditionalist: I know "truth" is a slippery word for any essayist, but as a fiction writer, I already get to lie professionally. If I'm turning to creative nonfiction, as either writer or reader, I want it to be a sincere effort to arrive at something true, however elusive that may be.

'MBRIAGO

Louise DeSalvo

A KNOCK AT THE DOOR

It would happen like this. A knock on the crackled glass of
the door to our tenement apartment in Hoboken, New Jersey.
My mother, not expecting a visitor, opening it as she would
for anyone who troubled to climb the four steep flights of
stairs. She had nothing to fear. She knew that if the visitor
was a stranger, by the time he got to our door, he would have
been stopped, thoroughly checked out, and granted passage
up to our apartment by one of the young men hanging out on
the corner of Fourth and Adam's in front of Albini's Drug-
store, by the old woman leaning out the window on the first
floor of our building, or by the old man sitting in the sun on
our front stoop.

So because there was nothing to fear from a knock on the
door (World War II was over, my father back home unharmed,
at work a few blocks away), my mother would put down her
mending, or turn away from her ironing board, or pull a pot
off the coal stove and open the door, hoping, perhaps, that it
was my father home from work early or Argie from down
the block—the only friend who could lure her away from the
punishing rounds of her daily household chores.

Outside the door, not my father, nor Argie, but an old
Italian man. Short, stooped, ruddy-faced from years of work
in the sun, wearing a cap like my grandfather's. Surprise on
his face. Then, shame. A slight bow, as he took off his cap.
"Mi dispiace proprio," he'd say. "I'm very sorry." He hadn't

known a woman would open the door. "'*Mbriago?*" he'd ask. '*Mbriago*, the drunk. My grandfather's nickname. The man had come to see him. He would be a distant relative from Vieste, my grandfather's village in Puglia, or a crony from his railroad days in upstate New York, or a pal from his years of working on the docks in New York City. And he would be needing a loan.

Ours was a neighborhood of nasty nicknames—"Joey the Fat," "Jimmy Goose Face," "Bobby Snot Eater." Even mine—"Miss Prim," "Miss-too-big-for-your-britches," or "Miss Smarty Pants"—given me by my father, were far from endearing, revealing my father's disgust at what he called my holier-than-thou attitude. So my mother never recoiled at her father's being called *Umbriago*. There were many old Italian men like my grandfather who worked all day, drank wine all day to fortify themselves for work, staggered home drunk, washed themselves at the sink, changed their clothes, poured themselves a little glass of wine to restore their spirits while they waited for their suppers, poured themselves a large tumbler of wine to accompany their meals, poured themselves a little glass of digestif so they would sleep all night. They, too, were called '*Mbriago*. And even the ones who weren't called '*Mbriago* were drunk much of the time.

"Next door," my mother tells the visitor, pointing. She knows that anyone who comes to see her father comes for a loan, the bargain sealed by a few glasses of my grandfather's homemade wine. My mother, worrying about how my grandfather will support himself when he retires if he gives money to everyone who comes to his door, and because she embraces the American doctrine of self-reliance, slams the door on the old man, shakes her head, and grumbles her way back to her work.

THE TABLE

In all the photographs, in all the moving pictures of my grandparents' table, there is always bread, just enough food for satiety, and always a flask of wine. But there is never water. Not a pitcher of water, nor a glass of water. My grandfather, so far as I know, never drank water. Nor did my grandmother, much. A little glass of water for her on the hottest of days is all I can remember.

When I am young, I never notice that my grandfather does not drink water, that he drinks only wine. And his nickname, *'Mbriago*, tells me nothing more about him than if he were called something else. For his drinking wine instead of water when he was thirsty was not something I questioned or remarked upon. It was as natural to me as the green of the trees in the park around the corner in springtime, the sweat of summer, the melancholy falling leaves of autumn, or the death of the soul in wintertime.

HOME MOVIE

In one moving picture, taken by my father, my grandfather is standing behind his kitchen table, miming drinking down an entire flask of wine. My grandmother looks annoyed, tries to take the flask from him. He pulls it away from her, mimes drinking the entire flask of wine again. She becomes annoyed again, grabs his arm, tries to take the flask away again. But he turns away from her. He is the hero in his son-in-law's home movie; he is enjoying playing the drunk that he is.

My mother sits at the table, looks away, cups her face in her hand, a gesture that I have come to understand indicates her displeasure at what is going on. There is an antipasto on the table. Another flask of wine. A cup of milk for me. But no water.

WATER, WATER

My grandfather began to work in the fields of Puglia when he was seven years old. When he worked in the fields, he was not given water to drink by the landowners or their overseers. Water was scarce; water was needed for the crops and for animals, who were viewed as more valuable than farmworkers who could more easily be replaced if they sickened and died.

In the fields of Puglia, as in fields all across the South of Italy, people working in the fields drank wine to quench their thirst, not water. Wine was abundant; wine was cheaper; wine was safer to drink—at least that's what the farmworkers believed. Even now, if you travel to the South, if you see a group of farmworkers stopping their work for a few moments to rest, you will see them passing a flask of wine among themselves, you will see each man or woman wiping the mouth of the flask before passing it on to a comrade. "Passing the saint," they call it.

And so, my grandfather began "passing the saint" when he was seven years old as he worked in the fields; he "passed the saint" each day of his farm work in Puglia until he left for America. And one of the reasons he left for America—one of the reasons many people of the South left for America—is because the South was arid, the South was drought-stricken, and because of this lack of water, farmworkers did not earn what they needed to support themselves during bad years. So, at the beginning of the twentieth century, when there were a series of droughts that left many unemployed, America beckoned. And by the time my grandfather left Puglia, the habit of drinking wine, not water, to quench your thirst was ingrained. Water was dangerous, he believed (and it often was); wine was safe (even though drinking wine long term would kill you, but this he did not know).

If my grandfather had lived in Puglia until 1939, if he had not emigrated to America very early in the twentieth century, he would have witnessed the completion of the great aqueduct that now delivers water to Puglia, albeit inadequately. It was begun in 1906 and encompasses 213 kilometers of subterranean tunnels built by eleven thousand workman. During the Roman Empire, eleven aqueducts served the imperial city. But the Pugliese people had to wait until almost the middle of the twentieth century for water to be brought to their arid land.

Perhaps my grandfather would have been one of the men building that aqueduct. But he was not. He lived in Puglia when water was scarce; when whatever potable water was available was sold to the poor at exorbitant prices; when much of the water of Puglia was tainted and undrinkable; when much of the water of Puglia was standing water, which bred mosquitoes, which gave the people of Puglia malaria, which killed the people of Puglia in astonishing numbers, especially the children and the old and the weak.

But the South of Italy was not always an arid land. The aridness and the lack of safe drinking water in the South when my grandfather lived there was caused by human beings and rooted in history and racism—the history of conquest, exploitation of the land and its people, and the refusal of the governments of the North to provide the South with the water it needed to sustain life.

The Englishman Norman Douglas traveled through Puglia and Calabria in 1922 to see how the modern South compared to descriptions of the region in ancient texts, such as those in the odes of Roman poet Horace (65–8 BCE), who was born in Puglia, and the *Iter Venusinum* of Lupoli, and the texts of Virgil, Martial, Statius, Propertius, Strabo, Pliny, Varro, and Columella. He wrote about what he discovered in *Old Calabria*, originally published in 1915. Everywhere he went Douglas looked for rivers, or streams, or springs mentioned in these ancient texts, and he discovered that virtually all of them had disappeared. He remarked upon how waterless the modern South is. How in the South, unlike the North, rains come during the winter when nothing is growing—in spring and summer, instead of rain, there is hot dry air, which makes it essential for the government to provide a system whereby water is captured when it's plentiful and distributed when it is not, only this isn't done. How the only water to be had is bottled from mineral springs and sold by vendors. How peasants and farmworkers drink wine, not water; how they're often drunk by midday.

But in Horace's time, the South was "covered with forests," and the forests were full of "hares, rabbits, foxes, roe deer, wild boars, martens, porcupines, hedgehogs, tortoises, and wolves," virtually none of which survive now because the forests have been cut down or burned by invading armies.

For Douglas, the South's poverty was linked to how despoiled the land had become; he attributes the lack of water to deforestation; he attributes the diseases that have plagued the South—cholera and malaria—to what has happened to the water in the South because of deforestation.

He tells of the "noisome" waters that exist in this generally "waterless land" of the South, of how little the government has done to drain the swamplands that breed mosquitoes. He writes about how prevalent malaria is in the South, how taking doses of quinine is necessary to prevent malaria, but how the poor can't afford quinine.

"I dare say," writes Douglas, "the deforestation of the country, which prevented the downflow of the rivers—choking up their beds with detritus and producing stagnant pools favourable to the breeding of the mosquito—has helped to spread the plague [of malaria]." He writes how cholera is increasing, and how the government's not providing adequate sanitation in the South has made its spread inevitable. He tells how, because of deforestation, there are more frequent landslides, and of how, after landslides, the threat of cholera becomes greater.

Centuries of invasion left their mark as well. Invading Turks burned down everything they encountered—towns, cities, forests—as they rampaged through the South. Spanish viceroys and Bourbons and Arab invaders destroyed the land. The Adriatic seacoast was depopulated during the Arab invasion, and villages and towns were destroyed, everything in the path of the invading army was burnt to the ground, and "the richly cultivated land became a desert."

And what the foreign invaders began, the government in the North completed. Northern and German industrialists acquired rights to the timber of the South, and Douglas saw the slopes of existing forests felled during his journey. To denude hillsides of trees in countries with abundant rainfall was one thing. But to do so in a country with insufficient rainfall was "the beginning of the end."

Douglas believed that politicians and industrialists were greedy and did not care that their practices would lead to disaster for the economy of the South in the future. Once hillsides were denuded, rainfall washed the soil away, exposing the rocks beneath, making reforestation impossible. But why should they care? They did not live there. The immense profits gained from these destructive practices went north, went out of the country, and often the workers that cut down trees were imported. So the people of the South did not profit from their country's abuse.

Centuries of conquest coupled with the ravages of exploitative capitalism left the South devoid of two important natural resources, forests and water, and turned the South into the arid land my grandfather left. These acts changed the character of the people of the South. It led to the kind of "bestialization" and "anguished poverty" that Douglas observed—until the 1880s, the poor sold their children by officially sanctioned contracts.

Douglas tells how haggard the people are, and how "distraught" from hunger and thirst. He believed that it was because the land could not feed its people, could not provide employment for its people, could not quench the thirst of its people, that the great emigration of the people of the South to America occurred.

Later in the twentieth century, Carlo Levi's observations were essentially the same as Douglas's. Levi spent time in Lucania, the desolate region between Puglia and Calabria, as a political prisoner. In *Christ Stopped at Eboli,* Levi describes the state of this region when he lived there.

Hills of clay had become its most prevalent geographic feature. Wondering how they have been formed, Levi asks a local and is told that the trees have long since disappeared and the once fertile topsoil has eroded, leaving clay. Now, because there are no trees to hold the clay during the rainfalls of winter, there are frequent landslides. "The clay," he is told, "simply melts and pours down like a rushing stream, carrying everything with it. ... When it rains, the ground gives way and starts to slide, and the houses fall down ... the clay simply melts and pours down like a rushing stream, carrying everything with it."

Because the earth can't support agriculture, many of the men of the region emigrated to America, destroying the family structure of the region. "For a year, or even two, he writes to her, then he drops out of her ken . . .; in any case he disappears and never comes back." The women form new attachments, but they cannot divorce, so that many of the children are illegitimate. But the children die young, or "turn yellow and melancholy with malaria."

Levi believed that the South became poor because "the land has been gradually impoverished: the forests have been cut down, the rivers have been reduced to mountain streams that often run dry, and livestock has become scarce. Instead of cultivating trees and pasture lands there has been an unfortunate attempt to raise wheat in soil that does not favor it. . . . [M]alaria is everywhere."

For Levi, the effect of chronic malaria has been inscribed into the character of the people of the region. Malaria has robbed the people of the South of their ability to work and to find pleasure in the world.

LUXURY TRAVEL

When I take my husband to Sicily for his sixtieth birthday, we stay in a fancy hotel in Agrigento, overlooking the famous Greek temples.

At the end of the day, I take a long, hot bath. It is the time of the winds that blow up from the Sahara. There is grit on my body, in my hair, on my clothes.

Later, in early evening, I take a solitary walk into a village. I hear old women complaining to each other about how, for yet another day, there has been no water. A thousand yards down the road, in our hotel, there is an ocean of water. Here, none. Why?

When I return home, I ask a Sicilian friend. He laughs at my ignorance. "The Mafia," he says. "They control the water." He tells me to read Mary Taylor Simeti's *On Persephone's Island*. There I learn that in Sicily's interior, very often there is water only once every five or ten days. This is not the fault of nature, says Simeti. For Sicily is "rich in water that flows to the sea unexploited" because of government neglect, and because the Mafia "controls the major wells and springs that tap subterranean water layers, and . . . sells its water at high prices" and interferes with any attempts to ensure a cheap, safe water supply for the people.

WORKING ON THE RAILROAD

My grandfather came to America when he was a young man. He came for a better life, yes. But he came, too, because he was afraid that if he stayed in Puglia he would die. Die from a bullet to the chest during the worker's rebellions. Die from thirst. Die from starvation. Die from malaria. Die from cholera. Or die for no reason at all.

And regardless of the stories we have been told of the people of the South leaving because they wanted a better life in America, it was terror, more than anything else, that propelled him and the scores of others like him up the gangplank to the ship that would take him to America. Terror, and, yes, a job promised him by a boss recruiting men from his village to build a railroad line in upper New York State. The deal was simple. If you put your mark on a piece of paper, you'd get free passage to America. When you got there, you worked until you paid off your passage. Until then, the railroad would take care of you. There would be nothing for you to worry about.

And so my grandfather came to America, and worked on the railroad, and slept in his filthy work clothes—there was no place to wash, no water to wash with—on vermin-infested bags of straw, covering himself with a discarded horse blanket, eight men to a roach-infested, windowless boxcar. He awakened at three in the morning, just like in Italy, and walked the line to the day's worksite, and worked from five to twelve without stopping. For lunch, there was bread, and sometimes there was water, but not always, because fresh water was in short supply. In a 1916 essay called "The 'Wop' in the Track Gang," Dominic T. Ciolli reported how the *padrone* of a gang like my grandfather's complained to him because the laborers complained that they had no fresh water, had had no fresh water to drink or to wash with for weeks, and how the *padrone* said, "These dagoes are never satisfied. . . . They should be starved to death. . . . They don't belong here."

But, like in Italy, my grandfather said, there was wine, there was always wine for the workers to drink. Wine: antidote to rebellion. Wine: pacifier of those plagued by injustice. Wine: quencher of the rage. By the time my grandfather paid off his passage and moved to Hoboken to work on the docks, he was an alcoholic. But that word does not describe who my grandfather had become: a wounded man who had lost whatever hope he'd managed to salvage from the rubble of his life.

When my grandfather talked about his days on the railroad, there was a rage in his eyes, a rage that could pummel a wife, that could start a riot, that could burn down a building, that could kill a *padrone,* but that did not. And so. He'd take a glass, pour himself some wine, and then some more wine. After his third glass, he looked for the rage, but it was no longer there. After his third glass, he'd miss his mother, his father, his *paisani.*

LAST SUPPER

"The day your grandfather dies," my father says, "he's digging out the basement in the house of one of your grandmother's relatives. And it's hot down there, and it's hard work because he's got to put all the dirt he digs into a sack and carry it up the stairs, and out to the back yard, and your grandfather is doing this to make a few extra bucks because his pension isn't enough to live on and because he's always giving his money away to anyone who comes to his door, and this pisses off your mother and your grandmother, but they can't do anything to stop it.

"And this day, he isn't feeling so good. He's tired and dizzy even before he starts working, and after a couple of hours, he wants to stop working, but they tell him a deal's a deal, and that he has to keep working. And to keep him working, those bastards gave your grandfather wine to drink. And, you know your grandfather, there wasn't a glass of wine he would ever refuse. So he takes the wine, quenches his thirst, forgets he's tired, and keeps right on working until mid-afternoon when the job is done. Keeps working through the heat of the day. Keeps working even though he's hot and tired and dizzy and feels like he can't breathe."

The rest of the day goes like this.

My grandfather comes home, washes himself at the sink, changes into a clean set of clothes, has a glass of wine and a bite to eat with my grandmother. After he finishes his meal, he pours himself another glass of wine, gets the spiral notebook that lists the money people owe him, sits down at the kitchen table, starts tallying his accounts using a system of his own devising—he's never gone to school, never learned arithmetic. He's scribbling away, getting angry, because it's a year later, and his wife's relatives in Long Island still haven't paid their debt, and he's tallying how much they owe him when he falls to the floor. He's had a massive heart attack.

A few hours later, my mother, my sister, and I come back home. My mother knocks on her father's door to ask for help. We've been shopping; she's tired of being with us; she wants him to take care of us while she puts her groceries away.

He doesn't answer. She panics: He's supposed to be home. She struggles my sister and me into our apartment. Tells me to climb through the open window out onto our fire escape. Tells me to climb through my grandparents' open window, tells me to unlock their door.

I do as I'm told. I've done this before when my grandfather's forgotten his keys. So this is why I'm the one who finds my grandfather dead.

LAST RITES
At the wake, I go up to the casket to see my grandfather's body. He is wearing his one good suit, the one he wears to my First Communion. There is the smell of flowers from a

few commemorative wreaths surrounding him, the smell of mothballs emanating from his suit, the smell of death.

"That doesn't look like grandpa," I say. "And it doesn't smell like him, either." A neighbor stands behind me. She is watching me, listening to me, awaiting her turn to view my grandfather's body.

I am kneeling down, as I have been told to kneel by my father. I am supposed to be paying my last respects to my grandfather, as he has told me I must do. I don't know what last respects are, just like I don't know what first respects are, so I don't know what I'm supposed to do. But I have watched the stream of visitors go up to the coffin, kneel down, touch my grandfather's hands frozen in prayer, make a hasty Sign of the Cross, kiss their fingers, and move on. My mother kneels in silence next to me. She hasn't said much since the day her father died; she will say even less in the years to come. Sometimes it will seem that she has followed him to wherever he has gone.

Everyone in the funeral parlor cares about how she is "taking it." No one is concerned about how I am "taking it." My grandfather, the man who took care of me whenever he could, who sang me songs, who told me stories I couldn't comprehend of a land where wild seas drowned fisherman, where rainfalls were so powerful they made the land slide away, rainfalls so relentless that they washed away all the good earth and made it impossible to grow anything to eat; of a land where wolves ruled the night and men and women walked to the fields in the dark and worked in the blaze of day without a tree to shade them during their precious few moments of rest.

"And what did your grandpa smell like?" my neighbor asks.

I remember my grandfather, at his table, drinking wine. I remember my grandfather at our table, drinking wine. I remember my grandfather crushing grapes in the basement, stomping on them with feet that would stay purple until late summer. I remember my grandfather drinking wine when he took care of me, drinking it, sometimes, right out of the bottle. I remember my grandfather giving me watered wine to drink when he took care of me when I told him I was thirsty. I remember my mother being angry at my grandfather when she came back home and found me drunk, asleep on my grandparents' bed, under the giant cross on the wall with Jesus Christ bleeding.

(In high school, I am the girl who drinks too much at parties. The girl who is always thirsty but who never drinks water when she is thirsty, only booze. The girl who drinks so much she can't remember how she gets home. The girl who drinks so much that she passes out on the way home, once, in the middle of a four lane highway.)

"And what did your grandfather smell like?" the woman asks again, for I have not answered her.

"Like wine," I say.

The woman laughs. "'*Mbriago*," she says. "That's who your grandfather was: '*Mbriago*."

"No," I say. "That isn't who he was. He was my grandfather. Salvatore Calabrese."

TRANSUBSTANTIATION

In Pier Paolo Pasolini's film *Uccellacci e Uccellini* (*The Hawks and the Sparrows*, 1966), a contemporary Italian father and his son travel into the past, to the time of Saint Francis of Assisi, and become monks. The father, Brother Ciccillo, prays for a miracle. He prays that all the wine in the world be turned into water. He prays that there be no more wine in Italy. He prays that there be enough water in Italy so that those who have become drunks because they have had no water to drink will drink water, for they will no longer need to drink wine.

I read about Pasolini. Learn of his belief that the workers of the world, like my grandfather, will save the world. Learn that his father, like my grandfather, was alcoholic. Learn that his father, like my grandfather, died because he drank.

Brother Ciccillo's hoped-for miracle: wine into water, not water into wine.

LOUISE DESALVO, winner of the Laura Pizer Prize in Creative Nonfiction, the Premio Speciale Giuseppe Acerbi Prize, and the Gay Talese Award, is the Jenny Hunter Endowed Scholar for Literature and Creative Writing at Hunter College. She has published five memoirs, among them *Crazy in the Kitchen* and, most recently, *On Moving*, and is currently completing *Slow Writing*, a sequel to *Writing as a Way of Healing*, and a new edition of her novel, *Casting Off*.

Louise DeSalvo on "'Mbriago"

In April 2004, I'd finished writing *Crazy in the Kitchen*, a memoir about my family's food history and emigration from Italy, and feared I'd never again write something worthwhile—a fear I have after completing each book. I'd been asked by Paola Corso to contribute an essay to an anthology about water by. I wasn't yet writing another book, and so I welcomed the opportunity to try my hand at a short piece.

Writing a short piece for an anthology, I had found, was the way I eased myself back into writing after the stress of completing a book. Virtually all my books had started this way, with writing an essay for someone else. For example, *Crazy in the Kitchen* had grown out of an essay, "Cutting the Bread," which I had written for an anthology called *The Milk of Almonds*.

These essays always felt like low-risk writing projects for me. Not that I didn't take them seriously—I did. But other people had conceptualized what they wanted me to write about. They'd given me a homework assignment, essentially, and I was good at doing homework, had been since my Catholic grammar school days. I didn't have to think up a topic; a subject was handed to me. All I had to do was put my own stamp on it. I'd found each of these assignments immensely freeing, and so, yes, I agreed to write something about water. But what?

Two years earlier, very much against my will, I'd visited my family's burial plot in Holy Cross Cemetery with my father. My grandfather, step grandmother, mother, and sister were all buried there. (My father is buried there, now, too.) I hadn't been there since my mother's funeral, and I hated going, but I had agreed because I was trying to mend my troubled relationship with my father.

It was a clear summer day, and I discovered that, from the vantage point of the family plot, which my father diligently tended as I wandered off, you could see across to New York City and where the Twin Towers had once stood. On a chain link fence nearby, there were the tattered remains—faded photographs, written testimonies, plastic flowers—of one of those impromptu shrines to the dead that had sprung up throughout the metropolitan area. I was transfixed by that shrine: anything was better than standing on the ground beneath which the bones of all those I'd loved now rested. There was still room for two more, my father said, as he cleared debris from around the headstone, a grisly one depicting St. Lucy holding the eyes that had been plucked from her head on a plate. Over my dead body, I thought, but didn't say, when he intimated he'd like me to be buried there, too.

When I got home, I started thinking of writing something about my grandfather as a way of honoring him. He'd helped raise me when my father was away during World War II. Over the next several weeks, I got to work. I began with the image of my grandfather in our home movies, picking up a jug of wine, tilting his head backwards, and pretending to swallow. I wrote about how my grandmother and my mother didn't think this was funny. But (perhaps because I found the subject uncomfortable) I soon abandoned writing about my grandfather's drinking and developed, instead, a description of his wedding photographs (he was married twice) and his death. At the end of the piece, though, I wrote about my grandfather's wake and how neighbors called him "'Mbriago," "the drunken one."

I soon abandoned that effort. Went back to work on *Crazy in the Kitchen*. The next year, in 2003, I returned to the subject of my grandfather's drinking again, got no further with it, and soon abandoned that effort, too. But then, when I was asked to write that essay about water, I decided that I would "try to unravel the mystery of my grandfather's life, and of his alcoholism." Intuitively I knew that my grandfather's alcoholism had something to do with water—I'd heard that wine was more available than water to the workers in the South of Italy—and decided to do some research before moving on. Some of it found its way into the completed essay.

As I wrote the essay I was calling "Water, Water"—the urtext for "'Mbriago"—I kept reading *New York Times* articles about the despoiling of Iraq by the invasion of the United States, so that the tragedy of how an imperialist power destroys another country's land was very much on my mind. I was sickened by photographs of Iraqi women standing on line for potable water; I was ashamed to be a citizen of the United States. And I decided that I couldn't write about my grandfather and about wine without discussing the colonization of the South of Italy and how its natural resources had been destroyed—something I hadn't been aware of and hadn't imagined including in the essay when I began.

For reasons I can no longer remember, I never completed that piece for Corso's book. But I revised the work seven times that I know of. Over time, I wrote a new beginning, changed the voice completely, rearranged the sections, eliminated some material, inserted other material, added section titles, and figured out a more memoiristic way of using my research. After I completed the final draft, I was satisfied with the results. Satisfied enough to begin writing my next book, *On Moving*, which discussed, in part, why my grandfather emigrated from Italy to the United States.

FAR, FAR AWAY

Pria Anand

Here is what islanders agree on when they tell the story of Kendrick Britton: he was beautiful, tall, and wrapped in muscles he earned breaking gravel for construction projects in the days before it was imported. He never wore a shirt. There was a white streak in the front of his Afro that he hated, plucking and dying it religiously. Of all of the blue-eyed Brittons in Southwest Bay, he had the most beautiful eyes, clear and light like the reef. Most days, Kendrick would swim out from the bay, past the cay, almost to the horizon, until all you could see was a dark stain in the Caribbean. He swam like a fish.

Kendrick was the third child in his family to be born deaf. On days he wasn't working, he sat on the beach and sketched sailboats in the sand and, with his hands, told tourists stories about ships and the sea. The tourists never understood, but every islander from Bottom House to Lazy Hill knew about Kendrick's dream. He stuck a steering wheel, pilfered from a broken-down car, into a dead tree and said that he was navigating a ship. He was leaving to be a captain, to go far, far away and bring back money for his mother.

Thirty years later, *far, far*—always with one hand waving at the wrist, out to sea—is one of few phrases that every deaf person on the island can speak out loud.

Islanders agree that Kendrick's destiny was out at sea. His first trip—to Cartagena and back, on a cargo ship, the *Doña Olga III*—was his last. The ship sank on its return, and Kendrick was lost to the sea.

This is where the stories diverge. Some people say Kendrick was asleep when the ship sank, that he never heard his crewmates sound the alarm. His nieces, also deaf, tell the story with their hands, fingers rolling like crashing waves and arms wheeling at the shoulders for the five men who swam away while their uncle with the freckled arms sank and died.

Some say Kendrick was killed for what he witnessed—drugs grown on the mainland and smuggled out on the *Doña Olga III*. When Kendrick's brother, Ares, signs the story, he mimes Kendrick's death with a blow to his own head. One night, his youngest sister whispers that she doesn't believe he drowned at all: three days after the boat sank, she dreamt of a voice that told her Kendrick was alive in Nicaragua. In her version, Kendrick made it ashore, but no one understood him well enough to help him find his way home.

Everyone says he was too strong a swimmer simply to have drowned.

After all, even before he was lost to the sea, Kendrick was of the sea: he was born and bred on Isla de Providencia, just seven square miles of lush mountain jutting out of the Caribbean and ringed by a barrier reef covering an area of almost a hundred square miles. For more than a century, the Colombian island—situated almost five hundred miles from the mainland—was largely ignored, and in its isolation, men like Kendrick were born: by 1953, the beginning of an end to Providencia's languid years of solitude, 12.5 in 1,000 children on the island were born deaf—between 12.5 and 25 times the worldwide rate.

In the tight-knit Britton family, Kendrick was one of three deaf siblings. He lived to meet the next generation, the two deaf daughters of his half-sister, but died without knowing that his niece, now thirty-six years old, would be the last member of the family to be born deaf.

For Providencia is changing. In 1953, the Colombian government opened the borders of a neighboring island for trade, and by the 1990s, the rate of deafness on Providencia had dropped to five in one thousand, diluted by immigration to and from the mainland.

For all of its islanders, Providencia is at once safe and stifling, but for deaf islanders—chief among them the Britton family—the tension is felt even more keenly. It's felt by Kendrick's brother, Ares, who lives in his mind to survive the loneliness of a place where everyone knows him just well enough to laugh at his longing for a wife and a family, and by his sister, Cillis, who gave birth to two daughters while she waited for a man who wouldn't be ashamed to admit he had fathered her child, even though Providencia has no secrets.

And by Kendrick, who left for the sea.

The details change each time it's told, but on Providencia, Kendrick's story is always about the tragic fate that awaits deaf men who dream beyond the safety of the reef. Providencia is a place where everyone shares a history that reads like a novel with a very small cast of characters. The island still has no school for the deaf and a sign language that is only half-formed, into which gossip, but not abstractions, can be translated. Here, everyone brags that they can understand sign language, no problem, but really they mean they already know any story a neighbor of theirs might have to tell. In a place like this, *far, far*—where people won't already know where you're from—seems like a dangerous place.

On sunny days, from El Pico, the highest point on the island, you can see the reef, with waves cresting at the outside like white cotton and the dark shadow of coral just under the surface. Inside the reef, the water is a quieter, darker blue, and the waves are still. Inside the reef, a man can dive down as deep as his lungs can hold and shoot lionfish and hogfish with a spear and eat for days.

Inside the reef is the safety and bounty of Providencia, and outside the reef is where boats sink, boats like the *Doña Olga III* and a ship called the *Betty Bee*, on which a deaf neighbor of the Brittons lost her mother. She signs *death* with her hands folded in prayer, shows the ship taking on water by sweeping her hands toward her face as if she's swallowing something.

Some days, you can hear the reef from any distance; always, you can hear it in the islanders' stories. Here is a story: Once, a man in Rocky Point had a deaf child, and his neighbor swore that if any of his children were born deaf, he would take them out to the reef in his launch and leave them to die. Just for the words he spoke, all three of his children were born deaf.

On Providencia, people believe that words have power. God made the world just from his words, and sometimes the words of the father are wrought upon his sons. Here is another story: Once, there was a married man in Old Town who was sleeping with another woman. When the man's oldest son tattled to his wife, the man wished that the rest of his children would be born unable to hear and unable to speak, and they were, down to the last one.

Almost two thousand miles away, at Javeriana University's Institute of Human Genetics in Bogotá, geneticist Marta Lucía Tamayo Fernández tells a different story.

Marta Lucía is a diminutive woman, who wears vinyl pants the color of military fatigues and tiny, solid brown boots. She is square-shouldered, with a limp that looks more like a swagger, and she always starts her sentences, "Seems to me . . . ," even though she's usually sure. She has little dimples and round ears and a sticker of a koala bear in her car window. On Providencia, people remember Marta Lucía as "*la pequeña*" or "*la doctora*." They remember that she talked a lot, but of what she told them about the deafness that runs in their blood, they remember only that it's inherited from older generations. But then, so are curses.

Marta Lucía has been studying hereditary deafness since she noticed that her first patients, after a decade of profound deafness, were starting to lose their sight, too. These patients were born with Usher syndrome. In a cruel twist of nature, many of the proteins that allow the inner ear to function are also integral to the function of the retina; a mutation in a gene that codes for any one of these proteins can mean that a child who is born deaf, who spends his childhood learning to communicate in Colombian Sign Language, will later find himself blind and completely isolated. Now, Marta Lucía travels around Colombia to institutions for the deaf, drawing blood from deaf children and their families, identifying causes of deafness and trying to prepare her patients for things to come.

From 1988 to 1998, drawn by the island's unusually high rate of congenital deafness, she did the same in Providencia, making five trips to collect blood and family trees, and analyzing them for genetic causes. She found two. The first was in a handful of Providencia families like the ones in Rocky Point and Old Town, in which profoundly deaf children had been born to hearing parents for the first time in anyone's memory. The underlying cause of deafness in these families is a piece of missing code, a mutation in the gene for a protein called connexin 26, which is part of a system that allows ions to pass quickly between cells. In the inner ear, it's this fast movement that turns the vibrations of sound into a biological signal.

Connexin 26 mutations are the most common cause of recessively inherited deafness in the world; children must inherit two mutated genes, one from each parent—both of whom are usually hearing carriers—to be born deaf. In the whole world, where just 3 percent of people carry the gene, it's generally unlikely that two carriers will have a child together. On Providencia, however, it was almost common.

Providencia's thin phonebook lists just a handful of last names, almost all reminiscent of its original British colonists—Robinson, Whitaker, Britton, Newball. Out of only seven pages, over half of one is devoted to the last name Archbold, which came to the island with the captain of an English slave ship at the end of the 18th century. To put it mildly, Providencia is—and has always been—a very small place.

Disorders caused by recessive mutations are often frequent in a place as small and isolated as Providencia, where everyone shares blood but people wind up together, recklessly, regardless. It's much, much more likely that two people who are related will carry the exact same mutation. Sometimes, people say that Providencia's deafness comes from a handful of ancestors foolish enough to couple with their own relatives, even though everyone there is related by now. It's akin to a curse, a sin that doomed the grandchildren of their grandchildren.

Sometimes, an islander can distance himself from deafness by claiming an ancestor from outside, unequivocally unrelated to anyone, a grandfather from the Cayman Islands or Jamaica who fell for a Providencia girl. Sometimes, though, people say that deafness came to the island, like mosquitoes, from the outside—on ships, with sailors who married and stayed. Ask about Kendrick Britton's family, descended on one side from an old Providencia family and on the other from Jamaican passersby, and you'll hear both.

The last name is a common one, but the Brittons in Southwest Bay are descended from just one hearing man, Kendrick's father, who fathered thirteen children with his wife, three of them deaf. He had a handful of children with other women, too. Although none of those children were born deaf, the youngest, Rosa, had two blue-eyed deaf daughters before Kendrick died.

In the Britton family, deafness is intertwined with other traits, including a white shock of hair and mottled skin and brilliant blue eyes. Almost everyone in the family, deaf and hearing alike, loses the dark from their hair while they're still young, but the blue eyes—wide-set in dark faces, with irises so bright they're almost impossible to capture on film—always herald deafness.

In communities as small as Providencia, it's so uncommon to find two distinct genetic origins of the same disorder that Marta Lucía first speculated that the albinism was something apart, that deafness among the Brittons was caused by the mutation in connexin 26 and just happened to co-occur with a mutation in a completely different gene, one for color.

Instead, she found a different cause for the Brittons' deafness, seventy times more common on Providencia than in the rest of the world, called Waardenburg syndrome. It's caused by dysfunction in the distribution or development of melanocytes, a type of cell involved in both pigmentation and inner ear function, and although she hasn't yet identified the exact gene, Marta Lucía knows that, unlike the recessive mutation in connexin 26, Waardenburg syndrome is dominant. A child can inherit Waardenburg syndrome from just one parent, and in theory, anyone who has the mutation will exhibit some of its characteristics. The gene is still inconsistent though, expressed in some as prematurely white hair and perfect hearing and in others as deafness and freckled wrists.

In the Britton family, blue eyes are so inexorably linked to deafness that when Kendrick's niece was born blue-eyed thirty-six years ago, her mother knew before the baby could even lift her head that she would speak only in sign.

To understand Providencia Sign is to understand how languages are born, unbidden, of a time and necessity.

It's a phenomenon that linguists once documented three hundred miles away and thirty years ago, before Kendrick was lost to the sea. In 1970s Nicaragua, deaf children who had previously been isolated from one another were brought together in a special-education school. In classrooms, they were taught spoken Spanish and lip-reading, learning to sign only the letters of the alphabet, but on buses and playgrounds, out of the informal and disparate gestures the children had devised at home to communicate with hearing family members, a sign language emerged.

As far as anyone knows, that's how a language happens: over time and generations, a hybrid vocabulary made consciously by adults develops a formalized syntax and a refined lexicon as children begin to learn it as their mother tongue. But in Providencia, despite generations of deaf islanders living in close proximity to one another, and despite the willingness of hearing islanders to communicate with signs, some part of the cycle stagnated, leaving the sign language incomplete.

In the 1970s, as sign language was beginning to evolve in Nicaragua, a sociolinguist named William Washabaugh, who had come to Providencia to study Creole, began to focus instead on what he called Providencia Sign Language. What he found were the kinds of inconsistencies that are weeded out of mature languages. Deaf islanders might use any of a number of signs to describe the same image—a ringing bell or hands folded in prayer for *church*, for instance. The Brittons sometimes sign *family* with two index fingers side by side and sometimes with one finger running up the inside of the other forearm, as in "blood." Washabaugh also found that the syntax of Providencia Sign Language—the order of nouns and verbs within a phrase, for instance—varied just as broadly as its vocabulary, sometimes varying even between two phrases signed by the same islander.

When deaf signers were shown a puppet performing a clear action and were asked to describe it to hearing family members, Washabaugh found that the family members understood the signs only half of the time. Perhaps it's not surprising: in the seven-square-mile world that the islanders inhabit, populated by characters and places that everyone knows, signers could rely on context to fill in the vagaries.

In short, Providencia Sign is a language of utility. It fulfills the practical requirements of communication between the deaf and hearing in a small community—conveying gossip, soliciting jobs—but in his time on Providencia, Washabaugh found no evidence of the abstractions that exist in languages like American Sign Language. Providencia Sign has no way to talk about Providencia Sign; there are no signs for *name*, *meaning*, or *word*. There are no puns in Providencia Sign, and there is no poetry.

In some ways, any understanding of Providencia Sign must be filtered through hearing islanders, though everyone agrees that when deaf islanders meet, something transpires in their signs, which are suddenly faster and more fluid, that no one else can follow. Perhaps PSL poetry exists in some form utterly opaque to even the most fluent hearing signers. But with no school for the deaf and no concept of a deaf community, deaf islanders are often firmly entrenched in the world of their hearing family members, who have Creole for poetry and puns, and need Providencia Sign only for practicalities.

* * *

It's not easy for an islander to disappear, but in Southwest Bay, there's a disappeared boy. Ask about him, and people will tell you that he's deaf and that he's not; that he's a Britton, but not one of those Brittons; that he's here, that he's in Panama, that he's in Barranquilla. You'll hear that he's smart. He knows English and Spanish, and he can sign with real signs, the official Colombian Sign Language. You'll hear he's a shut-in, that he might be on the island, but no one sees him.

The truth is, he's a cousin of Kendrick, and his mother left for Barranquilla so he could go to a school for the deaf, so he could learn to read and write, and so he could have a chance to leave and never come back. He did come back though, for a year and a half, while his mother looked for a job in Panama so he could finish high school there. He didn't miss Providencia. There was nothing for him here—no school, no friends. He missed the city, where he could be deaf and still dream of studying computers and finding a white-collar job. Providencia is a place for dreamers, but it's also the place where the boy's dream can't come true.

Most islanders make it only as far from Providencia as the Colombian mainland, but the island shares a great deal more with a handful of communities even farther away, similarly isolated places where genetic deafness once flourished. Most famous is Martha's Vineyard: at the end of the 19th century, before it became a summer colony for the presidents, the island had a rate of deafness almost forty times the national average and a unique, elaborate sign language that formed part of the basis for what is now American Sign Language (ASL).

On Martha's Vineyard, the stories go, everyone signed fluently, hearing and deaf alike.

Although the last deaf woman to be born on the island died in the 1950s, hearing islanders occasionally continued to use sign language for years, to send messages in places where spoken word wouldn't do: across wide fields and between the quiet seats of churches and schools.

Accounts of such "signing communities" have occasionally cropped up in linguistics literature for decades, just often enough to create a mythology of what one graduate student calls "deaf utopias": an isolated Balinese village that counts a deaf god among its deities; a tribe of Bedouins in Israel in which one hundred out of the three thousand members are deaf; and Providencia.

Things are changing in Providencia, though. Once, it mattered that Kendrick worked hard breaking rock. Now, it matters that one of his nieces dropped out of school before she learned to read and write, and that the other never went at all. It matters that you learn the things that help you to leave Providencia, to run drugs from the mainland to Central America or to work half the year on a cruise ship and send the money home.

Leaving matters the most—but for deaf islanders, with no formal sign language or literacy, and with no way to communicate with anyone off the island, anyone who doesn't already know their stories, who can't finish their sentences, it's a daunting prospect.

The trip from Providencia to the mainland starts with a trip to San Andrés, a larger neighboring island, either by a tiny airplane or a choppy catamaran ride. From the sea, Providencia looks impossible: a wet green mountain so verdant that the whole island seems alive—the mossy hump of a sunken giant that the island's original settlers, British Puritans aboard a sister ship of the Mayflower, deemed a divine providence. It is from these Puritans and their slaves that so-called "native" islanders are descended. Despite being claimed by the Spanish empire not long afterward, the islanders remained Protestant for hundreds of years, speaking an English Creole and nursing British traditions in the heart of the Spanish empire, as if the patch of the Caribbean on which they existed was transplanted from the Irish Sea.

Kendrick's older sister, Cillis, only ever left the island for San Andrés, to see the doctor and stay with family. On Providencia, she went out dancing on the beach in Southwest Bay and in town during the summer festival, when reggae music blasts out of speakers as tall as a man and as wide as two, so loud it fills your chest and buzzes in your ears the next morning. "She don't hear the music, but she keep the compass good," her neighbors would say. On Providencia, she could work, cleaning at the Catholic church clear across the island and bringing the gossip home to Southwest Bay.

But on Providencia, she also had two daughters with men who never acknowledged that they'd fathered children with one of those deaf Brittons from Southwest Bay, even though the whole island already knew, even though both men had deaf family members.

The Brittons, like Kendrick, are dreamers, and Cillis's dream was to have a husband, not just secret boyfriends.

But that's not how things go on Providencia.

She only ever left for San Andrés, but sometimes, she'd go to the tiny one-room airport with her money and bags. She'd say she was leaving for good, but everyone at the airport knew her, and they'd send for her family to bring her home.

Someone always came.

Up the hill, her brother, Ares, is parting his lips and moving his tongue from side to side, signing a story about a snake he saw up in the mountains. He's scared of the snake, he signs, clutching his fists. He shows its length with one hand cutting against the other arm, then puts his hands in a wide circle—it was so thick—and mimes coiling a rope, hand over hand. "Says he was tying a rope on a tree, and then a snake was there," his niece says.

A long time ago, Ares farmed his father's land, growing sweet potatoes and yucca and sugar cane. He used to farm, but people stole what he grew, knew he couldn't hear them rustling the trees and dropping the fruit, and he got so angry that he stopped.

Sometimes, though, he still works outside, chopping wood and gathering fruit—mangoes and pears and plantains and coconuts—up on the mountain. He can't count, and when he works others' land, they pay him far less than the value of his work, if they pay him at all.

He signs the story about the snake again and again, moving his tongue and pointing back toward the mountain. He puffs out his cheeks and spreads his arms wide, like a very fat man. He mimes cutting something, one hand hitting the other. "He said a big guy from down there kill the snake." They slit the snake down the belly; he makes a line from his chest to his stomach. Sometimes, it storms up on the mountain; Ares signs *rain* and *thunder* with his fingers shaking and his fists flung outward from his head as if he's pounding on something. He makes clouds with his hands loose, moving in a circle.

Like Kendrick, Ares wanted to leave Providencia on a boat for far, far away, but his father always made him stay put. Ares signs his father with the sign for *death*—eyes closed, arms stretched by his sides, body stiff—and a hand pointing toward Aguadulce, to the cemetery where his father is buried. He tells this story again and again, himself at sea and his father furrowing his brows and waggling his finger as if he's reprimanding a child. Ares has always said he'll leave Providencia someday, mimes packing his things into a suitcase and claps his hands past one another—*gone*.

But Ares is fifty-eight years old, and he hasn't yet left the island, not even for San Andrés. He lives off of his father's government pension, in a house on the hill. His hair and beard are white, and his eyes are watery and blue, and he leans into you and tips his head and murmurs as he signs.

Of all of the Brittons, Ares had the biggest dreams.

"His dream was to have family," his youngest sister tells me. "He wanted a beautiful woman, and he been waiting on that woman until now."

Ares dreamt of a wife and children. While Kendrick drew boats, Ares cut out pictures of women from old magazines. Sometimes he spends his pension money on Pampers and talcum powder and baby shampoo, and keeps them in a box under his bed for when he has a family. He used to pack boxes with baby supplies and money, and his siblings watched him to make sure he didn't send them away, even though he had nowhere to send them.

In the dark, swatting mosquitoes outside her aunt's house up the hill, Ares's sister says that out of all of her deaf siblings, Ares is the only one who is truly discontent in Providencia. "The only one that I saw that was all the time in torment was [Ares]," she says. "He all the time preparing the house because he's been waiting on that lady. It's just like the book that Gabriel García Márquez write: *El coronel no tiene quien le escriba.* The Colonel doesn't have anyone to write him a letter, and he's been waiting and going to the mail house for that letter— and for that letter and for that letter. Looks to me like it's my brother, waiting for the lady."

Ares signs a story about a boat. He had a girl on the boat, he says, miming two long braids swinging past his shoulders, and she had his baby, but she was studying, so she and the baby never came to Providencia, where he was waiting for them. His niece laughs at this, says he's dreaming again.

Sometimes, Ares has bad dreams, dreams that make him upset, that he can't seem to explain. When he was younger, they sent him into a temper, but now he murmurs and signs and waits for someone to understand.

He had other dreams, too. When he was younger, Ares dreamed of being a dentist before islanders even really knew the word. When he had a toothache, he pulled out his own tooth with pliers; when he noticed the gap between his front teeth, he tried to close it with homemade braces.

"The first one on the island to ever think about brackets was [Ares]," a neighbor remembers. "He took out those pliers and tighten, tighten, tighten. He got injured, you know? His mouth got swelling. But for me, he was the first dentist created this bracket things."

Sometimes, Ares dreams of becoming a cop like his oldest brother. He gave himself a blue tattoo on his right bicep, like the one he saw on a TV soldier. But his brother, who can hear, left Providencia to become a cop, and Ares almost never leaves the Brittons' land in Southwest Bay. Every year, though, when the children and the firemen and the military stationed in Providencia march on July 20 for Colombia's independence day, Ares fashions a cardboard gun and a striped uniform and marches with them.

Once, Ares dreamt of a Spanish man from far, far away playing a guitar in town, and he made a guitar for himself out of a broad plank, cutting away the rotting wood and imagining the details. There's a scrap of metal embedded in the neck, and it's strung with fishing line, curls from the spool pulled straight over a hole in the body. He put the hole in because he might like to make it electric someday, he explains, miming plugging two wires together. If it were electric, he could play more songs, he signs. He could have a microphone. He holds a fist in front of his mouth, and moves his lips like he's singing.

The wood is rough and warped, and the strap is a leather belt, attached only at one side because Ares doesn't have a screw to put in the hole he chiseled into the other side. For a time, he made wooden guitars again and again, each one truer to his dream than the last, but this is the only one he kept because the others are too tall for his little house. He takes it out to play whenever his neighbors have a party, nodding his head and tapping his feet and pressing down chords and strumming with his eyes closed, murmuring a song so softly you can barely hear it.

He signs that he's imitating the Spanish man he saw in his dream—the man, he signs, his hand waving at the sea, from far, far away.

PRIA ANAND lives in California, where she is a fourth-year medical student and an amateur pie-maker. Her writing has appeared in the *Bellevue Literary Review, Creative Nonfiction,* and elsewhere.

Pria Anand on "Far, Far Away"

It takes me two full days to reach Providencia, first a flight through Texas into Bogotá, then a puddle-jumper to San Andrés, and finally the choppy catamaran ride across the Caribbean and into Santa Catalina bay. I am staying alone, in a long house with no doors and a broken stove. I rent a motorcycle I'm not quite heavy enough to steer and get lost on the single road that winds and dips around the island, eroding into the sea. It is June 2011, the tail end of the rainy season, and at night, a crab as wide as a quarter-plate climbs my bedspread and watches me sleep.

In Providencia Sign, almost every islander has a name they don't know to answer to—one finger tracing a peculiar moustache, or a hand twisting the way their hair is braided and coiled close to the scalp. It's difficult to explain the ways in which Providencia is insular, how I become familiar to the island before Providencia feels familiar to me. I find the island's one beekeeper and tell him I've been searching for him, to buy a jar of Providencia honey, to see his thirty beehives laid out in a clearing on the mountain, and he tells me that he's been looking for me, too.

I stay in Providencia for two months, and I begin to feel at home because of the stories I hear again and again, some about deaf islanders, but others, too, about babies born on boats, lost at sea on the way to Panama, and a shipwreck that claimed whole families, and the assassination of a local bigwig in which the hit man escaped the island on a waiting motorboat before the pistol smoke had even cleared. I start to understand the island from a young doctor who, when I ask him what he has learned here, tells me he's learned how to suture a circular wound, the kind made by the crescent moon of shark teeth. I understand it from the men who make their living diving for conch and crawfish until their tympanic membranes rupture, becoming deaf as adults even as fewer and fewer deaf children are born on the island each year.

In Providencia, I learn that to be a physician and to write nonfiction are the same. Both are built on the idea that to observe a person is to know something of his or her story; both deal in personal details too familiar to be told.

There is too much to Providencia for me to come to know the whole island in just two months, but I gather enough details, enough hours of interviews and pages of notes, that "Far, Far Away" includes only those stories I hear again and again, those details that feel the most true. I feel comfortable with the story—comfortable sharing it with the Britton family, with the handful of friends from Providencia who somehow receive my snail mail—in part because of everything I chose not to include, those observations that felt flimsy or forced or out of place.

Months later, back in suburban Virginia, I share wine with a friend from the island, who is in town to visit her daughter. In Providencia, we celebrated our birthdays together—her 76th and my 23rd—over johnnycake and stewed plums, and she tells me now that she is aching to go home. She tells me the ends of stories that had only just begun when I was in Providencia, love affairs and burgeoning families and political intrigues, and she tells new stories, too, just unfurling, with the same cast of characters. The narrative of the island has changed since I left, and it will change again before I return.

NIGHT RHYTHMS

John T. Price

I leave Dean's bedside to make 2 a.m. rounds. His are the only lights, besides those in the nursing station, that are on. The in-patient unit at the children's hospital is dim and empty—silent except for a metallic hum that can be heard, just barely, in the air. I am in my nursing assistant uniform, white, except for the splotch of creamed ham I spilled on the leg during a now distant daytime meal. Besides Dean, there are ten other patients, all children, the oldest nineteen, only three years younger than I. They are all disabled—cerebral palsy, spina bifida, failure-to-thrive, hyperactivity. But that is during the day. They are asleep now, free from their daytime gnawings and spasms.

My job tonight is to go from one room to the next, checking diapers and catheters. There are not many to check this round. So I just listen to their breathing, and if it is too silent, I place my hand on their rib cage, gently, to feel the measure of their sleep. I am glad it is not the designated hour to reposition them, to wake them up, interrupt, and, if they have had surgery, to cause them pain. That time is two hours away. For now, I can just watch and feel for their breath, celebrating the trail of drool for what it means: peace. Sleep the elixir. I am extra quiet.

I return to Dean's bedside once again, alone. There is a blue swelling near his ankle where, earlier in the evening, Dr. Van Skeldt tried to insert an IV needle, again and again. It was clear then that we would have to transfer him to the main hospital, where they are better equipped to deal with him. Dr. Van Skeldt has left to make arrangements. The night nurse enters, her support hose rubbing and swishing, to register what vitals she can. "Why did he bring him here in the first place?" she says. "He knew we wouldn't be able to take care of him. He knew that." But the care facility won't take him back, I remind her. Maybe this is the only place he has. "Well, I don't know about that."

She is right in a way, our small unit isn't equipped to handle a patient like Dean. But nevertheless he is lying in a bed here. Dean won't live much longer. He has severe cerebral palsy, which means he choked during birth, which means the rhythm of the contractions were wrong. His lungs opened too soon. He has lived seventeen years, barely. I have been with Dean tonight for over two hours, just sitting on the side of his bed and watching his rib cage extend then collapse: up . . . down . . . up, up, up . . . down. His lips, dry, are collecting a thin film of mucus. His auburn hair shines with nearly three days' oil. He is so emaciated that when the fluorescent light casts blue upon his twisted limbs, it sends shadows in odd places, unexpected: pelvis, upper lip, ribs. . . .

An hour later I leave to clean the sunroom. This is the children's playroom, now empty. Around me the carpet, the plastic chairs and tables are covered with the daytime patterns of childhood, lingering. Toys and pieces of toys lay here and there, always everywhere, weaving together messy spirals and rhythms and textures. Yellow, red, blue. Mini-houses, Ken heads, Fisher-Price farms, hollow plastic bulbs—some together, some not. I pick them up, one by one, and put them in their designated places. I used to work the evening shift here, just after supper, when the sunroom is full of children, of wet hair and pajamas; movement and noise; tricycles, story-books, gossip; house, cops, robbers; tossing, chasing, shouting. John, John, John, they called from all corners, all sides. The supervisor's big butt, Dan's booger, Kara's farts. Faster and faster, the kinetic energy of their play seemed to raise the small hairs on my neck and arms. . . . But I'd forget. On the mat, near the television, would be the other patients like Dean. Quiet, except for tiny rockings from seizures or masturbation. Movement would flurry about them, balls would accidentally bounce off their heads as we nursing assistants played with the other children; all of us believing, hoping, that because these patients lay quietly, just breathing and rocking, they were pacified. With bright colors spinning around us, we would tuck them and their gnarled fingers into the back of our minds and forget them. But here on the night shift I remember.

I return to Dean's bedside. His steamer is stuttering. I lift off the top, and add another pint of distilled water. James, my only brother, is on my mind tonight. He was buried 15 years ago in soft blue, terry-cloth pajamas at a funeral I wasn't allowed to attend. A stillborn, lost during labor. I sometimes dream about that funeral, but not very often anymore. In fact, I haven't thought of James much at all recently. But tonight is different. From Dean's windows I can see a distant intersection, where the traffic lights are changing by themselves. Green, yellow, red, again and again . . . no one is awake to heed them except me. I am on the night shift, and I feel as if I am privy to the secrets of day existence; privy to the secret knowledge that pedestrian buttons on traffic lights are an illusion. There is no real control. The traffic lights change according to timers, predetermined rhythms that go unnoticed during the day like the regular seizures of children who lay on playroom mats. But at night I can see them changing while others sleep.

It seems unimportant, unless you realize that just over the curve of the earth, surrounding our sleep-time, are day-time lands and cities where people and machines are pounding and cars jam clover-leaf junctions and planes are landing and emerging through thunder. People barbecuing, starving, mowing lawns, riding camels or tugboats or the backs of lovers in pounding, ceaseless, pulsating patterns and rhythms that blend into palimpsestic nonsense until just once—just once—the synchronization goes bad, and you find yourself standing near a Dean and counting the number of times his

rib cage rises, watching as a doctor jabs and jabs and jabs
an IV needle into the tender flesh of his foot in the hope of
finding a vessel with a pulse. Or you find yourself a woman in
labor, in an empty hospital room in April, whimpering as you
feel the frantic kicking against your abdomen slowly dwindle
to silence. Or you find yourself a father standing outside your
remaining son's doorway, the night before Easter, letting the
heavy candy drop from your hand and onto the carpet, one
by one by one. Or, at seven, you find yourself alone, tearing
out your hair in fists because secretly, for some forgotten
reason, you had once wished the baby dead, and indeed it had
been born so.

Dean coughs, just a little, then returns to the wet labor of
his breathing. Softly, carefully, I slip my thumb into his small
velvet palm and caress the top of his hand with my index finger. I don't know if he notices, but I feel the need. The need to
shout him on, to set the pace of his life stream, to fill arteries
and lungs and heart with the measure of strong, rosy-cheeked
life. On my caress he'll live out the evening, keep breathing,
stop choking, become born. Or so I imagine. But who is this
boy to me, anyway? Why am I drawn to him? Perhaps because James was my brother, and because I was the only male
child, out of three, to survive birth. Perhaps because James
was born at night, and because it was a night nurse who left
my mother in a room alone. Perhaps Dean is what James
would have been if he had lived, a good portion of his brain
suffocated. Perhaps I am just unusually sensitive tonight. I
don't know. I don't know why I'm sitting here. Why, out of
the hundreds of children I've assisted in this place, some
terminally ill, I should feel the need to especially comfort this
boy on this night. I just do. So I sit and I caress and I listen,
beneath the hum of machines, for the breath of life, and the
secret rhythms of compassion.

Too quickly, Dr. Van Skeldt enters the room, and the night
nurse is with him. They have brought a cart for the transfer.
He has decided not to use motor transport, and I wonder why.

Why push him when you could drive him the short, bumpy distance to Main? I don't know a lot about Dr. Van Skeldt except that he arrived from Boston, is divorced, and lives alone, no children. Usually, he walks around the halls with a grave brow, checking a file or a patient or two, rarely going too far out of his way for patient or staff. He's considered rather cold.

But his relationship to Dean has been an enigma for everyone. Among staff, Dean is referred to as Dr. Van Skeldt's personal "project." He checks in on Dean every evening, meeting with staff in the process, courteously begging favors from us for his care: Could you put a pillow there please? And tonight, when Dean whimpered as the needle kept missing its mark, I thought I read, on Dr. Van Skeldt's brow, a wrinkle of pain. He has had to move Dean from one facility to the next, trying to find a place willing to take care of him until he dies. Now we can't keep him either.

Dr. Van Skeldt takes the two far ends of Dean's bed sheet, and I grab the near. Slowly we lift him, with the nurse's help, from his bed to the cart. Dean's eyes are moving back and forth, and his breath stretches to squeak out a whimper. He is crying, I can tell, and frightened. Slowly we start to move—Dr. Van Skeldt in front, me in back—past the nurse, out the door and onto the cracked sidewalk that leads to the main hospital. It is an Iowa summer at night. It is a time when the slopes and lulls of the river valley bear the thick steam of vegetable life, soaking the fur of rabbits as they nibble, calling witness to the indisputable fact that the earth itself breathes. In the air is the smell of damp earth, and the faint hint of late blooming lilacs. Suddenly, we stop moving.

"Now isn't that pretty?" Dr. Van Skeldt says to himself, or maybe to Dean. "I caught that scent earlier. I was hoping it would still be here for us. It reminds me of California when I was a boy. During those summers the smell from those blossoms filled the air. My mother used to say that if you breathed too much of it you would faint away or lose your socks or something. That's what she used to say then. There it is again . . . isn't that something?"

281

Dr. Van Skeldt pauses, then touches Dean's shoulder, lightly. He checks the IV pole. And then we move on, toward the bright fluorescent lights of Main.

JOHN T. PRICE is the award-winning author of three memoirs: *Daddy Long Legs: The Natural Education of a Father*; *Man Killed by Pheasant and Other Kinships*; and *Not Just Any Land*. A recipient of a fellowship from the National Endowment for the Arts, his nonfiction has appeared in numerous journals, magazines and anthologies, including *Creative Nonfiction, Orion, The Iowa Review, The Christian Science Monitor*, and *Best Spiritual Writing*. He lives with his family in western Iowa and is the director of the Creative Nonfiction Writing Program in the English Department at the University of Nebraska at Omaha.

John T. Price on "Night Rhythms"

The experience I write about in "Night Rhythms" occurred during my early twenties, while I was in my first year as a MA student in the University of Iowa's English Department. I wasn't sure what I was doing there, other than I liked to read. I certainly had no intentions of being a writer. For most of my undergraduate years, I'd been studying pre-medicine, but then (for reasons I didn't fully understand) I switched to literature, forever disappointing my grandmother and several other influential people in my family. I didn't have the credentials or the grades to earn a teaching assistantship, so I took out loans and continued to work as a nursing assistant at the hospital to pay the bills.

At the time this story takes place, I was working at the hospital all night and, in the mornings, attending a nonfiction class taught by Carol de Saint Victor. Sleep deprivation may have played a role in breaking down my usual resistance to the writing process; writing had always been a slow, arduous endeavor for me (and still is, to some extent), aggravated by what my freshman composition instructor had diagnosed in my writing as "chronic grammatical illiteracy." I think Carol's gentle enthusiasm for the beauty of the written word was also very helpful. More influential than anything, though, was the way Carol and the authors she assigned modeled an attentive, wide-open relationship with the momentary—the "bead of life" Virginia Woolf speaks of in "The Death of the Moth" (an essay which was a revelation to me when I first read it in Carol's class). Somehow this openness infected me, so that as tired as I was when I showed up for work that summer, I was in some ways more awake than I had ever been.

On that particular night at Dean's bedside, I became aware of something very *different* happening inside me, something I didn't understand. Just a few months earlier, I might have pushed those feelings and observations and questions aside, but instead I began to write them down, mostly on the backs of prescription slips because that's what was closest at hand. The language flowed out of me, and much of it would appear verbatim in the final essay—the traffic light reflection, for instance—which has rarely happened since. I must not have fully trusted that flow, its urgency, because it took me another year before I wrote the first draft of the essay, and then several more years of revisions and workshops before I found the courage to submit to an upstart journal called *Creative Nonfiction*. That was my start as a writer.

The people whose lives briefly intersected on that summer night have moved on, or vanished, but I can never quite seem to leave them behind—including the young author. I now see in his perceptions the almost naïve uncovering of a core mystery I would spend the next twenty-five years of writing trying to understand: the mystery of our kinship with one another, alive and dead and dying, as well as with the earth, and all that this kinship asks of us, demands of us. Part of what it demands, as that young author was just discovering, is what writing itself demands: that we be attentive, open to moments like the one in the hospital. Moments which, by their very nature, are without language, and because of that, create their own language, their own syntax beyond any notions of "grammatical illiteracy." It is the language of the spirit, the rhythms of which can become—though I hardly appreciated it then—the music we live by.

THE FINE ART OF LITERARY FIST-FIGHTING
Lee Gutkind

Creative Nonfiction's founding editor looks back on the unlikely series of events that inspired him to start a journal for a then-homeless genre and reflects on the rewards and heartbreaks of the literary life.

PROLOGUE

It's late at night, maybe midnight, and my student Marisha, who is also my son's babysitter, is standing in line at the supermarket checkout counter. The line is long and there's nothing to do but wait, so Marisha thumbs through the current issue of Vanity Fair *magazine. It is October 1997.*

Meanwhile, I am at home, in bed alone, as usual, watching a Law & Order *re-run—the best way I know to fall asleep. The phone rings. I pick it up. It is my ex-wife, Patricia.*

"I have something to tell you," she says. "I don't know how you are going to take it."

Marisha, she says, is afraid of my reaction, so she doesn't want to break the news to me directly. Flipping through the issue of Vanity Fair, *she came across an article written by the prestigious literary and cultural critic James Wolcott. She telephoned Patricia as soon as she returned home. Better my ex-wife telling me rather than my current student.*

"You are all over Vanity Fair," *Patricia tells me. "It's not pretty."*

I listen. Patricia doesn't really have the details, and she is pretty upset for me and subsequently kind of inarticulate. So I tell her not to worry, hang up the phone, and force myself back into the comforting predictability of Law & Order *and fall asleep.*

I. OUTCAST

Never did I intend to start a magazine or pioneer a literary movement—or any movement whatsoever. At the beginning of my professional life, I was focused on books, motorcycles, and German Shepherd dogs. A literary movement was the last thing on my mind. But life is funny: circumstances arise, opportunities are presented, insults hurled—stuff happens—and suddenly you are doing things that are totally beyond the scope of the deepest reaches of your imagination. Incredibly, this "stuff"—campaigning and crusading and fighting—becomes your raison d'être. That's what happened to me with creative nonfiction.

(I am not at all sure that I don't regret it all, by the way—but that's a conversation for another time and place, and anyway, as they say too often these days, "It is what it is.")

I won't bore you with the details of my early life, except to say that I grew up Jewish and attended grade school in a neighborhood of Catholics who were convinced that the Jews had killed Christ. That was true enough, I guess, but not really my fault . . . though good luck explaining that to Billy Sopira, the older boy next door, who made me his official punching bag, considering all of "you people" complicit. Later, I went to high school in a Jewish neighborhood with peers who were convinced that the fact that I lived with the Catholics—"mill hunkies," they were called in Pittsburgh's snobby Squirrel Hill section—made me a less than desirable recruit to the "in" group. My truancy and overall outlandish, boorish, "mill hunkie" behavior—not to mention my horrific grades—were such that I could not, after high school, get accepted into a college, and therefore I had no choice but to enlist in the military, where I was the fattest and more or less youngest recruit in the 60+ member boot camp company at that time.

This is what I believed back then: That everywhere I went, I was an outcast. I didn't fit in. I wasn't feeling sorry for myself; I was certain that this was true. Nobody paid any attention to me unless I called attention to myself, and I did that in many inappropriate ways—like hitting Rabbi Weiss at B'nai Emunah synagogue in the back of his black hat with a cream cheese bagel, or wearing pink pants and red suede shoes. Stupid stuff, which I only gradually realized brought me attention but did not attract much consideration or respect. It dawned on me only after high school, when I went into the military, that I needed to discover or re-shape my identity. More specifically, I had to fight for a mission and a position in the world. I hated being a loser—and that is what I thought I was. (I still do, to a certain extent, to this day.)

Anyway, I got out of the military sixty pounds lighter than when I enlisted and a hell of a lot more confident. I could do fifty push-ups without breaking a sweat. I came back to Pittsburgh, looking for some direction. I worked a variety of day jobs, including selling orthopedic shoes and driving a beer truck, and in September 1966, I wandered into the Cathedral of Learning, a massive forty-two-story monument to education, the tallest university classroom building in the United States, and registered for my first college course at the University of Pittsburgh: Freshman English. The following evening, notebook and pencil in hand, I went to class.

On the first night, the teacher—his name was Meyers—told us to write an essay. As I wrote about the time I spent sorting empty bottles or driving a beer truck for a few months between high school and the military, I felt exhilarated. I had written book reports in high school, as well as a few essays for science and history classes, but this—telling stories about my life—was fun. All awareness of time escaped me. When I looked up, I realized I was the last person remaining in the classroom.

I could tell Meyers, a goateed man in his late twenties with pock-marked cheeks, was getting antsy. He closed his book and exhaled sharply, smiling apologetically in my direction. Reluctantly, I ripped the pages from my notebook and handed the stack to him. It took me a couple of moments to pack up. Out of the corner of my eye, I could tell that he was reading what I had written. As I opened the door to depart, he said, "Wait." I went back into the room. "This is pretty good." He was pointing at my essay. "What do you do?" he asked. "I mean, in life. Or what do you want to do?"

I told him that this was why I had decided to start college: to build a life and find a profession. I was lost, I admitted.

"Well," he motioned at my essay, pausing to nod and purse his lips, "this is pretty good. Well-written. You ought to think about being a writer."

This was, I have to say, the first time anyone had offered me career advice that felt hopeful or exciting or unique. Despite the fact that I had never achieved a grade higher than C in math, my high school guidance counselor had recommended I become an accountant. This made no sense. Numbers made me sleepy. Even today—and even with a calculator—I have difficulty adding and subtracting. But this suggestion struck a chord. After all, I was reading all the time. My passion for reading had helped me get through the military, prior to registering for classes here, and partially rehabilitate myself physically and intellectually. I had devoted all my spare time to hanging out in the base library.

"OK," I replied, not knowing anything about a writer's world or what one did to make a living as a writer, except to tell stories and write. "I think I will."

My writing career started while I was still an undergrad. I got a job working for a public relations agency as an assistant account executive. I promoted a theatre in the round, a company that manufactured and sold industrial cement mixers, and other small businesses. Success came quickly, and after a while, I was awarded a special account: The Helium Centennial Committee for Government and Industry—an organization founded to celebrate the hundredth anniversary of the discovery of the element.

The cornerstone event was the unveiling of a monument in Amarillo, Texas, where helium was discovered in 1868. It was called the Helium Centennial Time Columns: three stainless steel time capsules came together like a tripod, supporting a fourth shooting straight up, six stories into the sky—a dramatic, erect shaft glittering in the relentless Texas sun. Before the lavish inaugural event, four helicopters lifted the corners of a gigantic black tarpaulin, hovered above the site, and dropped the tarp over the entire monument, thus concealing it from view. The corners of the tarpaulin were securely anchored.

The day before the official inauguration, dozens of large helium-filled weather balloons were attached to the tarp. Senators, congressmen, and government bigwigs came from all across the country. The airport was mobbed. Every visitor was personally welcomed by the Amarillo Greeting Club: two rows of twelve cowboys in red gabardine pants, white shirts, blue bandanas, white gloves, and hats, lined up like toy soldiers in front of the exit doors, waiting to shake each visitor's hand and thank him or her for coming to Amarillo: "Welcome to Amarillo. Thanks for coming to Amarillo." "Welcome to Amarillo. Thanks for coming to Amarillo." "Welcome to Amarillo. Thanks for coming to Amarillo," each visitor heard twenty-four times.

The ceremony featured high school bands playing the national anthem, the state anthem, and "The Yellow Rose of Texas." The three television networks sent cameras. At precisely noon, burly cowboys, stationed at the corners of the monument where the tarpaulin had been anchored, swung their axes, severing the ropes. With music playing and cameras rolling, the balloons began rising, first slowly but then ever faster, climbing higher into the sky until the tarp was lifted and the Helium Centennial Time Columns were dramatically revealed. The crowd hooted and hollered, then settled in for beer and barbecue, baked beans and Texas toast.

The monument was in the middle of the biggest slum in Amarillo. Down the road from the festivities were houses without plumbing and children playing in mud puddles in the middle of unpaved streets—a reality I subconsciously protested in a news release I wrote, which should have started with the following sentence: "People from throughout the country will have the opportunity to achieve immortality by nominating items to be included in the Helium Centennial Time Columns." Only after the release was sent to hundreds of newspapers and radio and TV stations nationwide did I realize I had omitted the *t* from the word *immortality*—an honest mistake I have never regretted.

II. LIVING THE CREATIVE NONFICTION LIFE

I quit my job after the Helium Centennial debacle and struck off on my own, freelancing.

I was, back then, a romantic, young and innocent, inspired by writers who took chances with their writing and in their lives. I read certain books over and over again: Kerouac's *On the Road*,

Baldwin's *Giovanni's Room*, Mailer's *The Naked and the Dead*. I could almost recite some of Hemingway's Nick Adams stories—"Big Two-Hearted River," "Indian Camp," and "The Three-Day Blow"—by heart. These writers were travelers, wanderers; their lives and writing were experiential, deeply spiritual, and maniacally spontaneous. As a young man—not, I suppose, unlike many young men—I found this incredibly compelling. As Dean Moriarty, Kerouac's crazy, nomadic, sleazy anti-hero, says, you choose your own road in life. "What's your road, man?" he says. "Holyboy road, madman road, rainbow road . . . it's an anywhere road for anybody, anyhow." I vowed I would give that road a try—in a couple of different ways.

My first real writing gig—I mean my first writing that counted, because it was widely published—came in 1969 when, in my powder-blue VW convertible, I drove to Wyoming to follow Hemingway's path across that state. I had read in Carlos Baker's biography of Hemingway, which was published that year, that Hemingway wrote parts of *Death in the Afternoon* and *A Farewell to Arms* in a cabin on an isolated ranch in the upper Tetons. Even in Baker's very thorough biography, not much had been written about Hemingway's Wyoming—although there was a short story, "The Wine of Wyoming," which, actually, wasn't one of his best—but this trip, I thought, would open another door to his life and perhaps a door for me. So I went there and lived for a while in a cheap motel. I tracked down the only remaining child of the family that had built and operated the ranch, now a woman in her eighties, a short, plump silver-haired widow. She was gruff but polite, and I begged and pleaded with her to take me up to the ranch and show me where Hemingway had lived. Incredibly, she agreed.

The going was slow. We bounced and banged in the surprisingly frisky powder-blue bug, with the top down, dodging rocks, fallen trees, and nasty ravines. It was an hour and a half up the "Red Grade Road" to the site of the ranch. It was surprisingly intact, considering it had been abandoned and reportedly uninhabited for three decades. The woman—her maiden name was Spear—led me through the property, a modest complex with a main house, a bunkhouse, a mildewed barn, rotting corrals, and a couple of guest cabins. She tired quickly and decided to return to the Beetle, but pointed at one of the two guest cabins.

"That's where he lived," she said. "That's where he wrote."

Amazingly, the cabin was intact. I could walk up the steps into the room and, with the light shining through the bare logs, see a table sitting by the window and facing a bank of lodgepole trees. I felt at that moment a sudden chill and a rush of emotion—a burning, exhilarating clarity. There I was, where the man had written—maybe even at that very table, surveying the lodgepoles! And this was not some tourist place, like his homes in the Florida Keys (or even the famous finca in Cuba), but it was a secret spot that few had visited. I owned it, so to speak. This was my experience. And I would write about it—which I did for a newspaper syndicate. It was published in various forms all across the United States. Since that time, I gather, the ranch has come back into operation as a dude ranch and, later, an educational facility. The last I heard, Hemingway's cabin still stands.

It was a remarkable event for me—like I said, I was a dreamer—which solidified the notion that I could simultaneously write and experience new things, subjects, ideas, barely touched. I could live it and write it, all at once.

Of course, lots of other folks were doing this and had been for a long time, I knew, like George Orwell in *Down and Out in London and Paris* (published in 1933), or Ernie Pyle in his dispatches from World War II, or Lillian Ross in *The New Yorker*, or Hemingway himself in his reports from the Spanish Civil War in the late 1930s and, even earlier, in the consummate and meticulous *Death in the Afternoon*. I could go on and on—Breslin, Dickens, Didion. But it was Gay Talese who really turned me on, whose work had actually planted the seed for my Hemingway odyssey. Not the classic "Frank Sinatra Has a Cold," which so many writers and critics have talked and written about, but actually *The Bridge*, a short book (it's only 147 pages) all about the building of the Verrazano-Narrows Bridge, a double-decked suspension bridge which was, when it was completed in 1964, the longest suspension bridge in the world.

Talese had camped at the site, more or less, for the duration of the construction, writing not only about the bridge, but more so about the people involved with the project, those who lived around the bridge and those who built it. The latter group called themselves "the boomers," which was the title of the first chapter, and the moment I read the first paragraphs, I honestly thought I was hearing music. That book and Talese's example of living with a subject and getting down to its very essence, combined with my own very singular and personal experience discovering Hemingway in Wyoming, immediately defined my life's direction, writing stories that were true, using all the terrific techniques available to novelists, like dialogue and flashback—all the tricks of the trade.

Here are those first paragraphs, so poetic, rhythmic, dramatic, profound, and inspiring:

They drive into town in big cars, and live in furnished rooms, and drink whiskey with beer chasers, and chase women they will soon forget. They linger only a little while, only until they have built the bridge; then they are off again to another town, another bridge, linking everything but their lives. . . . They are part circus, part gypsy—graceful in the air, restless on the ground; it is as if the wide-open road below lacks for them the clear direction of an eight-inch beam stretching across the sky six hundred feet above the sea.

Talese, I should say, is one of the most remarkable men I have ever met. He's charming, handsome, and quite fit for an octogenarian, and he outfits himself with an impeccable wardrobe. (His father was an old-fashioned Italian tailor in New Jersey, where the family lived after coming to the United States in the 1920s.) Under his smooth exterior, however, is steel: he is rigorous—a hard-ass—when it comes to his reporting and writing.

There's a classic scene in "Frank Sinatra Has a Cold" in which Ol' Blue Eyes confronts a young screenwriter in a private club in Hollywood and insults his work, calling it "crap," and his mode of dress, especially his Game Warden boots. Half a century ago, when the piece was published in *Esquire*, reporters typically downplayed such confrontations, but Talese recorded it brilliantly, insult after embarrassing insult, and it has become one of the most memorable and talked-about scenes in the history of the genre.

His 1981 book, *Thy Neighbor's Wife*, explored the sexual mores of the 1950s and 1960s, and precipitated an avalanche of insults and criticism (and jealousy?) from religious quarters and his journalistic colleagues for his raw and realistic, on-the-scene immersion research, which included living in Hugh Hefner's Playboy Mansion, visiting nudist colonies, and—what else?—sleeping with his neighbor's wife.

Yet the content of his book and his integrity as a reporter remained unquestioned. In one of his most recent books, *A Writer's Life*, Talese revisited some of the stories he had chased around the world but abandoned because they were unworthy of telling—or he found himself unable to write them. This insider's story of the frustrations and failures of a working writer is eye-opening and heart-rending—and required reading for anyone who wants to understand the true nature of this unholy, brain-breaking, chaotic profession.

When I was starting out as a writer, I understood that what Talese was doing in *The Bridge* and his other work was not new or terribly unique—although he could do it, then and now, better and more realistically than most anybody. What *was* new during the time I became aware of this kind of writing was that it began to receive a particular kind of critical attention; it began to coalesce as a genre in itself—not exactly the same as journalism, though not exactly capital-L Literature, either. Tom Wolfe, another inspiring figure along with Gay Talese, says he did not coin the term *new journalism* and actually did not particularly like it, but he certainly championed the label and led the bandwagon, beginning in 1973 when he edited, along with E.W. Johnson, the anthology *The New Journalism*. In his introduction to the collection, Wolfe proclaimed the new journalism a "higher journalism"—a style and an approach to nonfiction that "would wreak such evil havoc in the literary world . . . causing panic, dethroning the novel as the number one literary genre, starting the first new direction in American literature in half a century."

In some ways, his prediction was right, as we see today, but really, *new journalism* was mostly an inspired spin—Wolfe being Wolfe, making outlandish statements to call attention to himself. Make no mistake: Wolfe is quite learned—he has a PhD in American studies from Harvard, and his astute literary reflections and observations have been widely published—but he was and still is a masterful self-promoter, demanding attention not only with his words, but his presentation, most famously his white suit. Especially in his younger days, it seemed to me, he set out to create dialogue and controversy for his own ends—an endeavor in which he was pretty damn successful.

But all Wolfe and other new journalists were really talking about was writing in scenes, using a lot of dialogue, writing with subjectivity—allowing a point of view, whether it be the writer's or the character's—and including what Wolfe called "status details," meaning how people represent their positions in life through behavior and appearance (not unlike his own white linen suits!). Not that this wasn't revolutionary and a game-changer in some quarters—the journalism community has, historically, been painfully and self-destructively resistant to change—but when you get down to the basics, new journalism meant being a very good writer who was willing to apply the diligence required for first-rate reporting, as well as having the time, patience, and talent to put all the information together in a powerful prose package.

The one aspect Wolfe and others added, which was new to journalism, was their obsession with themselves; anything they felt, thought, dreamed, remembered seemed to be fair game, no matter how unrelated or uninteresting. Wolfe, in particular, loved the sound of his own voice, as in his "The Last American Hero" essay about stock car racer Junior Johnson, in which he sang:

Ten o'clock Sunday morning in the hills of North Carolina. Cars, miles of cars, in every direction, millions of cars, pastel cars, aqua green, aqua blue, aqua beige, aqua buff, aqua dawn, aqua dusk, aqua aqua, aqua Malacca, Malacca lacquer, Cloud lavender, Assassin pink, Rake-a-cheek raspberry. Nude Strand coral, Honest Thrill orange, and Baby Fawn Lust cream-colored cars are all going to the stock car races, and that old mothering North Carolina sun keeps exploding off the windshields. Mother dog!

This was cute—different—but such wailing wound through this essay and many others, including his book *The Electric Kool-Aid Acid Test,* and it sometimes wore thin, lacking the poetic clarity of Talese's riffs about the boomers. More troubling, it provided substance for attacks about the new journalists' self obsession and unnecessary verbosity and excesses, calling attention to their own voices rather than those they were writing about—thus distracting from the literary and journalistic value of the stories.

And these stories did have literary and journalistic value; they were rich in facts and carefully reported, but there was also a strong sense of style that was almost poetic in its vision. Wolfe sometimes took it a little too far; fortunately, the quirky innovations he introduced in some of his early work in *New York Magazine* and *Esquire*—writing in the accents of his characters, making up quotation marks like :::::::::::::::::::, yelling and screaming at his readers IN CAPS—were gradually discarded. But done with a little restraint, this writing could be incredibly effective. Take, for instance, Norman Mailer's incredible cataloging of characters and personas in *Armies of the Night*, for which he won the 1968 Pulitzer Prize in general nonfiction. Here we have Mailer describing the young people protesting the Vietnam War. He was appalled by their lack of a sense of history and how they treated political protest like a Halloween parade:

The hippies were there in great number, perambulating down the hill, many dressed like the legions of Sgt. Pepper's Band, some were gotten up like Arab sheiks, or in Park Avenue doormen's greatcoats, others like Rogers and Clark of the West, Wyatt Earp, Kit Carson, Daniel Boone in buckskin, some had grown mustaches to look like Have Gun, Will Travel—Paladin's surrogate was here!—and wild Indians with feathers, a hippie gotten up like Batman, another like Claude Rains in The Invisible Man—his face wrapped in a turban of bandages and he wore a black satin top hat.

Not everyone was as thrilled and enthralled with this new(ish) style as I was, however. As early as 1965, Dwight Macdonald, a writer, editor, and TV commentator, in reviewing Tom Wolfe's *The Kandy-Kolored Tangerine-Flake Streamline Baby* for *The New York Review of Books*, called it "parajournalism," which, he wrote, "seems to be journalism . . . but the appearance is deceptive. It is a bastard form, having it both ways, exploiting the factual authority of journalism and the atmospheric license of fiction. Entertainment rather than information is the aim of its producers and the hope of its consumers." Later, he complained, "We convert everything into entertainment," and maybe he wasn't too far off in his evaluation.

One could make the same argument today—that we value entertainment over information. Look, for instance, at the Internet, which puts an almost unimaginably vast world of information at our fingertips. I am not the first to point out that we have put a shameful amount of time into cluttering up this resource with videos and pictures of cats when, surely, we could be doing better, more important things with our time and technology. But, of course, entertainment and information needn't be mutually exclusive. We understand that nonfiction needn't be boring or laborious to be effective. It can and should entertain, inform, educate, and enlighten. Writing with truth and accuracy needn't force a reader to pop the periodic NoDoz.

I think that was the key to the success of new journalism—or whatever you want to call it. It was fun to read; it had energy, personality, authenticity, and pizzazz. And thanks in large part to Wolfe, this first-rate and sometimes experimental journalism had a name, whether he initially liked it or not, as well as a special persona—and that awakened nonfiction writers to the fact that the tools of our trade were limited only by our own inability or unwillingness to think and perform three-dimensionally. Wolfe's new journalism doctrine provided an anchoring foundation to those who were working in this genre in the dark. When people asked what I wrote, I would say, "New journalism." It sounded cool to me—and the thing is, it *was* cool. And it *is* cool.

After the Hemingway series, I wrote other essays and articles, often about eccentric, somewhat edgy subjects in which I could be an active participant, such as clowning for Ringling Brothers, wrangling at a rodeo, and transcontinental trucking. I profiled a one-arm blacksmith and a cooper who practiced his craft in the old way with a schnitzelbank; sparred with professional wrestling's heavyweight champion Bruno Sammartino; and hunted rattlesnakes with a mountain man named McCool. Once, in the hills of eastern Kentucky, I joined a group called Judo and Karate for Christ; members chopped, kicked, flipped, and hurled their fellow disciples in the name of the Lord Jesus.

There was, however, a problem, for me and others like me, turned on by this newish way of writing: what to do with it? There were few magazines interested in publishing such hybrid material. Writers had to think creatively, but so did editors, who had to provide writers with the space and time necessary to make journalism three-dimensional. *Esquire* and *The New Yorker* did this, and, to a lesser extent, *Harper's, New York Magazine,* and *The Atlantic Monthly*—and in San Francisco, you had *Mother Jones* and the now-defunct *Ramparts*—but it was very difficult to get a foot (or even a toe) in the door in any of those places. It was a limited market, and it helped if you had a political (primarily liberal) orientation or were well-connected—or both. I think of them as the "player" magazines. The "players" themselves included the names I have been bandying about— Joan Didion, Lillian Ross, Gay Talese, Tom Wolfe, Norman Mailer, Jimmy Breslin, Pete Hamill—the crew who got the best assignments or were able to create their own assignments, like

Wolfe. Editors gave them blank checks, at least as far as ideas went, and they were all part of a connected circle of writers in New York. It was (and still is) a very "in" group. Can you imagine "Radical Chic," Wolfe's essay about the cream of the New York cultural scene entertaining and raising money for the militant Black Panther organization, set in Denver or Milwaukee or Pittsburgh? Not a chance. Who would care?

Ironically, books were easier to publish in this new journalism genre back then—at least for me. For my first book, *Bike Fever* (1972), I traveled the country on a classic black BMW, chronicling the two-wheel experience and capturing the emerging motorcycle subculture. Two years later, I lived with a crew of National League baseball umpires for a season, sharing their isolation and alienation as the lone lawmen—villains in blue—in what was then our national pastime, an experience that led to *The Best Seat in Baseball, But You Have to Stand*. But the top magazines were basically dominated by this East Coast literary society.

It was not impossible to break into this group, but it was a lot more complicated than just putting a manuscript into an envelope, mailing it out, and hoping to be discovered. You heard about the rare breakthrough: Hunter S. Thompson did it, and as legend goes—I am told that there's more than a grain of truth in the story—the veteran editor (and brilliant baseball writer) Roger Angell was seen running up and down the corridors of *The New Yorker*'s offices, waving a manuscript he had snared from the slush pile and shouting, "Look at this!" It was a story by a young writer named Garrison Keillor.

Even so, and even as a published author, I wasn't holding my breath waiting for this to happen to one of the half-dozen profiles and essays I had sent to *The New Yorker*. It was frustrating. I suspected that there was some great work being done by writers like me in this narrative nonfiction form—outliers and outsiders who would probably never break down (or even slip through) the doors—and I guess, looking back now, that that was when the seed of the creative nonfiction movement, and the publication that might lead the way, began to germinate in me.

III. INTO THE ENGLISH DEPARTMENT

I regularly shared the stories I was writing with Monty Culver, one of my teachers at Pitt, and he eventually persuaded the department chair to allow me to teach part-time, a course in expository writing.

It was kind of amazing, actually, if you think about what an outcast I was—the only person in the entire department teaching without an advanced degree, and the only faculty member who was an obsessed with and a totally committed motorcyclist. (True, I did have a published book, my motorcycle book, *Bike Fever*, which gave me some credibility; even though I was a schlep, degree-less, I had published more than anyone else who was teaching writing courses at the time.) And the only person on the faculty who actually—can you imagine this?—*wanted* to teach nonfiction writing. I mean, honestly, you have no idea how ferociously my colleagues battled over who would teach the fiction courses—no holds-barred back-stabbing went on. But I was in the clear because I had no interest in fiction or poetry; I was the nonfiction guy. That's how I got my job; that's how it happened. Quite simply: I wanted to do what no one else had any interest in doing. It was my passion. Expository writing.

Well, that's a big lie. I mean, I had no interest in teaching expository writing. No way! What the hell is expository writing, anyway? It is basically a formula in which every essay contains the same features: the introduction, the thesis, the body paragraphs, and the conclusion. I mean, c'mon! Expository writing? It is a formula to produce boring, predictable, automaton students—clones of one another. If you want to make certain that your students are discouraged from being creative, reading edgy literature, being daring and spontaneous in life and in their professions, making an impact in this very challenging world, and if you want to prepare them to be ordinary and unremarkable, accountants and CPAs working for Ernst & Young, then teach them that expository writing is the best way to express themselves.

That wasn't me. I was not the expository writing kind of guy. That's not what I wanted to teach or write, and that's not how I wanted to think. But since I was the only person in the city of Pittsburgh (or so it seemed) who would actually agree to teach nonfiction expository writing, I figured I would take the job and then, like many faculty members I have known, spin it into exactly what I wanted to do—new journalism. If my colleagues wanted to call it expository writing, fine. (Today, there's actually a chaired professor in that department in "expository writing"—what a waste of a chair!) But it was all a bunch of bullshit. I wasn't teaching expository writing; I was teaching Mailer, Hemingway, Talese, Wolfe, and Thompson and calling it expository writing. I loved the job. The students were hungry for more participatory journalism, so that's what I taught them. And nobody in my department—at least at first, in the 1970s—really cared one way or the other as long as they didn't have to teach it.

At the time, creative writing programs were relatively new. Pitt didn't have one. Iowa, Stanford, and a few others had been around for a good while; these programs were not, interestingly enough, part of English departments. If you wanted to study creative writing—officially, that is, with a graduate degree—there weren't a lot of options, and perhaps with good reason. Writers were like painters and composers; they followed their muse and created literature—poems, stories, plays. Hemingway, Fitzgerald, Welty, Capote, and all the others, the immortal masters, did not learn craft from tweedy, pipe-puffing professors; they went out and lived life and poured their souls into their poetry and prose. There were apprenticeships and mentoring for artists and writers, of course. But courses? Who needed courses?

It's hard to imagine now, but there was a time when most writers were not affiliated with universities. They were much more a part of the world—driving taxis, selling insurance, teaching high school, thinking that you had to experience life in order to write about it. (Or the more fortunate few were living on trust funds or the good graces and hard labor of spouses.) But the establishment and growing popularity of creative writing programs became a lure and a safe haven; why struggle for health insurance and a certain amount of praise and prominence? Teach the craft and huddle under the protective academic umbrella, where young wannabes idolized you, for as long as possible.

I don't mean to sound condescending here regarding English departments and the academy; this is the road I have followed in my life, and it has served me well. Selling shoes, driving a truck, and creating advertising and public relations campaigns during the day while writing my first novel at night, in my twenties, was not an easy life. I tried it for a half-dozen years, and I learned about people and the worlds they inhabited, and that strengthened my writing and my passion to make a mark in the world. And it was often fun and rewarding in various ways. This was to me a great benefit, and it distinguished me from my English department colleagues who took the more traditional PhD route. Sure, I was an outcast again, now in the academy, the English department at Pitt, totally not belonging but feeling lucky to be there. But I also had a motorcycle, and this was good—every English department should have a motorcyclist, my colleagues agreed, especially one who rides a BMW.

And I do wonder if I would be writing this today—or perhaps not writing at all—if it wasn't for the support of the University of Pittsburgh specifically and the academy generally. Not that I appreciated everything about life in the ivory tower, but it made being a writer easier. It gave you a platform, a home base, and an audience to try out ideas on—and colleagues to drink beer and smoke dope with. But it was also very difficult to be a part of this world. Just like Billy Sopira, these guys could play rough, though their way of doing it was subtle but debilitating, so that a guy like me, coming from the wrong side of the tracks, could be ruthlessly frozen out.

During those years, the debate about creative writing—and creative nonfiction writing in particular—was intense, mean, and often nonsensical. I remember the editor of the university newspaper, *The Pitt News*, once went to see the department chair, requesting that the department offer a new journalism

course. He was a student in the "expository writing" course
I was teaching and the students, especially from the student
newspaper, were turned on. The idea of immersion—experiencing life and using literary techniques to make their work
cinematic—got them going. They wanted more.

So the editor—his name was Bill Gormley, and today he is
an author and professor of public policy at Georgetown University—made an appointment with Walter Evert, the chair of
the English department, and proposed something like "Basic
New Journalism 101," which I would teach. Like I said, it was
actually what I was already doing, but this would allow me
to come clean and could lead to other courses that were more
advanced, specialized, and challenging. Evert explained that
he lacked the authority to approve, let alone encourage, such
a course so out of the mainstream of contemporary literature.
But in the spirit of free speech and openness reflected in the
early 1970s, he allowed Gormley to make a presentation to the
faculty at its next meeting.

I will never forget the scene. Gormley was a little guy,
bespectacled, with straight brown hair hanging in bangs down
his forehead. Almost dwarfed by the podium, he stood reading
from the sheaf of notes he had prepared, about the history and
relevance of new journalism and its many practitioners, to a
totally silent collection of Birkenstocked, ponytailed professors.
There may have been a few questions—I don't remember—but
after Gormley's presentation, a big, balding, flat-nosed guy
named Don Petesch stood up, carrying one of those massive,
flat-bottomed leather briefcases that fold out like an accordion
so you can carry around half of your library, as well as lunch
and dinner. He plopped the case on the table beside the podium
and, facing Gormley, who had retreated to one of the back rows,
began pulling out books—Faulkner, Thurber, Fitzgerald, Thomas (not Tom) Wolfe, Welty, and on and on—holding each one
up in the air and providing us all with a succinct description of
its literary value and inherent brilliance and then slamming it
down on the table beside his briefcase, *kaboom, kaboom*, until
the massive briefcase was empty. And then, peering across the

room and addressing Gormley, he said something to the effect of: *Until you and the other* Pitt News *staffers read all of these books and learn to appreciate and understand them, this department should never support such lightweight and insignificant work as what you think you are calling writing that is "new" in journalism.* Like I said, I don't remember the words—but that was the gist of the finale of his illustrious presentation.

Listening to Petesch pontificate was actually too much for the other members of the department, who all burst out in debate over the books he had selected as classics—which didn't have anything to do with the subject at hand, but that was typical of the literary professors back then. And admittedly, Petesch's incredible rudeness also annoyed them. There was really no reason to treat an undergraduate, who had had the courage to present an idea to the entire department, in such a dismissive manner—especially the editor of the student newspaper, who could wreak revenge on Petesch or the English department should he choose to. You had to give the kid some credit, even though maybe his idea was worthless.

Finally, Walt Evert, the chair, stood up to tone down the rhetoric and move to another subject, reasoning, "After all, gentlemen, we are interested in literature here—not writing." We few writers paused for a moment to allow that to sink in. (There were, by the way, many women in the room who snickered but also held their fire.)

So this is the atmosphere in which creative writing existed—was forced to exist. Literature professors were willing to tolerate courses in poetry and fiction writing, but to discuss journalism and literature in the same breath? How dare you?

Well, Bill Gormley dared, and the faculty backed off after a while, and the following year, I was permitted to introduce a course called "The New Nonfiction." As bad as the term *nonfiction* was—according to my colleagues, "Nonfiction is a non sequitur! How can you describe what you do as something you don't do?"—at least it was better than the J-word.

A quarter-century ago, creative writing programs were rapidly being established in the United States, mostly in English departments, comprising primarily poets and fiction writers and a scattering of playwrights. On a graduate level, nonfiction was totally glossed over; undergrads could take essay writing or expository writing course electives, like the one I had been teaching, but without concentrations and majors. Since nonfiction was not poetry or fiction, it was not considered literary. If you wanted to write in a non-literary manner, that was okay, . . . but there were other places for that kind of low-end stuff: technical writing, PR writing, or basic journalism. Nonfiction was formulaic, like plumbing. It was the expository writing model—but worse!

I won't say that my poetry- and fiction-writing colleagues in creative writing programs across the United States opposed adding a third genre; they were mostly ambivalent. They were part of these programs as a shelter from the outside world so that they could write in peace; if you didn't bother them, you could write or teach anything you wanted, even if it is/was a "non"! They wouldn't take the time to complain or doubt or debate— as long as it didn't threaten their own comfort and position.

But the more contentious word was *creative*. Journalists hated *creative* because to them it meant that you made stuff up—lying, exaggerating, etc. But the academics in the English department also found it threatening. "Why can't my work be considered creative, too?" they whined and argued. Why, for God's sake, were their essays on Milton or postmodernism referred to as "criticism" while my prose about traveling the country on a motorcycle or hanging out with major league baseball umpires was artistic and literary and creative? This didn't seem fair.

The debate went on in our department for years—literally—and it may well still be going on, for all I know. It got to be very bitter. The MFA in creative writing for poetry and fiction was established at Pitt in the 1980s while an MA in nonfiction—perhaps the first advanced degree in nonfiction in the world—a few years later. A couple of us began campaigning for an nonfiction MFA, and at that point, the nonfiction writing students were harassed, intimidated, and threatened by literature and composition professors. One woman actually resigned her teaching assistantship under the constant pressure and torment. Simply put, the English department was a very dark and dour place to be if you wanted to be different and do something new, for it was all such a threat to the Petesches of this cloistered world. And the more my colleagues criticized and bullied my students, the more I came to believe, perhaps rightly so, they were also motherfucking me and the genre. At least, that's the way I took it. They were rejecting my ideas, and I didn't like it.

So, I found myself fighting back again, like in high school—not with my fists, but with my headstrong persistence and the originality of my idea. Not that I was telling anyone I had invented the genre—no way. You can't invent what already exists; you can only spin it and fight for it—and that was an opening and an opportunity made for me. I went wherever an opportunity presented itself and defended the idea that you could be literary and journalistic at the same time, that *creative* and *nonfiction* can stand together as a concept and a practice, and that you could write about yourself and how you feel and think and make it all work together without being sickeningly egocentric. Make it—the facts and the truth—vivid, passionate, beautiful, powerful, electrifying. I had found a cause to champion, in which I deeply believed.

And closer to home, I battled the hissing bitches, mostly male, inside the department at Pitt and gradually made headway. Eventually, we got a faculty line for a nonfiction position in addition to mine, and then, suddenly, dozens of unemployed literature PhDs who had written newspaper articles or op-ed pieces at some point in their lives were proclaiming themselves master nonfiction writers and applying for the position.

IV. SO WHY START A LITERARY MAGAZINE? IT'S COMPLICATED.
Let's go back to Hemingway and some of the other writers I have mentioned. Hemingway spent time working for newspapers. That's where he first began to develop the spare, crisp style for which he is known as well as his ability to capture and

recreate people and places with vivid and unforgettable detail. But the development of his "literary" career, in sync with his reportorial accomplishments and his maturation as a writer, was all about a bunch of magazines most people (including me) had never heard of. Most of them were defunct long before I was born—but a long line of these literary "little" magazines and journals supported and showcased Hemingway and others as they matured.

While he was still in his early twenties, Hemingway's work appeared in *The Little Review* (as did the work of Gertrude Stein and Ezra Pound); *The Transatlantic Review*, edited by Ford Madox Ford; and in another little magazine called *This Quarter*. Most of these little magazines were based in Paris, where many American literary ex-pats were hanging out at the time. Most of these literary magazines were start-ups that existed for a few years, supported by an impassioned writer or editor, made an impact, and then disappeared when the founders ran out of money or spirit (and sometimes both).

Literary or little magazines supported Hemingway at a key developmental moment in his career. Without their support and encouragement, and without the exposure they provided to critics and other editors, maybe Hemingway would not have ascended to such fame, might not have won a Nobel Prize for literature, might not be regarded as one of the most famous American artists ever to live. Perhaps I am exaggerating—but look: *The Little Review* was first to publish the Hemingway vignette "In Our Time," which was not long after reprinted with minor edits in Hemingway's second book, *In Our Time*. ("Big Two-Hearted River" was also in this collection.) Then *The Transatlantic Review* published Hemingway's brilliant short story "Cross-Country Snow," and *This Quarter* published "The Undefeated," a story about bullfighting that eventually was adapted into a screenplay. These stories had been turned down by *Harper's* and *The Saturday Review*, respectively.

I was vaguely aware of the importance of literary magazines when I came to work in the English department. And I discovered that my colleagues were appreciative of these "littles," as well—in some cases, more than I was. In fact, if you looked in the department's library or on the shelves in the offices of literature profs, you'd see some of these publications—*The Georgia Review*, *The Partisan Review*, and others were popular at the time. Interestingly, my colleagues did not display *Esquire*, *The New Yorker*, *Harper's*, or *The Atlantic Monthly* in their offices. Maybe these magazines were in their living rooms, bedrooms, and bathrooms at home—but not in the academic workplace. What was going on? I knew that many of my colleagues read these magazines, because we had discussions about them on a regular basis around the faculty mailboxes or over Iron City beer drafts at local pubs. I knew they appreciated the work— but it just didn't seem to count for much in the world in which they lived. There was a definite disconnect, much of which had to do with their public persona. Back then, in English departments, you had to be "tweedy" (unless, of course, you were the token chain-smoking motorcyclist.

So I began to make a plan. My colleagues appreciated literary magazines—maybe because they were called "literary" magazines—and they refused to consider new journalism as something students might want to study and write in a "literary" or literature department. But what if there was an actual literary magazine that published this stuff? Not something bold and brassy like *Esquire* or outrageous like *Rolling Stone* or *Mother Jones*, but something—how should I say it?—unpretentious, on nice paper—not glossy—and page after page of type. No photos, no ads, just words—lots of big words. It would have to be scholarly; the less style and personality, the better. Or so it seemed to me.

Of course, we weren't just talking about my colleagues at Pitt; it was the whole goddamned English academy in universities everywhere. They were boring. Conservative, uninspiring—despite their Birkenstocks and ponytails. So that was one thing I was thinking about.

I was also thinking about my role as a teacher—my impact. In the beginning, when I was first appointed at Pitt, I thought I would teach for a few years, get the feel of it, have the experience, all while writing a couple of books, then go off and do something else. Probably, I thought, I would write full-time, like Talese and Wolfe and their cohort. Being part of the academy, English departments in general, was a royal pain in the ass for writers generally and for nonfictionists like me specifically.

But we teachers can't easily deny the rewards of the academic life, chief among them the contact and interaction with our students. The thing was—and is—I liked teaching, liked coming into contact with smart and driven young people like Bill Gormley, from whom I could learn and for whom I could be influential. And as time went on, there were many others: Scott MacLeod, who became *Time* magazine's Middle East Bureau Chief, interviewed Osama Bin Laden and Saddam Hussein, and wrote a best-selling book about the death of Princess Diana; Michael Waldholz, who won the Pulitzer Prize for national reporting while working at the *Wall Street Journal*; the novelist Michael Chabon, who worked with me on the writers' conference that became the focus of his best-seller *Wonder Boys*; Jeanne Marie Laskas, whose work has appeared in all of the "player" magazines I once yearned to break into, like *Esquire* and *GQ*, and who is now the director of the creative writing program at Pitt, a position I once held. Later, there were other students who made good—among them Michael Rosenwald, also prominent in the player mags and an award-winning reporter for the *Washington Post*, and Rebecca Skloot of *The Immortal Life of Henrietta Lacks* fame. I could go on and on.

I am not saying that these incredibly bright and talented people would not have achieved what they have without my teaching—not at all. But I was privileged enough to have worked with them during their formative years. And perhaps I made a difference. They certainly made a difference in me and changed my thoughts about writing and life in general. Frankly, I did not want to give up teaching, that role which became so vital a part of my own identity.

Somehow all of this—my colleagues' awareness of the critical importance of literary magazines, and my own professional self-interests and desire to keep teaching—came together for me. I don't exactly remember a day—a light-bulb moment—when idea and inspiration turned to action and mission or purpose. It just nestled in the back of my mind for a while. It really wasn't too different from that time long ago when my teacher, Mr. Meyers, suggested I could become a writer. Or when I decided, for my first book, that I wanted to ride around the country on a motorcycle. The plan took shape slowly; I was only vaguely aware of it until, suddenly, one day: Commitment! This was what I was going to do—launch a journal, *Creative Nonfiction*—and that was that.

To call it a "plan" might even be too much. I just got started with it—thinking at the time, I have to admit, that the journal would be an integral part of the creative writing program at Pitt, helping to support the MFA and build a lasting community of nonfiction writers. Or at least, this was the way in which I might spin it in a department meeting, if ever called upon to do so.

I went to the English Department Chair. Walt Evert was no longer in power, and to be honest, I can't remember who I talked with about start-up money, but I thoroughly recall the answer—a resounding *No!* I did make follow-up requests from a long-time successor, David Bartholomae, who would also later decline, insisting that creative nonfiction was not significant, was just a fad, didn't belong in an English department. This didn't actually surprise me much. I was just going through channels, being political—trying to make an effort, touching all the bases so that potential supporters, and critics, could not say that I was trying to put something over on my department, going off on my own without considering the larger picture. And I did have loyalty to my academic home base; I really wanted *Creative Nonfiction* to have a home there. But I was pretty sure this was a futile effort, especially when it came to Bartholomae.

A leading figure in the world of composition, Bartholomae was the editor of a textbook, *Ways of Reading*, which would eventually be used in composition programs all over the world.

Perhaps it was a turf issue for Bartholomae—the work in many composition programs often parallels (or competes with?) the mission of many creative nonfiction programs. Suffice it to say, creative nonfiction was not one of the "ways of reading" (or writing) of which he approved. In a 1995 article in the journal *College Composition and Communication*, published by the National Council of Teachers of English, he wrote:

> *Should we teach new journalism or creative nonfiction as part of the required undergraduate curriculum? That is, should all students be required to participate in a first person, narrative or expressive genre whose goal it is to reproduce the ideology of sentimental realism—where a world is made in the image of a single, authorizing point of view? a narrative that celebrates a world made up of the details of private life and whose hero is sincere?*
>
> *I don't have an easy answer to this question. It is like asking, should students be allowed to talk about their feelings after reading* The Color Purple? *Of course, they should, but where and when? and under whose authority?*

Clearly, Bartholomae then believed that students should not be permitted to think or feel for themselves—at least not without a professor of composition to monitor them.

Bartholomae referred me to the director of development of the School of Arts and Science, to whom I made a presentation and who also, as expected, declined to support a journal. Creative nonfiction, as Bartholomae had stated, was simply not a serious discipline for a liberal arts college; it belonged in a journalism department. But the University of Pittsburgh had disbanded its "J" school in the 1960s. So that was that.

I wasn't surprised, and certainly I was in no way deterred by these rejections. I moved forward. I had a few dollars remaining from money I had raised to start a writers' conference—focusing on all genres, not just nonfiction—so I approached one of my former students, Paul Mathews, whose family owned a printing business in town. I explained my idea and asked if he would help by printing the journal, if I ever got it put together, just for the money I had, which was somewhere between one thousand and two thousand dollars. I figured I could supplement it out of my own pocket because I remained convinced—no kidding, I continued to hope for this—that once the journal was produced, the department would endorse and support it despite the obvious ideological resistance.

Paul was a good guy, a quiet, hard-working student who had once been an intern for the Pitt conference—the same annual conference Chabon had participated in. Over the course of the previous ten years, I had put on maybe a half-dozen writers' conferences—something that was pretty unusual back then. (As it turned out, the conference idea would be incredibly helpful in establishing the genre and the journal.) Paul had left Pittsburgh for Boston after graduation to work for the Boston *Phoenix*, but he was now back in town helping with his father's business. He remained fired up about the publishing industry and got very excited about the creative nonfiction literary journal idea. He would do anything possible to help whenever I was ready, he said.

But I was not ready quite yet. I had gathered some names of writers—a list of about 170 folks who I suspected had some interest in nonfiction—and wrote letters (real letters!) explaining what I wanted to do and asking for advice, comments, and, most of all, submissions. I got some nice return letters, telling me what a great idea an all-creative nonfiction journal was. And people sent submissions, too. I think I got about forty in all.

I won't say that most of the manuscripts sent my way—for not only that first issue, but the first few after word spread that there was a new journal seeking creative nonfiction—represented bad writing, whatever that is. I mean, lots of "bad writing" comes across the transom of any literary publication. But what people sent as creative nonfiction—what they thought the term meant—was difficult to fathom.

This debate about genre was going on everywhere in the early 1990s. I keep coming back to this war over acceptance of the form and its definition, but you have to understand that it was all-consuming and pervasive back then. You couldn't talk about the art or craft until you had explained what it meant. But no one had to explain what fiction or poetry or drama was, so why should creative nonfiction be any different?

By then, I should say, the term *creative nonfiction* was beginning to gain traction, maybe in part because the National Endowment for the Arts had adopted it. It wasn't a perfect term, and actually pretty much everyone hated it. But as with "new journalism," it was helpful just to *have* a term.

Still, as our slush pile made clear, that didn't mean there was consensus about what the term referred to. We got some poetry, for example, because the poems were true, the writers said. More often, we received submissions of poetry interspersed with prose. That was the "creative" part, the writers said when questioned. We got lots of fiction; the writers explained that the stories were based on fact, and more or less true, so why not just call them creative nonfiction? And then, of course, there were writers who sent whatever they had in their files and drawers—lots of newspaper clippings, and stuff unfinished or rejected a dozen times by other publications.

Sifting through these submissions and trying to figure out what to publish, I began to recognize at least one clear mission of the new journal: since no one could agree on the essence or meaning of creative nonfiction, we would publish work that demonstrated the core and fiber of the genre. We would select essays or articles or prose pieces—whatever you wanted to call them—that would help writers define and understand the parameters through example, not pedagogy. We would—as any good writer is supposed to do—show, not tell.

Fortunately, these are issues we don't need to deal with much anymore; the overwhelming presence of creative nonfiction as a genre (and a publication) is now fact, and while the exact meaning of the term remains somewhat cloudy and imprecise, I think we can say the same thing we say about fiction and poetry: it is what we say it is. The art defines itself. And the firm idea that we are helping define the genre by example continues to guide *Creative Nonfiction* today.

And when I say "we," I mean a pretty small group—even today, but especially at the beginning. Because Pitt had declined to sponsor the journal, I set up shop at home, on my dining room table in the Squirrel Hill neighborhood of Pittsburgh; I have vivid memories of working on the first issue of *Creative Nonfiction* there, with my wife (now my ex-wife), Patricia Park. Patricia was and still is a nurse, an avid reader, and a great editor. Also in the mix was our son, Sam, then only two years old. A favorite graduate student of mine, Kathleen Veslany, also contributed a great deal of time and energy to the project.

I won't go over all of the pieces we published in the first issue (the table of contents is available on the *Creative Nonfiction* website), but I want to mention two that stand out in my mind: First, Natalia Rachel Singer, then an assistant professor at St. Lawrence University, sent a manuscript based on a talk she had given when she was applying for the St. Lawrence position. It's a great essay, very informative and personal at the same time, but it was the title that caught my attention. It was like a proclamation, a definition of doctrine: "Nonfiction in First Person, Without Apology." It knocked my socks off, it was so apropos! I know Wolfe and Talese and Mailer and God knows how many other hotshots were saying this to the world, nothing new, but Singer was making this statement to some very judgmental folks. This was something I too could have said—and did say, frequently, to anyone who would listen—but it was much better coming from someone who was not such an avowed true believer. So we accepted and published her essay with pride and excitement.

Michael Pearson—like me, a lone wolf in a writing program, teaching creative nonfiction, more or less, at Old Dominion University—did not submit a manuscript; rather, he wrote a letter offering to conduct a Q&A with *The New Yorker* writer John McPhee. Pearson had interviewed McPhee once before for an academic article he had written, so they were acquainted. I needn't tell you how special McPhee is. For one thing, *The New Yorker* was a literary cut even above *Esquire*, *Rolling Stone*, and the other player magazines, and McPhee was also the author, at that time, of twenty or so books. And with rare exceptions—such as William Howarth's brilliant interview and profile of him in *The John McPhee Reader*—McPhee rarely discussed his work or his approach to writing. So this would be a gigantic coup for the journal if Michael could make this happen—and he did. It was quite a feat, not least because when Michael arrived at McPhee's office, tape recorder in hand, for his "20 Questions," McPhee told him to put his tape recorder away: "You'll get a better story without a tape recorder. Besides, the question-and-answer format is the most primitive form of writing, you realize. Writing is selection. It's better to start choosing right here and right now."

So Michael had a conversation with McPhee and wrote a profile of the writer whose work I admired more than anyone else's, except maybe Talese's. We published it in that first issue: "Profile of *New Yorker* Writer John McPhee" was right on the cover. Connecting the respected reporter, McPhee, to the ill-regarded, much-maligned genre of creative nonfiction was a big deal, I thought. And eventually, McPhee started teaching a course at Princeton which he called "Creative Nonfiction." He still offers it once a year for freshmen wanting to write true stories. For a writer of his distinguished reputation, this was a significant event for creative nonfiction writers—a boundary crossing in many respects. It was, in fact, those writers pushing the boundaries, going beyond the traditional limits, who fostered the growth of the field.

V. READY FOR TAKEOFF

We launched the first issue of *Creative Nonfiction* at the 1994 meeting of the Association of Writers and Writing Programs (AWP, which then stood for Associated Writing Programs), which was held in Tempe, Arizona.

I had been to AWP conferences before. Now, of course, creative writing has turned into a big business, and during AWP thousands of writers and wannabe writers swarm convention centers and hotels in the host city, attending readings and pedagogy and craft sessions, drinking too much and networking like crazy. Looking for jobs. Looking for someone to publish their poems. Looking for a one-night stand. But back then, the conferences were quiet, casual, and fun, with maybe a thousand people attending in all. People mostly knew one another, and it was a great time to get together and share war stories about colleagues, publishers, or whatever else. It was a lot more fun—and easier to get a drink in the hotel lobby bar.

Still, AWP was then, as it is now, the biggest event in the academic creative writing world, and because of that, I had made a promotional plan around it. I decided I could make the biggest bang for our buck by officially launching the first issue of *Creative Nonfiction* there. To help bolster the journal's image as the voice of the emerging genre, I designed a panel on creative nonfiction—"Creative Nonfiction in the Academy"—the first ever held at AWP.

I was very nervous; I had no idea whether anyone would show up. I had recruited some good panelists: both Michael Pearson and Natalia Rachel Singer had agreed to speak, and I had also invited Jane Bernstein—author, at the time, of a novel and also a wonderful memoir, *Loving Rachel*, about her developmentally challenged daughter. Jane was in Tempe at the time, researching a memoir about the murder of her sister when she was an ASU student in Tempe in the 1970s. We all met before the panel to make certain we were on the same page, joking all the while that we might be talking to ourselves. We figured no one would show up—either because they didn't know what creative nonfiction was or because they thought they knew what it was but were appalled by the thought of it.

The morning of the panel, I made certain I steered clear of the designated room and kept myself occupied with other matters. Even though I was the moderator and the initiator of the event, I intended to be if not late, then right on time. Not early, for God's sake, because I feared that standing there with my fellow panel members, watching an empty room not fill up, would make me crazy. So I walked around town and drank an extra coffee, with my heart literally pounding with anxiety. Patricia and our son, Sam, were at the table at the book fair, displaying and selling the journal. At that point, a few people had come around to look us over, but although there was a lot of interest—which was encouraging—we had made few sales.

Anyway, to make a long story short, I waited until the last minute and then hurried to the conference room. I couldn't get in; I had to push and shove to get through the door, explaining to those fighting for seats that I was the panel moderator. The place was packed. People were flopped on the floor everywhere. It was amazing. Many of the attendees knew exactly what we creative nonfictionists were all about, and others were intrigued by the idea, thinking that they had all along been writing and reading this stuff, or wishing they could write this stuff if there was a place to publish it. It was an eclectic, curious, and enthusiastic crowd.

I took it as confirmation of my theory that creative nonfiction was the way in which many writers had always wanted to write—if only they had a place to publish it or a classroom in which to learn more about it or a community with which to discuss or debate it. Or even just a name—an official label—to give it.

In my introduction to the panel, I made a pitch for the journal. I tried to be sincere and passionate. Now there is a potential home for your work, I said, an exclusive place. It is the new journal I started: *Creative Nonfiction*. Come and see it at the table at the book fair—buy and subscribe and give to the cause. Your commitment now is crucial. Patricia and Sam were at the table, ready to show and sell, I said.

After the panel, the conversation continued, with people jamming the podium and lingering in the hallway in front of the room as we cleared out. People were all over the place, incredibly excited, and it was hard to break away—and I did not really want to break away, if truth be told. I was enjoying this feeling of making a connection. It was like coming out of a dark alley, having wandered aimlessly, seeking an exit. I can't tell you what emotion I felt more at that time, elation or relief. Either way, it was great and glorious.

When I got back to the book fair table, most of the copies of the journal that we had shipped to the hotel had been sold. The event, the panel, the launch—it had all been a big hit. Like I said, my emotions were mixed. I knew that something really good had happened, and I wished that all of my doubting colleagues in Pittsburgh had been around to witness it. But it didn't matter in the end. The genre and the journal were on their way to establishing something significant to writers and readers everywhere.

VI. THE POET AS NONFICTION SOLDIER

As we began to receive a growing number of submissions—sent to us in the mail, hard copy, of course, back then—we could recognize patterns having to do with the writer or the subject being written about. I remember reading all of the submissions sent to us after our AWP debut, picking out the pieces I liked the best, spreading them out on my living room floor—the dining room table could no longer accommodate all of the work we were getting—and suddenly realizing the amazing connective tissue that linked them all: They were mostly poets, writing prose! I thought, What the hell is this? I mean, one of the primary reasons I launched the journal was to give journalists and other nonfiction (and fiction) writers the opportunity to be creative and use literary techniques to be more evocative and cinematic. But here were poets! This was very unexpected, but very exciting.

Contrary to popular belief (and mine, as well, at the time), poetry is much closer to nonfiction than one might imagine. On the most basic level, many poems are, in essence, nonfiction: spiritual and literal truth, presented in free form or verse. In addition, the skills and objectives of the best poets are the skills and objectives most vital in the writing of "fact" pieces. For example, one of the most formidable challenges of the nonfiction writer is to learn to develop a narrow and targeted focus. We devote weeks, months and sometimes years to the study and observation of different subcultures, places and ideas. In any given piece, journalists and essayists can tell many stories, go off on dozens of tangents, while gradually concentrating on what all of their research, ideas and interviews mean. Poets seem as consistently aware and in control not only of the structure of essays, but also the scope and range of vision. They translate and communicate complicated ideas with compact specificity while being informative and dramatic, which is what good creative nonfiction is all about. And many poets are oriented toward the subtle (and sometimes not so subtle) propagation of social causes—another trait associated with the deepest and most noble journalistic traditions.

Another point: previously, I mentioned Tom Wolfe's riffs in his early pieces of new journalism. I admit, I found them somewhat tiring and overblown, but I came to realize that some of that work is poetic in content and vision; in fact, it's much more powerful as poetry than as narrative. Ultimately, I think, divisions in genre are much too arbitrary and unnecessary. Like I keep saying—and I keep saying it only because people keep asking for definitions of creative nonfiction—art defines itself.

Who asks for definitions of poetry? Poetry is what it is and poets are what they are—and thus perhaps I should have realized what might take place when a literary journal (the kind of place where the work of most poets most regularly appears) began to accept and encourage out-of-the-box nonfiction prose. It was an opportunity for poets to achieve more with their literary pursuits. Early in her career, the writer Diane Ackerman told me that she often doesn't know what genre she is going to work in when she sits down to write—poetry or creative nonfiction. She writes for a while and decides at one point or another what she needs to do to achieve her literary or intellectual objectives—what the subject and the focus demand, prose or poetry. I don't believe that fiction writers are so flexibly oriented. They write or want to write magnificent stories and create characters that may (or may not) have societal or intellectual missions—but stories and characters often run away from writers, and some of the best fiction clearly arrives and makes its greatest impact when the text takes over. Not so with creative nonfiction because the facts and ideas determine depth and direction. I believe that poetry is much closer to that model than fiction.

I was also a long-time fan of W.S. Merwin's memoir *Unframed Originals*, which, I am embarrassed to say, I thought was his only nonfiction book, though I discovered when I looked back into his bibliography that it was actually his third. Now he has written five more nonfiction prose books. I wasn't a poetry reader and I had rarely spent time with poets, until I joined the Pitt faculty and met a few poets and discovered that poets were not as breathless and purposely exotic in person as when they were up at a podium reading from their work. In fact, they were much more fun to be with than the journalists I tended to hang out with; poets, I quickly learned, could smoke and drink and swear and womanize the average journalist under the table. But that's another story.

I also remembered an interaction I had observed a decade earlier between a young and successful poet confronting graduate student writers and scholars—challenging them, to no avail, to write nonfiction. We were in a conference room on the 5th floor of the Cathedral of Learning, discussing with a group of graduate students in writing and composition—I think they were all teaching assistants—potential summer support, or lack thereof. Let's face it, English departments being English departments, there's never a lot of money to go around—and in the summer, there's a lot less. That was especially true twenty or thirty years ago, when the third term was not such an essential income-generator for universities. And if anybody got paid any decent amount for summer or third term work, it was (and still is) the full-time faculty. Grad students are invaluable teaching assistants, or they help out in the department office, tutor challenged students, especially from other countries, and perform a number of support jobs during the academic year. But the summer is tough, and these people, mostly ranging in age from their mid twenties to early thirties, were feeling pressured and panicked.

"We are in a crisis mode. We are desperate," said one woman working on her PhD in composition during this meeting, as she made her tearful plea for funding. And a young man with shoulder length hair and a stringy beard commented—jokingly, but clearly unhappily—"I better call my dad."

This was one of those meetings we are all dragged into from time to time—obligatory, but in actuality unnecessary because there was really nothing to say. There was no money to promise to these students; we all knew it, even the grad students themselves. The real purpose of the meeting was that the grad students could voice their frustrations and the faculty members who felt obliged to attend would listen and sympathize, although I admit that I was not particularly on the same sympathetic wavelength as my colleagues, as I soon found out.

Remember, I put myself through school selling shoes on the road, as a traveling salesman, and subsequently in the advertising and public relations business, promoting helium for the U.S. Department of the Interior. (My big joke at the time was that whenever anyone would ask me if I liked my job, I would say, "It's a gas!") Among other accounts, I had a company that manufactured a line of ready mix concrete machinery. For some reason the name of this company, American Elba—in the office and out of earshot of the client, we called them "American Elbow"—just popped into my mind now, though I haven't thought of them in many years. I actually had fun working on some of this stuff. I hired a female model in a bikini to sit on top of the machine at a trade show in Cleveland, and I can tell you that the Elbow folks got a lot of attention from the visiting construction company executives; the Elbow guys took this girl out for dinner, and God knows where else. I haven't the slightest idea, since I quit that job soon thereafter, whether any of those very expensive Elba concrete mixers were sold. But it was a job—and a slice of life that most writers would never experience, either by choice or coincidentally. But the more varied the life a writer lives, the more there is in the memory bank to offer the reader, whether the vehicle is prose or poetry.

So I sat there during the meeting at Pitt with my mouth shut, wondering (and wanting to ask, but not asking, out of my own discomfort from not belonging) why they didn't just get jobs—like at the local McDonald's or the famous Pitt Tavern around the corner from the Cathedral, where they could pour 15-cent drafts all night for minimum wage plus tips and drink for free after hours with the regulars. Or get in a car and drive across country, doing odd jobs. Or stick out a thumb on some back road in Amish country and see where it led. Do something to prepare for life in the world at large—which, for a writer, might be the perfect start to a path back into the academy later on.

But I was especially annoyed at the time, I admit, and maybe overly and unnecessarily sensitive for, while I was teaching during the day, I was actually researching a book at night across the campus at the medical center on top of what Pittsburgh natives have long called "Cardiac Hill" because it is such a steep hike from the lower campus where the humanities and social sciences were embedded to the upper campus where medicine and science prevailed, that people had coronary episodes from time to time as they made the climb. I am exaggerating, of course, but it was known to happen, so it was only half a joke—and I think you get the point.

The book I was working on was about real desperation; the people I was writing about were actually seeking support to *live* through the summer. In fact, the chances of half of them living from then, the late spring, to the early summer were considerably dimmer than the slim-to-none likelihood of these grad students being rewarded a summer stipend. For the book, I was profiling the world of organ transplantation through immersion, trying to live in the shoes of all of the actors involved in the transplant experience. This was long before today's HIPAA laws, which protect patient privacy and make things challenging for writers seeking close and intimate observation; at that time, I had access to everything and virtually everyone, from the patient wards to the operating rooms. I Lear-jetted through the night on what were then called "organ harvests," when surgeons would fly thousands of miles to retrieve a heart or liver or heart-and-lung from a brain-dead donor, pack it into a cute little red Igloo cooler and jet back to the transplant center to sew it into a waiting recipient whose heart or liver or heart-and-lung block had already been removed and who was living and breathing on artificial life support.

I will never forget the danger and the drama. Each recipient had a diseased organ (or organs) that was killing him or her and perhaps had caused suffering and destroyed the patient's quality of life, until he or she was sick enough to qualify as a transplant candidate, and then after qualification waited months or years more for an organ of the right size, age and blood type to become available, "available" meaning that some-one had to die in order for the patient to have the opportunity to live, that it was finally the patient's turn on the transplant list. The organ was on its way to save a life, maybe . . . if it all worked out in the end, if the organ remained viable in the cute little red Igloo cooler, if the patient's body was strong enough to with-stand the trauma of a surgery that could easily take 10–12 hours, not to mention the hours prior to that on artificial life support. And then, if everything went smoothly and there were no mistakes or glitches from the time the harvest team removed the organs, left the transplant facility, returned to the medical center up there atop Cardiac Hill, implanted the organ—even then, the patient had only a 50% or 60% chance of living a year! (This was at the beginning of the transplant era; the survival rate is much higher now and the surgical and immu-nosuppressive processes have been magnificently improved. But it is not a picnic today, either.)

Most of the transplant surgeries were at night since most people who were viable as transplant donors died during the day in auto accidents, drownings, etc., and since the surgery took so excruciatingly long to perform, and the operating rooms were open and unscheduled at night. Just think of the loved ones, the friends and family members of the potential transplant recipient, sitting, sipping black coffee, chain smok-ing—you could do that in hospitals back then—numbly watch-ing television in the dark waiting rooms, listening for the clap-clop-clatter of the helicopter landing on the roof of the medical center having transported the harvest team back to home base from the airport with the organ, and then counting the hours and trying to image what was going on in the surgical suite, waiting for a surgeon or a nurse to appear with an update, news about their wives, husbands, parents, children.

I had been working in the book for two years at that point. I had witnessed plenty of suffering. Think of all of this awfulness, this hope and unfortunate despair these people lived through, which I had observed and in a small measure had lived through with them, since I came to know some of these patients and families (and the surgeons, with life and death of patients weighing on their shoulders and their consciences), and then listen to the young woman in the Cathedral of Learning conference room down at the bottom of Cardiac Hill, where the humanists were located, pleading for help for summer financial support so that she needn't get a job, a real job, and watch as she becomes tearful upon learning that the English Department bank is empty and the faucet temporarily turned off until the fall semester. I sat there, watching and listening, stewing, but afraid to speak for fear of revealing my anger and my sadness over the agony I had observed and experienced.

The conversation went on—and on—until the young poet spoke up. She would not be on the faculty for very long; her exotic style and manner and her outspokenness did not make a good fit in the conservative confines of the Cathedral of Learning English department, and she left after only two years. She was a prominent young poet then, having published two collections that had been well reviewed by critics and were popular with readers. Who was to know then that she would remain a respected poet, but become best-known for her many *New Yorker* profiles and best-selling and highly literary books in another genre—creative nonfiction?

She once showed me the books she was reading about science, wildlife, and philosophy—lots of environmental stuff, also—to prepare to write a profile for *The New Yorker*. She prepared in a similar way to write poetry. Her library and her reading list were impressive, but the scrawling annotations in the margins of each of these books, page after page, astounded and impressed me. The way in which she prepared to write would shame the average journalist, although, to be fair, the poet is not writing a poem on deadline, and in most cases the creative nonfiction writer will have a week, a month, a decade, a lifetime, to do the work. When you are writing for *The New Yorker*, on assignment, you do have deadlines, but they are months away, unless the piece is time sensitive, which is not so often the case in creative nonfiction, or at least it was not often the case back then. (Times and expectations have changed, as long form narrative has become more popular.)

Her long black hair wild and frizzing out with electricity and her arms waving dramatically, the poet addressed the young people sitting in that room with a simple suggestion. *Why not write nonfiction—creative nonfiction? You can be poetic, informative—and you can make a living that way. It's a perfect avenue for young people, poets especially. This is what I intend to do. I won't give up poetry; I can do both.*

I am obviously paraphrasing, but that was the gist of her message. And the students in that room, quite honestly, to my deepest recollection, looked at her like she was speaking in tongues. They would have laughed if they were not so surprised and so traumatized by their fear of leaving the confines of the university and finding other avenues of support. Nonfiction? Was this poet crazy? Had she lost her pride and her literary presence? For journalism? Like plumbing? Writing nonfiction was not an option at that time—not for these kids. The meeting ended soon thereafter without resolution, as everyone had known it would from the very beginning.

As I said, this English Department was not a good fit for this young poet, named Diane Ackerman, who departed the following year, moved to a different university, and became a model for other poets and fiction writers, encouraging them not to be afraid to cross genres and experiment. Diane was ahead of her time.

VII. EMERGING

I've been fortunate enough to work with many writers who have been ahead of their time—misfits, in some way. One of them was a young writer who spotted *Creative Nonfiction*'s second issue, "Poets Writing Prose," and began thumbing through it in the Harvard Book Store in Cambridge in 1994.

I have to say, it was absolutely amazing to me how quickly we were able to find a national distributor for *Creative Nonfiction* and get it placed for sale in key prestigious locations, like the Harvard Book Store and Border's and Barnes & Noble. Interestingly enough, there was no creative nonfiction, narrative nonfiction—not even a nonfiction section in most of these bookstores; some bookstores then and now have "Essay" sections, but they tend to be very narrowly defined and non-subject oriented. If the essays collected in a volume have an over-arching theme, then the prospective reader will find them by matching the theme to the sections—like healthcare, science, technology. This is not an awful way to do it, although how-to books, inspirational books, highly technical manuals, and other misfits are invariably lumped together. Someday, I hope, bookstores, if there are any left, will find a way to catalogue the genre more appropriately. This has been a long-time issue with me—that the prospective reader can more easily browse fiction and poetry than nonfiction. But at the beginning, in the 1990s, I was happy enough that *Creative Nonfiction* had a place on the magazine racks of a few bookstores, nationally.

Not many months earlier I would not have known—or cared—how magazines got from publishers to book stores and magazine stands; the publications I wanted were there, available on the shelf, for skimming or purchasing when I wanted them, and that was good enough for me. For many people, congregating around magazine sections in bookstores or smaller racks of magazines or newspaper sales counters brought great pleasure and entertainment. Sometimes you would stand there (or sit on the floor!) for hours, sampling a dozen terrific magazines before deciding which one to buy and take home. It's a nice memory. Times have changed as far as purchasing and reading magazines these days, and many of us more mature readers miss the way things used to be.

The young woman who stumbled upon *Creative Nonfiction* that day in Cambridge was an unpublished writer, a striking woman, tiny and delicately bird-like with a chiseled, pointed chin, pale white complexion and a shy, reluctant smile. I can just imagine her reaching down, picking up the journal, flipping through it, reading an essay or two, feeling the quality of the paper. (We had upgraded the paper for our second issue, in an act of purity; we didn't want the type shining through from one page to the next.) And then I imagine her lifting her eyes in recognition, nodding slowly and thoughtfully, like this is something really special—it is speaking to her, eureka!—and then heading home to pack up her manuscript and send it to us at *Creative Nonfiction*.

I wasn't there at that important moment at the Harvard Book Store, but the writer told me this story many years later when I visited her in a town not too far from Cambridge. She was no longer so tiny; she'd put on weight over the course of raising a family and now, in addition to writing fiction and nonfiction, she paints, sculpts, gardens, builds stuff with her hands. She's had a controversial career, to say the least—international criticism about her writing and research in relation to the psychiatry community and ghost writing for the stars, like Rosie O'Donnell. But her work remains brilliant and revered. And it started, in some respects, at the Harvard Book Store twenty years ago—with *Creative Nonfiction*.

I don't for one moment want to give the impression that we inspired her or that if it wasn't for *Creative Nonfiction* this writer (I'll tell you her name in a moment) would not have made an impact in the literary world. To the contrary, she made an impact with me—first, because she sent her book manuscript to me and I had the chance to read it before anybody, almost, and second, because she reminded me of the great work literary magazines were publishing from unknown writers deep into the past, and got me excited again about what gold there was waiting in them there creative nonfiction hills. I knew there were unknown writers out there, laboring alone, confronting the keyboard, not necessarily knowing what they were writing, or even what genre they were working in—Is this fiction? Nonfiction? Is it neither? What *is* it?—or where the work would be published once it was finished. (Not that any writer really knows when the work is finished.)

Anyway, you will remember that early on in this narrative I referred to an incident at *The New Yorker* when the longtime editor Roger Angell went running down the corridor, waving a manuscript up in the air with the sheer joy of finding a new writer who had done something really significant—and this happened to me, too. I received a big box in the mail from somewhere near Boston, and I put it on the corner of my desk, recognizing it as a book manuscript. This actually annoyed me to a certain extent; I had said I would read essay manuscripts— I mean, I wanted to read essay manuscripts, that was what *Creative Nonfiction* was all about, and I guess it was also what I was all about right then, and I had encouraged people to send, even if they weren't sure what they had written was creative nonfiction, which was, at that time, often the case.

But I was already getting weary plowing through all of this stuff—and reading my students' work at the same time. If I recall correctly, I was teaching a five-course load—two and three—that year. And most of the work received over the transom, as any editor will tell you, isn't too good, but you feel obliged to read the pieces all the way through most of the time; maybe the writer will surprise you and pull something out of his or her hat at the end, or for one reason or another it projects some faint promise, and even if an essay is too flawed to publish and can't be saved with any moderate intervention, you might be able to help the writer out with some comments and encouragement and a nice note asking him to send you something better the next time around. I admit that over the years I have lost a lot of that enthusiasm and willingness to plow through obviously mediocre material. I still do it on occasion, but I have to be highly motivated; I mean it's got to really show me something.

But anyway, we are talking here about a night, a Friday night, I remember, although I don't know why the day is so clear in my mind. I remember I had been at it for a very long time, reading submission after submission, working my way through the slush pile, which, it seemed, was getting higher by the day, no matter how diligently I was reading. I was in my office on the third floor of my house in Squirrel Hill, a cozy attic I loved but a place that I would soon have to vacate because of my impending divorce from Patricia. Maybe, in fact, I was upstairs hiding out for so very long because I did not want to come down into the living room or kitchen—and certainly not into the bedroom—and maybe have another fight about who knows what with my wife.

So I was up there, bored and restless but not ready to make a move from my desk and my hideaway, and my eyes fell on the box that had come in the mail earlier that day, and just for a change, a diversion, I cut open the paper it was wrapped in, lifted the manuscript, maybe 300 pages, out of the box, and, well, you know what happened next. My incredible Roger Angell moment. Eureka! Holy shit!

I won't hold you in suspense any longer: The manuscript was *Welcome to My Country*, the first book by the brilliant memoirist and psychotherapist Lauren Slater, who eventually sold the book to Random House for a substantial six-figure advance. Michiko Kakutani would rave in *The New York Times*: "Ms. Slater writes about her patients with enormous compassion and insight, making the emotional and physical realities of their illnesses palpable to the lay reader. At the same time, *Welcome to My Country* gently unfurls to become a revealing memoir and thoughtful meditation on the therapeutic process itself." Slater went on to write *Prozac Diary* and the brilliant bestseller *Lying: A Metaphorical Memoir*, among other great work.

Anyway, I went crazy, read all six of the long essays in the book that night, mostly about her work as a psychotherapist treating schizophrenic and borderline personality patients. It was a powerful, real-life narrative made especially vivid because the author, the doctor, also suffered so severely from her own borderline personality diagnosis that she had been institutionalized for many years as an adolescent. So I stayed up half the night reading the manuscript, slept fitfully into the early morning, then phoned the author up on Saturday, offering to publish the book—telling her of course how brilliant it was, repeating it again over the phone.

Judging by the way in which she responded, she must have thought that I was going a little overboard in her praise. But I thought that my enthusiasm for her work would be at least partially offset by the fact that I wanted to publish the book, but could only afford to offer her a $1,000 advance. And even that was going too far, a real stretch, since I knew even less about book publishing than I did about magazine publishing. But I had been talking with a small press from nearby Duquesne University about starting a creative nonfiction book series, and I figured maybe *Welcome to My Country* would be the first book. It was an exciting possibility—until a few weeks later when Lauren phoned to tell me, quite apologetically, that on the advice of friends, she had also sent a copy of the book to a New York agent, who, of course, recognized the work for its power and brilliance. The agent was amused—sort of—for she knew the moment she read the manuscript that she had discovered gold, a real treasure, and she wasn't going to allow this young, unknowing writer to give it away for $1,000 to a no-name press. Although she had agreed that I could publish her book with Duquesne, Lauren called a few weeks later and broke the news. The agent was about to present *Welcome to My Country* to publishers in an auction situation—which is how Random House eventually got it, weeks later, by outbidding dozens of other houses.

But Lauren was grateful for my encouragement and enthusiasm, and offered first serial rights for the publication of any of the essays in the collection. I chose a piece called "Three Spheres," a narrative that begins with Lauren's boss assigning her a patient with borderline personality diagnosis, and a call from the treatment team meeting at a hospital in the suburbs of Boston where the patient has been voluntarily committed. The reader finds out in the narrative that Lauren has been anxious to avoid visiting this hospital throughout her career as a therapist, and she tries to refuse the patient.

In the end, she capitulates and accepts the assignment. What else can she do? And then, as the narrative progresses, the reader discovers the biting and frightening truth: that Lauren herself spent time as a patient in the hospital as an adolescent. Midway through the story, Lauren and the treatment team take a bathroom break, and Lauren wanders out in the hallway, ending up at a bathroom in one of the patient wards. A nurse notices, and Lauren fears being revealed, stripped of the professional demeanor she has fought so hard to attain.

When we published "Three Spheres" in Issue #3 of *Creative Nonfiction*, we also wrote a news release and sent it out. Here I was using my skills as a public relations expert; most literary magazines then and now don't really publicize their issues to target markets. We sent the press release to *The Boston Globe* and other media in the area. Amazingly, it sparked some interest and a subsequent feature story in the *Globe* about Lauren, the patient turned therapist, and suddenly, the telephone in our tiny office was ringing off the hook with calls from readers who wanted to order the journal, buy a subscription, and learn more about it and the genre, generally. I can't count how many people said to me over the telephone the week that the Slater story appeared in the *Globe*, "Gee whiz, I have been writing this stuff all of my life and I never once knew what it was called."

VIII. WOMEN IN THE BATTLEFIELD

The third issue of *Creative Nonfiction* was notable for another reason, as well. Not only did it include Lauren's wonderful "Three Spheres" piece, but all of the pieces in the issue were written by women. We had discovered, as we sorted through and screened the growing number of submissions to *Creative Nonfiction*, that more and more of the stuff we were getting was written by women than men. This, I have to say, was another surprise. I honestly thought—assumed, really—that we would be inundated with work from the journalism world, which was then and continues to be male-dominated. All you would hear when talking to reporters was that they were sick and tired of writing in inches, which is what newspapers compelled them to do, and of being formulaic, all the while attempting to maintain the guise of objectivity. But there weren't many journalists in the stacks of manuscripts we were receiving.

I thought we would also hear from advertising copywriters, who expressed similar frustrations—mostly, these were men, trying to write the great American novel at night after the wife and kids had gone to sleep and they were finally alone. Hadn't Joseph Heller written *Catch-22* in his office during lunch hour as he worked as a copywriter in an advertising agency? Well, maybe. But we were not getting stuff from the advertising community any more than from the journalists. Either they didn't know that we existed—or, perhaps more likely, we weren't *Esquire*, *Playboy* or *The Atlantic*, and thus were simply not worth wasting the paper their manuscripts were printed on.

But we were getting a lot of great work by women, and so the third issue, "Emerging Women Writers," reflected that discovery. We published my old friend Jane Bernstein from the AWP panel and my student Kathleen Veslany, along with an in-depth Q-and-A with Diane Ackerman. (Our twelfth issue also featured all women writers—"Emerging Women Writers II.")

I mentioned previously Lillian Ross and Mary McCarthy as early women practitioners of the new journalism, but they were working in the 1950s, mostly, and with some exceptions—Joan Didion, Susan Sheehan, Annie Dillard, and Janet Malcolm come to mind—women got much less attention than men for their narrative nonfiction work in the 1960s, 1970s, and 1980s.

Clearly, however, there are (and were) a lot of women writing serious nonfiction; they're just not getting the attention they deserve. Perhaps one reason men still seem to dominate the "player" magazines, with their long-term immersion assignments, is because being "in the field" and doing the necessary immersion work presents many challenges—for any writer, but probably more so for women than for men, particularly if they have children. In a recent interview, the novelist Geraldine Brooks told me that she transitioned from nonfiction to fiction in part because of the responsibilities and demands of having and raising a family. "It doesn't suit the mothering of young children, because, in the pursuit of nonfiction, you have to follow the story wherever it leads you for however long it takes," she said. Similarly, Susan Orlean observed that most of her editors at *The New Yorker*, where she is a staff writer, are women, and they work just as hard as the writers they edit—only on a more normal schedule. "Editors don't travel," she pointed out. "They don't go to weird events at weird times, places where you wouldn't take a child."

Keep in mind that Brooks and Orlean were discussing the journalistic end of the creative nonfiction spectrum. At the other end of the spectrum, of course, there's memoir and other more personal writing, the writing of which can be less demanding—physically, at least—and may be, for this reason, more attractive to women writers. (Which, in turn, might contribute to the lack of respect memoir gets in certain quarters.) The memoir allows you to look back from your desk to the past or look straight ahead at the present and capture it. You needn't have the experience at the moment; it could be an experience from a month or a half-century ago, relived on paper. And while memoirs are necessarily factual, they deal with feelings, ideas, and intimacies, which journalists didn't and to a great extent still don't allow. First person is ok in long form journalism today, but you still can't get too personal—unless the personal stuff involves the person you are writing about and not yourself.

IX. ME, MYSELF, AND I

But let's get back to Wolcott and *Vanity Fair* and what he did to—or, rather, said about—me.

Early the next morning after Patricia called to tell me about Marisha's discovery at the grocery store, I went to the nearest convenience store, bought a copy of the magazine, and read the four-page article. "Me, Myself and I," it was titled. I was shocked to see my name and image in the form of a large caricature. (Me, a poor, fat, Jewish ne'er-do-well from Pittsburgh, in *Vanity Fair!*). Mostly, I was mortified by what the article said about me and about what I had been working for.

Wolcott lambasted most creative nonfiction writers as "navel gazers" writing "civic journalism for the soul." Creative nonfiction, he said, is a "sickly transfusion, whereby the weakling personal voice of sensitive fiction is inserted into the beery carcass of nonfiction."

I was stunned. Flummoxed. I felt like Henry Fonda in the movie *The Wrong Man*, suddenly and inexplicably accused of the murder of people he had never known at a place he had never been. There was my name and the name of the journal—Wolcott knew where I taught and what I had written, sort of—but surely, I thought, he couldn't be talking about me as the spokesperson for memoir. This couldn't be the same Lee Gutkind my students complained about, who forced them into endless journalistic immersion situations and made them write essays and articles without once using the word "I" in reference to themselves.

Wolcott assigned me the especially interesting role of "the godfather behind creative nonfiction." He deplored the fact that I traveled and talked about creative nonfiction all over the world, that I wrote books about creative nonfiction, published a literary journal, directed a creative nonfiction writers' conference, edited a series of books for new writers in creative nonfiction and taught creative nonfiction in a creative writing program. He called me a "human octopus"! And, he argued, all of these activities were ruining the audience for fiction. Because of the proliferation of creative nonfiction, he lamented, "the short story has become a minor arts and craftsy skill, like Indian pottery."

Now, I should say that most everything Wolcott wrote in that article was factually accurate. But in his attempt to be cute and clever, the piece was quite one-dimensional and skewed; it didn't really say anything of substance or significance, nor was it really fair to the subject he was approaching. This was journalistic ambush at its best—the cultural critic and contributing editor of a magazine with a circulation of 1 million bludgeoning the unsuspecting editor of a journal with a total circulation of 4,000. Wolcott hadn't interviewed me or anyone else for the article. He got me where it hurt, and I had no way to defend myself. How was this right?

Like I say, I was mortified. I felt awful, exposed, naked. All the work I had done over the previous half-dozen years fighting for the legitimacy of the genre—not to mention my books about baseball, organ transplantation, children with serious mental health problems, for which I had received prestigious awards—seemed suddenly to be diminished by Wolcott's sudden slamming of me. Or so I imagined, at least.

I remember thinking that my colleagues would find a great deal of satisfaction in the roasting of the genre and the interloper in their department who had been promoting it. "Promoting" was a bad word, with a horrible connotation, in English Departments, and in most of the Academy, at that time. Now everyone blogs and Tweets and Tumblrs, building "platforms," but in 1997, you had to be a little more subtle. You didn't *promote*; you waited until you were noticed, accepting acknowledgement with gracious (if obvious and sometimes calculated) reluctance. That was the pose and façade.

On the day I read the article, there was a meeting scheduled for members of the writing program—maybe seven or eight of us in all—and I wrestled all morning with the thought of not appearing. Would it be better for my colleagues to laugh at me and glory in my humiliation behind my back, or (if they had the courage) to my face? I was obviously being paranoid—I knew it—but knowing your imagination has run wild doesn't usually make a difference when you feel so wounded.

I remember that day well. My colleague, the poet Lynn Emanuel, was featured on the cover of the current issue of *The American Poetry Review*, a popular publication produced uniquely in newsprint, and in the meeting the director of the writing program, Ed Ochester, also a poet, commended her, the fine and impeccable poetry that had led to this honor, and the way the cover story enhanced the image of the Pittsburgh writing program. I braced myself, waiting for reference to the negative image I had brought to the program through the Wolcott roasting. But for the entire hour the meeting went on, not one word was mentioned about *Vanity Fair*, creative nonfiction, or me.

What was going on? Did no one in this room know about what happened in *Vanity Fair*? Or were they too disgusted to even mention it? All these years later, I remain unsure of the answer. As the meeting ended, I felt on the one hand relieved and on the other hand confused and unsatisfied. All I knew for sure was that I felt awful and betrayed. Wolcott didn't know me. He didn't know how hard I had worked, or how intimidated I often felt in the English Department, or how much I tried to carve out a place for myself, and for creative nonfiction, where I obviously didn't belong—and he obviously didn't care.

I will say, however, that the experience was a good lesson in how much power we have as wordsmiths and how easy it is to take advantage of that power. Years later, I did a terrible thing to a cousin of mine by writing about—if we're being honest, making fun of—his son's bar mitzvah. My cousin, Larry, had done absolutely nothing to me to deserve the ambush I thrust upon him, except to invite me to celebrate a momentous occasion in his son's life.

Nothing I wrote about that day was untrue—nothing was made up, just as nothing Wolcott wrote in *Vanity Fair* was made up—but what I wrote was exaggerated, a one-dimensional observation, the work of a writer trying to be clever at the expense of his subjects, an ambush I will forever regret. I have subsequently apologized to my cousins, but the damage is done. The book remains in print and as much as I can try to take the words back, they are indelible.

I haven't the slightest idea whether Wolcott is aware of the impact his article had on my life and work, but I am pretty certain he would not care to take back his words and observations. In fact I e-mailed him recently, knowing that I was going to write this history, asking him for an interview to talk about the genre. After a couple of follow-up e-mails, Wolcott declined my interview request, saying that he had pretty much said all he wanted to say about the subject and had nothing to add.

If he had agreed, I was hoping to talk to him about his work in the genre. In my response to "Me Myself & I," published in the 10th issue of the journal, I joked—or thought I was joking, at least—that he would someday write a memoir. And in fact, Wolcott later joined the "Me, Myself and I" generation in spectacular fashion, writing three memoirs (so far) and starting a very navel-gazing blog about the life and times of the great critic and cultural historian James Wolcott. I have always hated that cliché, "What goes around, comes around," but sometimes it is quite appropriate.

But back to the day after Wolcott's dirty deed—the ambush that changed my life. Suffering silently, I left the meeting and walked to the elevator in the Cathedral of Learning, heading to my office. I pressed the button, waited for others to walk on, and contemplated the awfulness of the day as we began moving upward. Then the elevator doors slid open and there standing before me was my colleague Bruce Dobler, a short, broad-shouldered fellow with a toothy smile. When he noticed me, he raised his eyebrows and then suddenly did something that completely changed my perspective about the *Vanity Fair* roasting. Bruce looked at me, paused thoughtfully, and then dropped to his knees, grabbed my hand, and said, with breathless reverence, "I kiss your hand, Godfather." And then, as I watched, confused and astounded, he did just that—with a loud, wet *smmmmmmmack!*

With that simple gesture, Bruce helped me remember the Oscar Wilde quip: "There is only one thing in the world worse than being talked about, and that is not being talked about."

It's true; to a certain extent, it's good just to be noticed, and being lambasted in *Vanity Fair* did bring attention to the genre. In 1997, when Wolcott disparaged me as the godfather, many people were writing and reading creative nonfiction, which, of course, is why it was a topic to target. But Wolcott didn't realize that few people knew what to call the form, how to write it, or where to try to publish their work. With Wolcott's article and *Vanity Fair's* million-plus readers, people began to understand that what they were reading and writing had a name—a label. From that time on, creative nonfiction—the literature of reality—became the genre to contend with in the literary world, an expanding literary movement with unbridled momentum. After that, for me and for the journal and the genre there was no turning back.

X. A MISSION AND A MANIA

Looking back now, I find this all quite amazing. How can twenty years have passed? What happened? Promoting true storytelling, creating the journal, keeping it alive . . . I thought this was just something I would do for a while before moving on to other projects and adventures, other books, other immersion experiences. (Not that I have stopped writing and living the creative nonfiction life; to the contrary, I have written or edited thirty books—so far.) But because I began to care about it and appreciate the form and the challenges of writing, teaching, and editing, creative nonfiction became a mission and somewhat of a mania for me. I couldn't quite stop doing it. And now, all these years have passed, and so much has happened in this nonfiction arena. There were nine issues of the journal published at the time Wolcott roasted me, and at this writing we are putting the final touches on issue 52. In fact, *Creative Nonfiction* was redesigned in 2010 and re-emerged as a full sized magazine—no longer a staid, boring journal—a reflection of the growth and popularity of the challenge and rewards of true storytelling.

I said at the start of this piece that I was once a romantic, a dreamer. Now, looking back, thinking of what has happened to me, to the magazine, and to the genre itself, I can only conclude that I have never stopped dreaming—about the power of true stories, the impact they can make, the way they can unite cultures, generations, and professions, even within the academy. Creative nonfiction's presence in creative writing programs continues to expand, and it is also spreading and taking root in many disciplines beyond English and composition and journalism. It's a real movement.

We—and I mean that in the broadest possible sense, including the writers I've been talking about, and the academics who have fought to establish programs around the country and even in other countries, and the magazine and book publishers who have supported and nurtured writers—have changed the way in which people are writing, and maybe even the way they think. True storytelling—narrative, memoir, long-form journalism, creative nonfiction, whatever you choose to call it—has become the dominant way in which thought leaders, as well as ordinary people with stories to tell and information to communicate, reach and affect their audiences. More than that, I would argue that this focus on true storytelling is helping people think more clearly and empathetically.

In the end, it is our stories that define us to the world at large and to ourselves. Writing is a challenge, but it is also a privilege. My story is my life—and you've just read my story or, at least, the first part of it. And here's something weird but totally true: until I told the story I am telling you here (and I have worked on many drafts over the months), I did not really understand it myself. I had never quite put it all together until now. I can't say whether my telling it has changed how you think or feel—but I can tell you that it has changed and enlightened me. That's pretty amazing, I think. And it's why creative nonfiction—or whatever you want to call it—is so vital, so invigorating, and so thoroughly addictive.

LEE GUTKIND is the founder and editor of *Creative Nonfiction* magazine. He is Distinguished Writer-in-Residence in the Consortium for Science, Policy, and Outcomes and a professor in the Hugh Downs School of Human Communications, both at Arizona State University.